ROUTLEDGE LIBRARY EDITIONS: ALCOHOL AND ALCOHOLISM

I0124904

Volume 18

RESPONDING TO DRINKING PROBLEMS

RESPONDING TO
DRINKING PROBLEMS

STAN SHAW,
ALAN CARTWRIGHT,
TERRY SPRATLEY
AND
JUDITH HARWIN

Routledge
Taylor & Francis Group

LONDON AND NEW YORK

First published in 1978 by Croom Helm

This edition first published in 2024
by Routledge
4 Park Square, Milton Park, Abingdon, Oxon OX14 4RN

and by Routledge
605 Third Avenue, New York, NY 10158

Routledge is an imprint of the Taylor & Francis Group, an informa business

British Library Cataloguing in Publication Data
A catalogue record for this book is available from the British Library

ISBN: 978-1-032-59082-0 (Set)
ISBN: 978-1-032-61148-8 (Volume 18) (hbk)
ISBN: 978-1-032-61155-6 (Volume 18) (pbk)
ISBN: 978-1-003-46226-2 (Volume 18) (ebk)

DOI: 10.4324/9781003462262

Publisher's Note
The publisher has gone to great lengths to ensure the quality of this reprint but points out that some imperfections in the original copies may be apparent.

Disclaimer
The publisher has made every effort to trace copyright holders and would welcome correspondence from those they have been unable to trace.

RESPONDING TO DRINKING PROBLEMS

STAN SHAW, ALAN CARTWRIGHT
TERRY SPRATLEY and JUDITH HARWIN

CROOM HELM LONDON

© 1978 Stan Shaw, Alan Cartwright, Terry Spratley and Judith Harwin
Croom Helm Ltd, 2-10 St. John's Road, London SW11

British Library Cataloguing in Publication Data

Responding to drinking problems.
  1. Alcoholism — Treatment
  I. Shaw, Stan
  616.8'61'06   RC565

ISBN 0-85664-525-7

Printed in Great Britain by
Billing & Sons Ltd, Guildford, London and Worcester

CONTENTS

THE MAUDSLEY ALCOHOL PILOT PROJECT

Stan Shaw, M.Sc., B.A., (Medical Sociologist), now Research Sociologist, Detoxification Evaluation Project, The Maudsley Hospital, London.

Alan Cartwright, M. Phil., (Psychotherapist/Medical Sociologist), now Administrative Director, Detoxification Evaluation Project, and Psychotherapist, Mount Zeehan Alcoholism Treatment Unit, Canterbury.

Terry Spratley, (Psychiatrist), M.B., B.S., M.R.C.P., M. Phil., M.R.C. Psych., now Consultant in Psychological Medicine, Mount Zeehan Alcoholism Treatment Unit, Canterbury, and Senior Lecturer in Psychiatry, Guy's Hospital, London.

Judith Harwin, B.A., (Senior Social Worker), now Lecturer in Social Work, London School of Economics.

ACKNOWLEDGEMENTS

The Maudsley Alcohol Pilot Project was funded by the Department of Health and Social Security, whom we thank for their financial support. The views expressed in this book are the authors' and do not necessarily reflect the Department's views.

We owe our main debt of gratitude for help in the production of this book to Mrs Diane Harding, who has cheerfully and skilfully nurtured the book through its many drafts and who organized the preparation of the final manuscript. We would also like to express our deep appreciation of the secretarial and administrative skills of Miss Beryl Skinner who worked with us throughout the research phase. Additional thanks for secretarial assistance go to Mrs Clare Newington and Mrs Cathy Gay.

For help in initiating the project and giving freely of his time and knowledge in encouraging us along, we owe special thanks to Dr Griffith Edwards, Director of the Addiction Research Unit, Institute of Psychiatry, University of London. Dr Edwards also generously allowed us permission to use data from his own population survey in Camberwell for purposes of comparison.

Two research workers also contributed much to the development of the project: Mrs Yvonne Salter, research psychologist, who worked as a member of the project during its first year and contributed greatly to the research design and the preliminary analysis of the data, and Dr David Robinson, Senior Lecturer in Sociology, Institute of Psychiatry, who worked in partnership with us on many areas of mutual interest.

Invaluable assistance in planning and conducting the experimental training courses was provided by Dr Beno Pollak, Sister Cathy Loft, Ms Helen Reeves and Mr Denis Powell.

Statistical advice on various aspects of our work has been provided by Mr Peter Nicholls and Mr Alan Smith of the Institute of Psychiatry.

Helpful comments on initial drafts were contributed by Mr R. Maxwell of McKinsey & Co. Inc., and Ms Linda Hunt, Lecturer in Social Work, University of Manchester.

For help in the hospital services study, we thank Mrs R. Pickard, Mrs R. Jackman, Ms J Hurry and Ms M. Towse.

The general population sample were interviewed by the Greater London Council Social Survey Team directed by Mrs J. Owen.

For permission to carry out interviews, questionnaires and training courses, we gratefully acknowledge the co-operation of the Planning Department and the Social Services Department of the London Borough of Southwark, the Inner London Probation and After-Care Service, the Inner London Medical Committee, the Royal College of General Practitioners and especially Mr Marcus Grant and the staff of the Alcohol Education Centre.

Last, but by no means least, our thanks go to all those people who so kindly gave of their time to complete our questionnaires and interviews.

INTRODUCTION

The work culminating in this book began as a consequence of a research proposal put by the Maudsley Hospital in London to the Department of Health and Social Security in 1971. The proposal was called 'Designing a Comprehensive Community Response to Problems of Psychotropic Substance Abuse', and in 1973 the Maudsley Alcohol Pilot Project was established to concentrate on problems of alcohol abuse in particular. The initial objects of the project were to evaluate the local situation in Camberwell, an area in South London comprising half of the Borough of Southwark, and to make practical recommendations to the Department for an improved local response to drinking problems and any recommendations which might be of value nationally.

The project, therefore, had to adopt a much wider perspective and to attempt a greater diversity of research operations than would be usual for such a relatively small team of four research workers. The studies involved attempts to explore the extent and nature of drinking problems; the ways in which these problems were perceived; how people with drinking problems felt about getting help in comparison to the responses which hospital and community services felt they could or should make, and lastly to consider ways in which these responses could be more effectively and appropriately matched to the prevalence and perceptions of the problems. What the variety of required studies might have lost in terms of intimate detail was more than compensated for by the comprehensive overall understanding gained of the prevalence and nature of drinking problems and the responses made to them. For this reason, our title, *Responding to Drinking Problems* was purposely chosen as a suitably open and flexible term. By 'drinking problems' we refer to the whole range of problems associated with drinking, from the problems of persons exceptionally damaged by alcohol to those affected only indirectly such as, for instance, people who feel disapproved of socially because they abstain from drinking. By 'responding' we also refer to a range of responses, from the minutiae of face-to-face counselling to, say, government policy on controlling the sale of alcohol. It was only through adopting such a wide focus that we were able to draw together the many different strands of thought about drinking problems and their treatment into a consistent and coherent viewpoint. To consider all the areas involved we had to undertake

varied forms of data collection with an equally varied range of subject
areas and samples. It would, theiefore, prove too unwieldy to include
here a full description of all the methodological details involved. Indeed, a full account of the sampling procedures and research methodology of all the studies mentioned would probably take as long as the
book itself. In any case, each individual study has been documented in
detail elsewhere and the reader interested in any particular study is
referred to the documents mentioned below. For the moment, we shall
briefly outline the studies undertaken in the manner which they will be
referred to in the text.

The work of the project fell into two main phases. The comprehensive overview of the range of problems and responses was conducted in
four major studies between 1973 and 1975. This phase was followed by
a further two-year period in which experiments in improving the response were tried out in accordance with the findings of the first phase.

Phase 1 Studies

(a) *The 1973 Summer School Study*

This study examined the attitudes of 112 students who attended the
1973 Summer Schools on Alcoholism in Britain organized by the
Alcohol Education Centre. These students comprised members of
various professional and voluntary groups involved in responding to
drinking problems. For the sake of brevity, all these kinds of different
worker — generalist and specialist, professional and voluntary — will be
referred to throughout the book as 'agents'. The agents filled in self-
completion questionnaires which contained forty-one attitude items
concerning the aetiology and treatment of drinking problems. This
study was basically designed to explore how the agents' ideas about the
nature and causes of drinking problems influenced their attitudes
towards working with clients with such problems.

The results of this study have been written into a paper (Cartwright
et al. 1976) available from the authors. The methodology and results
of the other studies in Phase 1 have all been thoroughly described in
our 1975 Report, *Designing a Comprehensive Community Response
to Problems of Alcohol Abuse* (Cartwright *et al*. 1975). This report
covered:

(b) *The 1974 General Population Survey*

A one hour interview and self completion questionnaire was administered to a random general population sample of 286 Camberwell adults.

The sample was taken from the electoral register but employing the Marchant-Blyth self-weighting random sampling technique to include non-registered adults (Blyth and Marchant 1972). The effective completion rate was 79 per cent and the sample was adequately representative both of the total Camberwell adult population and also the general population of England and Wales.

The interviews and questionnaire were based on schedules with open and closed ended questions which involved screens for excessive drinking and drinking problems, assessing attitudes to drinking, drinking problems, and potential sources for help with drinking problems and investigating respondents' contacts with these potential sources of help.

The epidemiological aspects of this survey mentioned in Part 2 of this book have been documented in a series of papers (Cartwright *et al.* 1976, Cartwright *et al.* 1977, Cartwright 1977, Cartwright and Shaw).

(c) *The 1974 Agency Survey*

This was a study of 'general community agents' by which we mean agents operating in the community who do not specialize in responding to drinking problems. Persons being helped by these agents, whether in medical or social services, have been referred to throughout as 'clients'. A one-hour interview and self-completion questionnaire was administered to 85 general community agents working in Camberwell, comprising 31 general practitioners (GPs), 28 local authority social workers and 23 probation officers. The questionnaire involved 47 items somewhat similar to those in the 1973 Summer School study. The interview schedule, which was virtually identical for all three groups, covered their attitudes towards drinking problems, their feelings about their own and other agents' responses and their attitudes and behaviour to treatment and referral of clients with drinking problems. In addition, to elicit how these agents operated in practice, they were asked in detail about their response to the last client they had seen whom they perceived to have drinking problems.

(d) *The 1975 Hospital-based Services Study*

This study comprised two record searches and one sample study. Statistics were gathered firstly on clients of the local specialist psychiatric alcoholism services over a 12 month period, and secondly on all local residents who had been labelled as alcoholics by a primary or secondary diagnosis in 1965, 1969 and 1973. In the sample study, the same interview schedule and self-completion questionnaire which had been used in the general population survey were administered to 18 clients attending the local alcoholism out-patient clinic.

Phase 2 Studies

Apart from experiments in improving the response of individual agents, which are reported in Part Five of this book and which have been more fully described in the research report which concluded the project (Cartwright, Harwin *et al*. 1977) the studies in Phase 2 were largely based on one research instrument – the Alcohol and Alcohol Problems Perception Questionnaire (AAPPQ). This questionnaire was constructed specifically to test out the hypotheses derived from the Phase 1 studies, and in so doing progressed through three different versions. The areas covered at various times by the questionnaire included agents' clinical knowledge of drinking problems, their techniques in dealing with drinkers, their feelings about their rights and responsibility in responding to drinking problems, their anxieties in working with drinkers and their sense of professional self-esteem in responding to drinking problems in comparison to their self-esteem in general. A full account of the development, methodology and results of the questionnaire studies has been documented in a paper written by one of the authors (Cartwright 1977b). Studies using the AAPPQ mentioned in this book include:

(e) *The 1976 Probation Officer Study*

This examined the responses of 46 officers from the Middlesex and Inner London Areas of the Probation and After-Care Services, before and after a three day training course.

(f) *The 1976 Detoxication Centre Staff Study*

This examined the responses of 17 staff members including social workers, nurses and care assistants, working in the first community-based detoxication centre in England. The AAPPQ was administered on three occasions: before and after a training course preparing them for the opening of the centre and again three months after the centre had been opened.

(g) *The 1976 USAFE Staff Study*

Examined the responses of 58 personnel from the United States Air Force in Europe whose work included helping servicemen with drinking problems. These agents included Social Actions staff, chaplains and doctors.

(h) *The 1976 and 1977 Summer School Studies*

Examined the responses of 175 students attending the 1976 Basic and Advanced Summer Schools run by the Alcohol Education Centre and of 187 students attending the 1977 Schools.

Besides the overall analysis of these studies (Cartwright, Harwin *et al.* 1977, Cartwright 1977b) reports on each individual study are available from the authors, together with appropriate versions of the questionnaire.

Before evaluating the responses made to drinking problems by the many different agents studied, we must first explore the extent and nature of drinking problems. This in turn requires us to begin by examining the nature and properties of alcohol itself.

PART ONE   ALCOHOL: ITS USES AND ABUSES

1 THE GOOD AND BAD EFFECTS OF ALCOHOL

Most books and pamphlets on drinking problems begin with an account of the nature and properties of the substance alcohol. This is not so much a convention as a reflection of the odd fact that millions of people throughout the world regularly drink alcohol but remain ignorant of its effects except for the more obvious physical and psychological sensations. Throughout history, alcohol has been man's favourite psychotropic substance yet most people's knowledge of it is no more than a combination of their personal experience and the myths of their particular time and culture.

The Constituents of Alcoholic Beverages

What then is alcohol? Alcohol is a compound of carbon, hydrogen and oxygen. Different chemical combinations of these three elements produce different types of alcohol such as ethyl alcohol, methyl alcohol and propyl alcohol. What we refer to as alcohol – the alcohol we consume in alcoholic beverages – is almost exclusively ethyl alcohol. Ethyl alcohol is sometimes referred to by the shorthand term 'ethanol'. It has been the most widely used because it is the most suitable for production and consumption compared to the other alcohols and indeed to any other intoxicating sedative. Some alcoholic beverages do contain minor traces of other alcohols, but the only other alcohol consumed as the main alcohol in a beverage is methyl alcohol or 'methanol'.

Ethyl alcohol rarely occurs as an absolutely pure chemical compound because it tends to dilute itself with the water vapour in the air. It has neither colour nor smell. Alcoholic beverages such as beer and wine which have a colour or an aroma owe these properties to substances in the drink other than the ethyl alcohol. However, ethyl alcohol does have a very strong taste experienced almost as a burning sensation; yet this taste is also mediated by substances in the beverage other than ethyl alcohol itself. Taste therefore varies with production techniques. For example, the whisky drunk in the United Kingdom in the early nineteenth century tasted more like modern vodka. These other substances in alcoholic beverages which add taste, colour and smell are often referred to as 'congeners'. The term is ambiguous since it may refer to other alcohols besides ethyl alcohol, to anything other than ethyl alcohol or just to non-alcoholic constituents. These latter may include glucose, carbon dioxide and various minerals, salts, sugars and acids (Leake and Silverman 1974). The different combinations of congeners with ethyl alcohol and water create the differences between types of alcoholic beverage.

History of the Types of Alcoholic Beverage

Presumably, Stone Age man first discovered alcoholic beverages as the by-product of fruits, berries, cereals and other plants mixed with water and left in the sun. Fruits and berries fermented in this way produced the first wines, fermented cereals the first beers. The earliest evidence of man shows alcoholic beverages considered by him as a food, a drug and a medicine, and alcohol use was well established in almost all Stone Age societies. Rules were passed about the sale of alcohol in Babylonia in 2,000 BC, and in China in 1134 BC (Anderson 1967). Alcoholic beverages are referred to in the Bible and in many of the ancient writings of India, Persia, Greece, Rome and Egypt.

After the fall of these societies, the use of alcoholic beverages changed little, except that the drinking habits of other cultures began to spread. For example, the Scandinavians introduced mead into the British Isles. Our word 'honeymoon' derives from the ancient Scandinavian custom of holding a thirty-day feast in honour of a wedding, at which the primary activity was the consumption of mead, a wine made from honey (Anderson 1967).

The drinking of distilled spirits has been a relatively recent innovation. St Patrick has been credited with the first production of whisky, but this would indeed have been a miracle had he achieved this centuries before the process of distillation was first carried out. The word 'alcohol' and the first spirits date from the invention of distillation by Moslem alchemists around AD 800 (Roueche 1960). 'Alcohol' literally means 'finely divided spirit' — referring to the distillation process by which the 'spirit' of the alcoholic beverage was removed invisibly from wines and beers, thus increasing the alcohol content of what had previously been fermented beverages. The discovered principle was that the boiling point of alcohol is lower than that of water. Thus when wine or beer were heated in a vessel, the steam would at first contain a higher percentage of alcohol than had been in the beverage, so when condensed, distilled spirit had a correspondingly higher concentration of alcohol. The first distilled beverage was brandy, which means literally 'burnt wine'. Distillation was first practised in Europe in the Middle Ages, when it was primarily conducted by physicians and monks, who intended their beverages to be medicinal.

Ironically, some authorities believe that before distillation was invented for 'medical' purposes, drinking problems were relatively rare and that it was the invention of much stronger beverages through the process of distillation which marked the beginning of drinking problems on a widespread scale, particularly when they came to be marketed widely in the period of industrialization and urbanization. Hogarth, for example, compared the degeneracy of 'Gin Lane' with the prosperity of 'Beer Street'. Hogarth's assumption that beer drinking does not lead to drinking problems, whereas spirit drinking does, is still a common attitude amongst people in modern societies. Doctors, for example, often consider heavy whisky drinking to be more 'serious' than heavy beer drinking and some people believe that people who just drink beer would be unlikely to become addicted to alcohol. Such ideas usually reflect inaccurate knowledge of the relative strengths and differing effects of the various alcoholic beverages.

Strengths and Types of Alcoholic Beverages

There are now basically five types of beverage in which ethyl alcohol is incorporated:

1. Beer
2. Table wines
3. Fortified wines (also known as dessert or cocktail wines)
4. Liqueurs (also known as cordials)
5. Distilled spirits

These different types of drink differ in their components, their characteristics and, to an extent, their toxic effects. But most obviously, they differ in strength. This can be worked out in terms of the amount of 'absolute alcohol' or 'pure alcohol' which they contain. The notion of 'absolute' or 'pure' alcohol is only a conceptual one as it is impossible to produce 100 per cent ethyl alcohol. Nevertheless, we can conceptualize an alcoholic beverage as containing a certain volume of absolute alcohol and a certain volume of water and other substances. The strength of the alcoholic beverage can then be theoretically expressed as the volume of alcohol in the drink as a percentage of the total volume of the drink. The table below presents the approximate percentage of alcohol by volume in a series of well known beverages.

1.1 The % Strength of Alcoholic Beverages

Beverage	Approx % of alcohol by volume
British lager	3.5
British keg beer	3.8
Stout	4.0
American bottled beer	4.5
Mexican pulque	6.0
Cider	3 − 12
Table wine	10 − 12
Champagne	12
Japanese sake	12 − 16
Vermouths and appetizers	17 − 18
Fortified wines (sherry, port, muscatel, Madeira, etc.)	16 − 22
Advocaat	26
Most liqueurs, (Benedictine, Kirsch, Cointreau, Curaçao, etc.)	30 − 40
British vodka	37.5
Most scotch, brandy, rum, gin	40
Bourbon	40 − 50
Polish vodka	47
Green Chartreuse, applejack	55

As can be seen from the above table, beers tend to be the weakest in terms of their percentage volume of alcohol. Brewed beverages are based on cereal starch, converted into sugar by adding malt. The sugar subsequently ferments through the action of yeast, a microscopically small plant which produces an enzyme which breaks down compound sugars. Most European and American beers tend to be made from cereals such as barley, while Japanese sake is based on rice. Mexican pulque is produced from fermented leaves of the agave cactus and cider is made from fermented apples.

Table wines are the next strongest variety of alcoholic beverage, containing around 10 to 12 per cent volume of alcohol. Wine can be produced by the fermentation of part or all of any sugar-containing vegetable fluid, such as fruit juice or coconut milk.

Fortified wines like sherry and port are made by adding distilled spirit, usually a form of grape spirit or brandy, to previously fermented wines. The added spirit increases the alcoholic content to around 20 per cent.

The precise strengths of beer, table wines, fortified wines and liqueurs can never be set exactly. There are relatively few legal definitions of their strength, and strict constraints would be impractical anyway since these drinks may change their strength over time within the bottle or barrel. However, the strength of distilled spirits can always be designated by their 'proof'. The term comes from the former process of estimating the alcohol content of drinks by moisturizing gunpowder with alcohol and then applying a flame. The strength of the flame 'proved' the strength of the alcohol. The lowest alcohol concentration which allows ignition is 57 per cent of alcohol by volume, and this therefore came to be designated as the baseline of 'proof' spirit. Other concentrations were then 'over' or 'under' proof (Leake and Silverman 1974). The United Kingdom and Canada still use this standard, and so the actual content of their distilled spirits is 57 per cent of the proof marked on the bottle. A 70 degrees proof whisky distributed in the United Kingdom contains 57 per cent of 70, or 40 per cent by volume of alcohol. The American system is to have a proof value exactly twice the alcohol content by volume. Therefore, a bottle of Scotch containing 40 per cent alcohol would be marked 70 degrees proof in the UK but 80 degrees proof in the USA.

The higher the percentage of alcohol content, the less the beverage tends to contain other elements besides alcohol and water. Many beers and wines contain minor traces of vitamins and minerals. Distilled spirits contain little but alcohol and water with only certain volatile remnants of the previously fermented beverage.

These considerable relative differences in the strengths of beer and wine compared to distilled spirits lead many people to assume that beer and wines are 'safer' than spirits. In some senses this is true, but people often forget that the volumes in which beer and spirits are normally drunk also differ considerably. Although beer is by volume much weaker in alcohol than distilled spirits, it is also usually drunk in much greater quantities. Because of the much greater total volume of a glass of beer compared to a tot of whisky, a half pint of British beer and a British legal standard tot of whisky in fact contain almost exactly the same amount of alcohol — about one centilitre by volume.

The Physiological Effects of Alcohol

The same amount of alcohol consumed in a pint of beer or in a double whisky might not have the same physical effects. Because the alcohol in beer is less concentrated, it does not irritate the stomach as much as the more concentrated alcohol in spirits. The low concentration of alcohol in beer makes it unlikely that anyone could drink a great enough quantity of beer to cause an acute alcoholic death. To achieve a fatal intake of alcohol a drinker might have to consume as much as five gallons of American beer. But in more concentrated beverages ethyl alcohol can be consumed in quantities large enough to lead to coma and death.

However, ethyl alcohol is not as dangerous in this respect as methyl alcohol. Methanol has some fanciful names like Colonial Spirit or Manhattan Spirits, but is more associated with methylated spirits, paint strippers and anti-freeze than with alcoholic beverages. Yet as late as 1910, wine and whisky being sold in New York's East side was between 24 per cent and 43 per cent methyl alcohol (Ziegler 1921), and it is still used by some drinkers even in its crude forms, because it is less expensive than ethyl alcohol and tends to produce longer periods of intoxification. Unfortunately methyl alcohol is more toxic. A Welsh science mistress recently added methyl alcohol to the punch she was making for her party. It killed herself and her fiancé and partially blinded some of her other guests (*J. Alchoholism* 1976).

Yet ethyl alcohol is not without its deleterious physiological effects. Even lager and beer of 3 to 4 per cent strength, whilst causing virtually no irritation at all to the throat or stomach, can still affect the liver and other bodily functions.

In whatever beverage form it is consumed, ethyl alcohol is absorbed through the stomach and intestines into the blood. This process of absorption can be slowed down by the presence of food in the stomach. Alcohol is gathered into veins and flows to the liver, then to the heart from whence it is distributed out to the rest of the body including the brain. Alcohol is lost to the body by oxidation, which breaks it down into carbon dioxide and water, from the bladder by urination and from the lungs by breathing out.

Alcohol as a Medicine

The physiological effects of alcohol on the body have sometimes been seen as beneficial. For example, alcohol can both boost the appetite and stimulate digestion. It increases saliva flow, excites the secretion of the gastric mucosa, and can inhibit emotional upsets which may prevent normal digestion. Alcohol can also help end constipation. This latter is particularly true of beer, although it may simply be the large amount of fluid rather than the alcohol which washes out the system.

At one time alcohol was thought to have a wider medical application. It was once used as a crude anaesthetic, but this was risky since the amount necessary for anaesthesia was not far short of lethal. It was thought not too long ago that because alcohol caused the blood vessels of the heart wall to dilate it might be of value in treatment of persons with a high risk of heart attack, but this evidence is now thought to be unreliable. Many old people continue to use alcohol because it appears to have the effect of warming them up. This is probably because alcohol increases the size of the blood vessels on the body surface, which makes the skin feel warm. Yet this is probably a misleading effect since alcohol is actually more likely to lessen the body's temperature. Neither is it true that whisky or rum help to cure colds or flu, although they may apparently relieve some of the symptoms such as backache. Ethyl alcohol might make you feel more comfortable, but it has no actual effect on the course of the illness. The clinical administration of alcohol *per se*, is now nearly extinct except for its psychosomatic value to some patients, and its occasional usage as a sedative. Yet unknown to many people who take them, and even to many doctors who prescribe them, a surprisingly large number of common medicines such as 'tonics' and 'cough mixtures' contain quite large amounts of alcohol (Bailey 1975). However, this probably says more for its anaesthetic and sedative properties than its curative power.

Alcohol as a Food

Because alcohol can aid the digestion and because it provides energy, it is sometimes defined as a food. It is true that alcohol is rich in calories — one pint of American beer usually contains over 200 calories. The reduction of alcohol into carbon dioxide and water releases energy. So in this sense alcohol is a food, but it is an incomplete food because it provides little else but calories. It contains no proteins, no fats and no vitamins. Alcohol cannot be stored in the body; it is oxidized as long as it is present. If there is any nutritional value in an alcoholic beverage it is provided by the substances in the drink other than the alcohol itself. Beer and wine contain a few vitamins but modern pasteurization and filtering processes have tended to remove most of the B vitamins which used to be present. Distilled spirits have never been of much nutritional value, because vitamins are not carried through in the distillation process. Moreover, alcohol itself does not merely lack nutritional value, it actually tends to deplete the body of nutrition it had before ingestion. Alcohol tends to deplete the body of vitamins A, B and C.

There are other ways in which alcohol can affect the nutrition of the body. It may interrupt the digestion process by interfering with the absorption of food or by causing the drinker to vomit up food. Alcohol may make the drinker lose his appetite, either by causing upsets such as gastritis or simply because it has provided calories, thus making him feel less hungry and precluding the consumption of more complete foods. By spending money on drink the impoverished drinker may be unable to buy food. An alcoholic patient once remarked to one of the authors that he had spent most of his money on wine, women and song, but had 'wasted' the rest of it. The combined effect of the resultant nutritional deficiencies, together with the direct toxic effects of alcohol, causes damage to the brain and nervous system and to the liver and stomach.

The Physical Consequences of Excessive Drinking

It is difficult to tease out how far physical damage associated with a pattern of excessive drinking is due to the alcohol *per se* or due to the common accompanying factors of heavy smoking, poor diet, disturbed sleep, unhealthy accommodation and so forth. Nevertheless, many of these other facets of the excessive drinker's lifestyle are attributable directly or indirectly to his alcohol consumption and so it is reasonable to consider the following aspects of physical damage within the bad effects of alcohol.

The most prevalent physical consequences of excessive drinking are probably gastro-intestinal, manifested as chronic diarrhoea and gastritis, peptic ulcer, pancreatitis, hepatitis and diseases of the liver including cirrhosis and cancer. These malabsorptional and stomach disorders tend to aggravate the vitamin deficiencies described above, which can sometimes progress to conditions akin to scurvy and beriberi, and which in turn are sometimes associated with congestive heart failure. Other disorders typically associated with excessive drinking are neurological (neuropathy, polyneuritis) haematological (megablastic anaemia), muscular (myopathy) and metabolic (hypoglycemia) (Kissin and Begleiter 1974).

Certain groups of excessive drinkers run extra risk of physical damage. Drinkers whose consumption is mostly in the form of wine and beer are more vulnerable to obesity due to excessive calorie intake. Women possibly suffer more than men from vitamin deficiencies, especially during pre-menstrual periods. Women also seem both more vulnerable to liver disease and more unlikely to recover. Amongst the offspring of women who drink very heavily, there seems to be a high risk of foetal death, malformation, growth deficiency and mental retardation. Research into this 'foetal alcohol syndrome' (BMJ Editorial 1976) has only recently begun in earnest, and as yet it is difficult to disentangle the causal role of alcohol from other aspects of these women's lifestyle. The same diagnostic difficulty applies to heavy drinkers who live unstable lives in poor accommodation, and who, in addition to the other illnesses described above, seem particularly vulnerable to skin disorders such as pellagra and cutaneous ulcers, and also to injuries and accidents, which sometimes result in infection (however, all excessive drinkers are prone to frequently sustain injuries when drunk). Drinkers whose general lifestyle is unhealthy and who also smoke heavily are probably particularly prone to develop tuberculosis, pneumonia, and various other pulmonary infections.

Intoxication

Although many of the physiological effects of alcohol on the body are now well understood, the effects which alcohol has on the brain are not as clear.

There are two major types of psycho-active substance. Some accelerate the activity of the brain — they are defined as stimulants; others slow down the activity of the brain — they are defined as depressants or tranquillizers. Ethyl alcohol is technically defined as a depressant. In normal dosages it relaxes the drinker and causes sleepiness. Of course, paradoxically, at other times it appears to do exactly the reverse and makes the drinker noisy, aggressive and over-active. However, drugs are not defined as depressants because they depress behaviour, but because they depress thought and perception. It so happens that alcohol tends to depress those brain centres which seem to apply the social and personal rules of behaviour. It depresses our inhibitions, and it often seems then as if the alcohol has increased the drinker's activity. In fact, it has depressed the ability of the brain to control behaviour.

Generally speaking, the higher the concentration of alcohol in the blood the more intoxicating effect there is on the brain. The concentration in the blood is in turn determined by the amount drunk over a given time and the rate at which it was absorbed. Therefore factors which affect the rate of absorption, such as the presence of food in the stomach, also affect the degree of intoxication. It is thus true that alcohol will have less intoxicating effect if food has been taken before, with, or shortly after drinking, especially if the food contains fats. Milk, or better still, yoghurt, is particularly helpful in slowing down the rate of absorption. These variables mean that the same amount of alcohol consumed at different occasions, may appear to have completely different effects.

But besides these physiological factors which cause different effects on the brain, the intoxicating effects of alcohol also vary because, like

all psychoactive drugs, alcohol relies for much of its effect on socially
and personally induced expectations. Before a drinker takes even the
first sip of an alcoholic drink he has some preconceptions about its
possible effect on him. These preconceptions channel the interpretation of subsequent sensations. Drinkers have different expectations of
drink at different times, according to the circumstances. The effects of
alcohol vary with the mood of the occasion, with the company present,
with the drinker's emotional state. This is perhaps most pronounced in
the possible range of moods and behaviours associated with drunkenness — a range neatly characterized in ancient Hindu legends which
defined the 'impish', the 'garrulous', the 'tearful', the 'belligerent' and
the 'stupid' types of drunkenness. This simple taxonomy still fits
contemporary variations in the mood and behaviour of persons when
drunk. The considerable differences between these states, which can be
produced from drinking the same amount of alcohol, demonstrate the
complexity of the interaction between pharmacological factors and the
psychological and social circumstances surrounding the drinking. Not
surprisingly, few of the theories and hypotheses about the intoxicating
effect of alcohol have been amenable to strict scientific testing.

The terms drunkenness and intoxication are often used inter-
changeably, but technically intoxication is any effect of alcohol upon
the brain manifested in mood and behaviour. This may not amount to
an alteration of mood and behaviour; alcohol may just emphasize or
exaggerate the pre-drinking state. But just a small dose of alcohol can
affect the brain. Experimental work shows that intoxication has less
effect on tasks which are familiar to the drinker. The more complex or
unfamiliar the task, the more alcohol disrupts task performance.
Typically, intoxication impairs by slowing activities and reflexes,
eventually leading to lethargy and possibly sleep. Again, this may be
interpreted as a good or a bad effect at different times and in different
drinkers. Jellinek (1960), one of the major researchers into the effects
of alcohol, believed that the intoxicating effect of alcohol was of most
benefit to people who, when sober, were over-cautious, anxious and
inhibited. For alcohol leads the drinker to be less self-critical, it breeds
self-confidence and promotes chance-taking. On the other hand, this
might also be associated with decreased alertness and the prevention of
logical thinking. This is not always obvious to the drinker at the time
or even upon reflection when sober. We all know someone who thinks
he can 'drive much better after a couple of drinks'. The more correct
interpretation is probably that either this person becomes less critical
of his driving after a few drinks, or that being aware of having had a lot

to drink, he makes a much greater effort than usual and over-compensates. Because alcohol deadens the central nervous system and slows down reactions, it often appears to the user at the time of intoxification to be acting as a stimulant. Some people believe that alcohol helps them think more clearly.

What alcohol actually does is to sedate some of the faculties of mental activity, particularly the experience of self-perception, self-criticism and fatigue. Thus whilst the person appears to himself to be operating more efficiently, in fact his performance is being impaired. But when the task in hand is carrying out a social function or making conversation, trying to impress someone, or coping with an anxiety-provoking situation, the deadening of self-criticism may be highly beneficial. Alcohol may often relieve anxiety which might have impaired performance altogether. Since alcohol depresses our inhibitions, the shy person may become forward, the quiet person become talkative and the uncertain person become confident.

Two interpretations are commonly made of this apparent personality change. One view is that intoxicated behaviour is a meaningless travesty of the drinker's normal personality. The sober Dr Jekyll is taken over by another personality, the intoxicated Mr Hyde, and the influence of alcohol is seen almost like a form of demoniac possession — 'it's not him, it's the drink talking'. The contrary interpretation is that alcohol brings out the 'real' personality freed from its usual social restraints and personal camouflage. Drink is not seen as 'taking over' but rather as releasing underlying facets of the drinker's personality, which are normally suppressed — 'it brings out the worst in him'. Both views probably contain some element of explanation, but by themselves they are incomplete interpretations. The mood and behaviour of the intoxicated drinker is created both by depressed cognitive functioning and also by the drinker's expectations about how he should behave in the particular circumstances, including cultural expectations about how he should behave when intoxified.

For example, respondents in our 1974 general population survey expected intoxification to have quite different manifestations in men compared to women. When the sample were asked what effects they thought 'regularly drinking too much' might have on men, they mentioned physical illness and disinhibited behaviour, such as getting into fights. They thought that women who regularly drank too much were likely to suffer marital difficulties, a loss of self-esteem and to be open to exploitation. Out of 286 respondents in the survey, only 43 thought that the effects of drinking on women would be the same as on men.

Respondents tended to believe that the underlying physically aggressive and violent nature of men 'comes out when drunk'. They 'hit their wives and drag their children out of bed', 'smash windows and run people over' and 'get very troublesome and start to fight'. On the other hand, women were expected to become vulnerable to moral temptation. They 'neglect their children and their housework'. 'A woman who drinks too much can often become free and easy, lose faith in herself.' In general, respondents considered that drinking had worse effects on women than on men, for the effect of drink on men was seen as an exaggeration of their normal positive and aggressive role, while drinking was expected to lead women into indulging in moods and behaviour contrary to the maintenance of their socially expected image of being demure and reserved. 'I think one is ashamed of one's own sex when this happens because it is usually in public.' Therefore the public was more critical of the effects of drinking on women than on men. 'It is disgraceful – bad enough for a man, but a woman to drink is dreadful.' 'It's bad to see women drink too much. It never looks as bad in a man, I don't know why.'

Straus and Bacon's study of American college students particularly noted that male college students believed alcohol led to violence in men and promiscuity in women, whilst the females believed drinking led to promiscuity in both men and women (Straus and Bacon 1953). But the effects of alcohol may create a promiscuous mood, but simultaneously preclude promiscuous behaviour. As the porter in Macbeth commented,* 'lechery, Sir, it provokes, and unprovokes; it provokes the desire, but it takes away the performance; therefore, much drink may be said to be an equivocator with lechery'. Like many drugs, the good and bad effects of alcohol often balance each other out.

Tolerance to Alcohol

We have noted that there are various physiological, psychological and social reasons why the same amount of alcohol consumed on different occasions can produce quite different psychological effects and levels of intoxification. But if alcohol is consumed regularly more of a pattern begins to emerge.

If a man at first gets drunk after an average of 5 pints of beer, a year later he might be getting drunk after an average of 6 pints, and then after 7 pints and so on. So although he will not experience exactly the same effect on each occasion he drinks, there is a progressive general

* Act II, sc. 3, 133-60.

tendency to become more resistant to the intoxicating effect of alcohol. This process is referred to as the development of 'tolerance' to alcohol.

Tolerance is often just considered in terms of drunkenness. The more alcohol it takes to make a man drunk, the more 'tolerant to alcohol' we say he has become. Yet just as intoxication refers to the range of sensations besides drunkenness itself, so the phenomenon of tolerance applies to a variety of effects. A person who uses alcohol regularly to achieve some specific effect, say, relaxation or the ability to make easier conversation, will gradually need more and more alcohol to achieve this effect. There is also a distinction between 'innate' tolerance — the degree of intoxication due to the drinker's weight, age, and other personal characteristics, and 'acquired' tolerance — the degree of intoxication due to the drinker's gradual ability to cope with more alcohol. The degree of acquired tolerance is directly related to his previous life's consumption.

Acquired tolerance seems to have two main dimensions — metabolic tolerance and functional tolerance (Gross 1977). Metabolic tolerance is the body's gradual ability to deal with alcohol more rapidly, particularly in the liver, which means that over the years the same intake of alcohol produces a gradually less concentrated blood alcohol content, and hence gradually less effect on the brain. Functional tolerance is a learning process by which the regular drinker comes to anticipate the effects of alcohol and the reactions of others to them, and to compensate for these effects; to cover them up and to learn to cope with impaired functioning. A person less used to alcohol has not learned these coping mechanisms and he cannot control his behaviour as easily. The tolerant drinker can appear to others as sober, healthy and efficient after gradually larger amounts of alcohol; he seems unaffected, he 'can take it'.

In some ways then, a developed tolerance is good for the heavy drinker; he can keep up his appearances, keep his job, carry out his duties. On the other hand, the highly tolerant drinker is like someone who can feel little pain — the need to drink more alcohol to maintain the desired effect escalates consumption and the toxic effects of alcohol cause more and more damage to the liver, heart and brain. When the drinker abstains from alcohol for a period and then returns to drinking, his high tolerance level is quickly regained. Successive periods of abstinence will be followed by increasingly rapid reinstatement of tolerance. Eventually the toxic effect of the continually larger amounts of alcohol the body has to process, combined with commonly associated nutritional deficiencies, becomes so harmful that the

functioning of certain parts of the body may be irreparably impaired
and become unable to sustain the level of tolerance. The system decom-
pensates and becomes less and less able to cope with alcohol. Eventually
the drinker may be quite intoxicated after a tiny intake of alcohol.

Withdrawal from Alcohol

Withdrawal is the end of the process by which the body deals with
alcohol and marks the reaction of the body and brain to having been
intoxicated. The same principles therefore apply to withdrawal as applied
to intoxication. The actual course and severity of withdrawal are
affected by many other factors besides the drink itself, although in
general the more alcohol consumed, the more severe the withdrawal
from it is likely to be. Therefore, the highly tolerant drinker who is
likely to consume very large amounts, is also more likely to experience
severe withdrawals. Symptoms of withdrawal can last from a few hours
up to a few days. Withdrawal takes the form of a 'rebound' effect of
the body and brain. Whereas the very heavy drinker, when intoxicated,
acts in a slow and lethargic manner, in withdrawal his body over reacts
and he may experience fits or become hyperactive. And whereas his
mood was calmed and tranquillized by the sedative effects of alcohol,
in withdrawal he may instead experience gross anxieties and fears,
sometimes of a hallucinatory nature. If his mood when intoxicated had
been euphoric, his mood during withdrawal may be one of deep depression, sometimes referred to as 'boozer's gloom'.

    Although these are extreme forms of withdrawal, a similar though
much milder 'rebound' effect follows any intake of alcohol, however
small. As the sedative effects wear off, the body becomes slightly aroused.
This is typically manifested in disruption of sleep 'the morning after'.
For although the sedative effects of alcohol produce heavy sleep at
first, withdrawal will later produce restlessness and sweatiness in the
early morning. Such withdrawal effects are typically accompanied by
the after-effects caused by the toxicity of alcohol such as headache and
nausea. The combination of the withdrawal effect and the toxological
effect is commonly referred to as a hangover, but technically speaking,
withdrawal effects can be assuaged by a further intake of alcohol
whereas toxic effects will only be made worse by more alcohol.
Although a hangover can be produced by alcohol alone, its severity is
usually exacerbated by factors such as disturbed sleep, smoking,
indigestion and regret for behaviour the night before. Moreover,
different symptoms and severities of hangover can apparently be produced by the same amount of alcohol contained in different types of

beverage. In some experiments, these different effects have been attributed to the 'congeners' in the drink, i.e. the constituents of the beverage other than ethyl alcohol and water. There is some evidence which shows that drinks which contain more congeners, such as whisky and rum, tend to produce worse hangovers than do clear spirits such as vodka and gin (Chapman 1970).

But this does not necessarily mean that 'mixing drinks' will produce a worse hangover. This idea probably arises because if a person has mixed a few drinks, he has probably drunk quite a lot anyway, including some drinks which seem more likely to produce hangovers.

Neither is there any evidence to support the popular notions that hangovers can be cured by alternating warm and cold showers, by vomiting or by drinking black coffee (Maling 1970). There is no scientific evidence to show that any of these remedies will actually accelerate the rate at which alcohol disappears from the body. If these remedies work, they must be relying on a psychosomatic expectation that the severity of the hangover will be reduced.

Drinking Behaviour associated with Increasing Tolerance and Increasing Withdrawal Effects

As a drinker becomes increasingly more tolerant to alcohol, he gradually requires more and more alcohol in order to achieve the blood alcohol concentration at which he experiences the good effects. He also comes to require more alcohol to stave off the increasingly severe withdrawal effects which may occur as his blood alcohol concentration falls. Thus not only does his overall consumption continue to increase, but the concern to prevent blood alcohol concentration falling can become a gradually more important reason for drinking than the usual factors like mood, company and social situation. Thus his pattern of consumption tends to become heavier, and more regular and consistent. He may begin to orientate his day and his arrangements around acquiring and consuming alcohol. He may begin to keep supplies of alcohol always near to hand, particularly to safeguard himself against experiencing withdrawal symptoms. Such symptoms may be quite mild, but nevertheless cue the drinker that more severe symptoms might follow if he does not consume some alcohol. The drinker may begin to engage in 'relief' drinking even in the middle of the night or in the early morning.

To achieve and maintain the good effects and to ward off withdrawal effects, the highly tolerant drinker has to consume a much higher amount than other people. This pressure to consume much more than others forces the drinker into deviant behaviour. Before going out to meet other people, for example, he may stoke up with some drink beforehand in case he cannot achieve the desired blood alcohol content later. He may begin to drink between rounds bought by the company he is in. The drinker may gradually become guilty about such behaviour and try to hide it. He may begin to lie about his drinking, claiming it is not as high as it is; sneak drinks when others are not looking; or conceal his supplies of drink about the house, in the office or in the car. The combined effect of his guilt and the pressure rapidly to achieve a higher blood alcohol level may cause him to gulp drinks much quicker than the more restrained drinking of less tolerant drinkers. To offset his guilt about drinking so heavily he may begin to associate with other excessive drinkers in whose company his drinking behaviour does not appear deviant.

The Psychological Consequences of Excessive Drinking

For the drinker who seeks to prevent his blood alcohol level falling, obtaining and drinking alcohol may become his most important activity. He begins to put less value on his other activities. A man who begins to drink at lunch-time may become less concerned with functioning well at work in the afternoon and alcohol reinforces this attitude by sedating him and making him less self-critical of his work performance. Another may have begun to go to the pub at night to avoid being upset by his wife's nagging. The tranquillizing effects of alcohol may contribute to him gradually putting more value on the atmosphere of the pub as an increasingly attractive alternative to his home. 'Typically, a patient relates that he used to be proud of his house but now the paint is peeling off, used always to take the children to football matches but now spends no time with them, used to have rather rigid moral standards but will now beg, borrow or steal to obtain money for alcohol' (Edwards and Gross 1976). As drinking increases, the person may begin to lose his commitment to his previous interests, hobbies and sports, choosing instead to spend his time and money on drink. His whole outlook on life may alter. A married man might come to put much less value on his home and family; the ambitious man might lose his drive and become uninterested in promotion.

The drinker often experiences guilt about these changes and begins to rationalize his behaviour. He may come to reject the values he formally held and to claim that he no longer considers his home or his work to be of importance. He may also attempt to offset his guilt and maintain his self-esteem by trying to influence other people to drink as heavily as he does himself. He may try to persuade other people at work to join him in lunchtime drinking sessions, or prevent them going home when their wife is expecting them. If he fails to influence them, he may decry them as unsociable, unmasculine, or 'under the thumb'. An alternative means of maintaining self-esteem while engaging in excessive drinking is to blame the effects of drinking on bad luck or more commonly on other people. The excessive drinker may rationalize losing his job on the grounds that his boss 'had it in for him', or feel his wife 'doesn't understand' him.

Such growing suspicions of other people can often be associated with jealousy. Jealous feelings of a most obsessive nature are common in marriages and relationships in which one or both of the partners drink excessively. In many cases, this jealousy is bound up with psycho-sexual problems such as impotence and inadequacy. These problems may be of an acute nature, such as episodes of 'brewer's droop' or more continuous chronic effects. Sexual problems can result from chronic disharmony associated with excessive drinking and longstanding feelings of inadequacy and of unfulfilled expectations. Impotence can also result from the neurological effects of alcohol. The more impotent a man becomes, the more inadequate he comes to feel and he becomes increasingly anxious that his partner will seek satisfaction elsewhere, and his jealousy will become obsessive. In these situations excessive drinking can itself become a substitute expression of masculinity, but its effects will only tend to worsen psycho-sexual problems.

It is not only sexual performance which may deteriorate due to excessive drinking. High alcohol consumption can be accompanied by gradual deterioration in the functioning of the drinker's brain. The drinker who used to be bright, alert and intelligent may begin to appear dull and lethargic. The drinker gradually suffers a decline in his faculties of judgement, perception, initiative and cognition. This impairment is not always obvious, especially as it tends to be of a slow insidious nature, but in some cases the impairment is quite perceptible, and the drinker may appear like a punch drunk boxer. This damage can be irreversible. Perhaps the most noticeable effect of excessive drinking on the psychological processes of the brain is the effect on memory. Acute memory loss is quite common, involving just a slight fragmentation of the previous evening's activities. As consumption becomes more re-currently high, the brain cells become increasingly disturbed and more serious amnesias begin to occur. Sometimes the excessive drinker can become almost like a demented old person, able to remember the distant past but unable to recall the immediate past or even to under-stand his place in the present. Such disturbance can be exacerbated by accidents which frequently occur when drunk, and which in turn can cause further damage to the brain.

Increasingly heavy drinking is often also accompanied by increasing use of other psychotropic substances. Heavy drinkers are very likely to be also heavy smokers (Dight 1976). Some excessive drinkers become polydrug abusers, mixing alcohol with both tranquillizers and stimulants. The pattern of alcohol consumption with other drugs varies amongst different groups of excessive drinkers. Middle-aged excessive drinkers, particularly women, tend towards taking barbiturates, Valium and Librium, often prescribed to them by their family doctors, who may be unaware of their patients' heavy alcohol consumption. Young people's mixing of alcohol with other psychotropic substances tends to be more hedonistic and often conducted in groups. Whatever the pattern and the substances taken, the aims of polydrug consumption are usually either to increase the good effects or to offset withdrawal effects such as depression, anxiety or disturbed sleep. Consumption of alcohol with other drugs creates a high risk of overdose, both accidental and deliberate. The rate of suicide amongst excessive drinkers is high and consumption of alcohol with other drugs is the most frequent method. Suicide is probably an extreme outcome of a pattern of emotions and feelings which often develops with excessive drinking into an all-pervasive sense of guilt, shame and inadequacy, marked by a chronic erosion of self-esteem as the drinker becomes gradually less capable of functioning as a parent, spouse, breadwinner or in any other role.

The Social Consequences of Excessive Drinking

The pattern of social harm associated with excessive drinking usually reflects the pattern of drinking itself. A man who drinks very regularly may experience chronic financial difficulties or marital disharmony without ever experiencing acute intoxication. Another drinker who drinks very heavily but only on intermittent occasions may suffer more from accidents. Nevertheless binge drinking can still cause chronic financial or marital problems and since excessive drinkers usually drink both heavily and regularly, they invariably experience both acute and chronic social problems.

Both the acute and chronic effects of excessive drinking tend to fall into five interrelated problem areas, involving the family, accommodation, occupation, finances, and legal problems.

The excessive drinker does not only cause difficulties for himself. As he spends increasingly more time and money on drinking, he increasingly neglects his partner, home and children. He becomes gradually detached from the realities of family life. This begins to exert more and more pressure on the partner and children. The wife of an excessive drinker is often forced out to work even when the children are still young, while the husband of an excessive drinker may have to look after all the housework and care of the children besides his usual occupation. The children can become neglected; they do not get regular meals, they may not have enough clothes, their performance at school may begin to deteriorate. Because one of the parents has to do more work than usual, or if both parents are excessive drinkers, the children themselves may have to take on adult roles such as shopping and running the home, which in turn forces them to take more time off school.

The growing pressure on the family results in chronic disharmony, manifested in endless rows and arguments. Sometimes these break out into violent episodes of child battering and wife battering, which are often related to jealousy. These rows and fights can cause depression and anxiety in the spouse and emotional disturbance and bed-wetting in the children. The children are frequently drawn into the rows them-selves, and usually take sides. Frequently they side with the drinker, perhaps because they feel sympathetic or because they blame the other parent. They may feel that they do not get enough attention from the non-drinking parent, who may be over concerned about the drinker and doing so much work and housework that they have not enough time to spend with their children.

The pressure on the family may also cause them to withdraw from relationships with others. The embarrassed spouse of a drinker may withdraw from the neighbours. The husband or wife of an excessive drinker may turn down invitations and avoid any social gathering such as parties, meetings or weddings, where they fear they may be publicly embarrassed by the drinker's behaviour. The children stop bringing their friends home because they expect one or both of the parents may be drunk or because they are embarrassed about the neglected state of their home. In a sense, the whole family can become as deviant and as affected by the drinking as the drinker himself. The whole family be-comes drink-orientated, and sometimes they begin to drink excessively them-selves. Spouses sometimes begin by joining their partners' drinking sessions, perhaps to try and control their consumption, but eventually they may start drinking heavily. This tendency to drink as heavily as their partner is also created by the pressures under which they find themselves. As the children grow up, they too frequently adopt a similar pattern of heavy drinking, following their parent's model as a response to their disturbed and neglected upbringing.

Sometimes the social problems and pressures caused by the drinking combine to break up the family. If the drinker is a woman, the family unit is particularly vulnerable. The man may leave her and she may be unable to look after the children properly, and they may have to be taken into care.

However, in the case of the second major problem area — accommodation problems — it is the male excessive drinker who is more vulnerable. If such a drinker loses his family due to the break-up of his marriage, he also tends to lose his accommodation as well. For his wife is more likely to be awarded the home or to retain the tenancy, because she gets legal custody of the children. If the family remains together, they may at least get some cheap or council accommodation. The problem of accommodation tends to be worst for the single male excessive drinker. His strained finances and unkempt appearance may prevent him from getting good accommodation, whilst his drunkenness, bed-wetting, noisiness and fighting may soon get him thrown out of any accommodation he does manage to acquire. A large proportion of single homeless men have alcohol problems and this is particularly true of migrant casual workers.

The third area of social problems which may be caused by excessive drinking are occupational problems. Episodes of acute intoxication may cause absenteeism or accidents at work, but a pattern of regular heavy drinking will lead to recurrences of these difficulties, together with a general decline in efficiency and ability to either hold down any job or to gain any promotion. Frequently the excessive drinker's occupational standard and skills drift downward, and he often ends up in a job well below his former capabilities.

Fourth, the money spent on alcohol combined with a decreasing income force the excessive drinker to live at a standard below the one one would expect. He comes to spend an increasingly greater proportion of his income on drink, and he often becomes saddled with debts. The excessive drinker's finances are often further strained by other relatively expensive habits such as smoking and gambling.

Fifth, excessive drinking may often lead to legal problems. There are certain legal problems typically associated with episodes of acute intoxication such as drunken driving, taking and driving away, drunkenness offences and disturbing the peace. A number of such alcohol-related crimes are often committed in groups, particularly hooliganism, assaults, fights, rape and certain types of theft. However, over a period of years, excessive drinking may have a more insidious effect, particularly as the drinker's financial difficulties pressurize him into stealing drink, the money to buy drink or to steal goods which his spending on drink have precluded him buying. Shoplifting becomes a recurrent activity, particularly for female excessive drinkers, the wives of excessive drinkers or for homeless men with very low financial resources. The financial pressures often lead persons who had not previously had any legal problems to become involved in various criminal activities such as fraud and embezzlement. Thus the age of first offence of convicted persons who are diagnosed as alcoholics is usually much later in their life than non alcoholics.

Alcohol-related problems rarely occur alone. More typically they co-exist and interact with the excessive drinking to make each other more and more difficult. For example, a company representative who drinks heavily may lose his licence because of driving while intoxicated, and in turn he may lose his job. This may cause him and his family financial problems and they may be forced into poorer housing. In turn, the pressure on the family may begin to cause rows, and he may begin to drink still more heavily as a result. He may thus find it increasingly more difficult to get another job, and may try to acquire money fraudulently. This may then also involve him in legal problems.

It is rare for excessive drinking to only occur with one type of harm. In most cases, different forms of problem become inter-related, and often in turn cause the drinker's consumption to increase still further. In many cases, the whole of the drinker's life becomes a morass of physiological, psychological and social harm.

The Value of Alcohol

Alcohol is thus associated with a variety of personal and social problems. But just as individual drinkers put up with the bad effects of alcohol in order to obtain the good effects, so it seems that societies throughout history have likewise gone on using alcohol despite its undesirable consequences.

As Jellinek (1945) noted:

> The use of alcohol has persisted through ages in which great cultural changes have taken place . . . it was used in greatly divergent cultures, . . . and it has persevered in spite of the observed dangers of excess.

To him, this observation 'suggests that alcohol fulfils some function which man, rightly or wrongly, values'.

But we have seen that many of the supposed 'functions' of alcohol such as a food, a medicine or an aphrodisiac, have little basis in fact. The social and psychological benefits of alcohol are almost all symbolic and/or attributable to its action as a tranquillizer and intoxicant. The value of these effects has led to false claims for other uses of alcohol and an underestimation of the bad effects it may have. But if the good effects of alcohol had not seemed so important to man, and had they not appeared to outweigh the bad effects, alcohol would not have been used by so many people over so many centuries.

Its current place amongst contemporary 'necessities' suggests a high valuation of the good effects of alcohol in modern society. In the UK in 1976, the average person aged 15 and over drank approximately 265 pints of beer, 8½ pint bottles of spirits and 14 pint bottles of wine (Brewers Society 1976). This accounted for around 10 per cent of all consumer expenditure, despite the fact that most of this outlay went in tax. Total receipts from Excise and Customs Duties and purchase tax (VAT) on alcoholic drink in 1976 amounted to a staggering £1,953,100,000. In the USA, too, spending on alcohol is thought to outstrip spending on education, health, and religion combined. Even during the Prohibition era, people went on making, purchasing and consuming alcohol, whatever the risk. So ingrained a social custom as drinking behaviour cannot be easily changed by mere legal or fiscal measures. Moreover, alcohol's functions as a promoter of social intercourse or a remover of tension and pressure could not easily be replaced by any other substance. Other widely used tranquillizers like Valium have no social connotation; whilst alternative psychotropics around which sub-cultural meaning has developed seem alien and dangerous to most people. They have no social reinforcement or well-known sets of rules about how to handle them. Learned attitudes exaggerate their bad effects and ignore or deny their good effects, whilst making exactly the reverse interpretation of the effects of alcohol. The use of alcohol has been approved for many centuries and is associated in most people's minds with enjoyment and conviviality. Its bad effects tend to be ignored, denied, underestimated or brushed away in jokes. This strongly affects the type of response people think should be made to the bad effects of alcohol, as we shall now proceed to discuss.

2   CONCEPTS OF ALCOHOL ABUSE

As we have seen, the good and bad effects of alcohol lie on complex
physiological, psychological and sociological continua. Alcohol can
produce a range of quite different effects and consequences. Concepts
of use and abuse have therefore been open to equally wide interpretations. Not only are there variations in our personal experience of the
effects of alcohol, but there are also contradictions in the information
and attitudes provided by parents, peers, media and other sources. Thus
there are inevitably variations in what different societies and even
people within one society consider to be alcohol abuse.

It is hardly surprising then that no consensus has ever been reached
on how one could define exactly what constitutes 'alcohol abuse' or a
'drinking problem'. For there is no dividing line where alcohol use ends
and alcohol abuse begins; where drinking stops giving benefit and starts
creating problems instead. Alcohol can have good and bad effects at
the same time; it can in some senses be both used and abused simultaneously.

It might be assumed then that there would be little point in trying to
make strict distinctions where none really existed. Yet people have
gone to inordinate lengths to construct definitions and typologies
which attempt to definitely distinguish alcohol use from abuse and safe
drinking from problem drinking. Infinite schemes of classification have
tried to categorize types of drinker and problems. Alcohol addicts have
been distinguished from problem drinkers, alcoholics from controlled
drinkers, excessive drinking from addiction, addiction from dependence,
dependence from harm and so on. The very fact that so many attempts
have had to be made shows that no criteria have ever been established
to support these distinctions satisfactorily.

For example, one well-known text book on alcoholism tried to distinguish between excessive drinkers, alcoholics, alcohol addicts and
chronic alcoholics (Kessel and Walton 1965). Excessive drinkers could
be distinguished by 'the frequency with which they became intoxicated
or by the social, economic, or medical consequences of their continued
intake of alcohol'. But not all of them are 'alcoholics', who 'are people
with a disease that can be defined in medical terms and requires a
proper regime of treatment'. It is not explained in what way this is
different from the 'medical consequences' of excessive drinking. Then

again, 'alcoholics are addicted to alcohol', but they are somehow different from 'alcohol addicts' who 'are unable to spontaneously give up drinking'. This is also distinguished from a later stage 'where their brains or their bodies have been so harmed by alcohol that the effects persist even when they are not drinking'. This stage is called 'chronic alcoholism' — a term which 'should only be applied when the body has been physically damaged by alcohol'. It is not clear how excessive drinking with 'medical consequences of their continued intake of alcohol' is distinct from 'when the body has been physically damaged by alcohol'.

This particular attempt to classify types of alcohol abuse is certainly no worse than many other such attempts. It merely serves to illustrate the inappropriateness of imposing divisions on continua, and selecting definitive criteria for conditions whose constituent elements overlap. Drinking behaviour can have all sorts of 'social, economic, or medical consequences', or may have virtually none at all.

The non-appearance of any cut-and-dried account of alcohol abuse has often been bemoaned by people in the field who believe 'the lack of firm definition has been a stumbling block to understanding and progress' (Office of Health Economics 1970). Perhaps it might be more pertinent to say that attempts to impose firm definitions on a conceptual area where they are either inappropriate or indeed impossible has been the real stumbling block to understanding and progress. These issues are not just points of academic nicety. How drinking problems are defined has the greatest impact on who is deemed responsible for responding to them, and in what way. It is therefore important for the reader to consider these arguments over definition. Furthermore, tracing the changing conceptualization of drinking problems helps us to re-examine our own views and prejudices about alcohol and alcohol abuse.

The History of Concepts of Alcohol Abuse

Controversy over what constitutes alcohol use and abuse is not just a contemporary phenomenon. Throughout history, some commentators have praised the effects of alcohol whilst others have criticized the very same effects. Neither has the concern to distinguish types of drinker been just a recent development. As long ago as the first century AD, the Roman philosopher, Seneca, tried to make the distinction between 'a man who is drunk' and one who 'has no control over himself . . . who is accustomed to get drunk and is a slave to the habit' (Jellinek 1942). This concern to make a distinction between heavy drinkers on the one hand and 'slaves to the habit' on the other has continually recurred in attempts to classify the effects of alcohol, as has the notion that being a 'slave to the habit' is some form of mental illness or disease which somehow differentiates people with this condition from other sorts of drinker. Equally so, there has always been opposition to these ideas.

In the seventeenth, eighteenth and nineteenth centuries, there was considerable argument as to whether excessive drinking was a disease, a sign of moral weakness or the inevitable outcome of a combination of poor social conditions and plentiful cheap drink. In mid-seventeenth-century Britain, drunkenness was widespread. The taverns and inns of the day were often meeting places for criminals and drinking and drunkenness became associated with crime and immorality. The situation worsened considerably with the invention of cheap distilled spirits, particularly gin. Excessive drinking of cheap gin probably reached a peak by the mid-eighteenth century when heavy taxes on spirits were introduced and consumption dropped markedly.

It was in this period, when consumption had been reduced and the Industrial Revolution had not quite accelerated, that the first major works on drunkenness as a disease were published; in 1785 by Rush (Rush 1785, 1943) in America and in 1788 by Trotter in Scotland (Trotter 1788). They referred to drunkenness as both a disease and an addiction. But at the turn of the century, mass urbanization relaunched widespread excessive drinking and this turned attention back to the association between alcohol and crime and social disorder. At the same time in America the absence of many forms of social control exacerbated the problems of increased urbanization and industrialization and the feeling grew there too that drinking was causing social, health and moral problems. On the eastern seaboard, temperance groups were formed to promote moderation in alcohol drinking, but on the more chaotic western frontier, groups associated particularly with religious denominations formed temperance movements which preached total abstinence for the individual and prohibition for society. Anderson (1967) has characterized this movement as 'convinced that beverage alcohol in all forms was evil in itself and that only evil can come from its use, and further that anyone that used beverage alcohol was evil, and therefore these groups insisted that total abstinence was the only way to civilize and Christianize the barbaric frontier west of the Appalachian Mountains'.

Yet at the same time that the temperance movement was trying to stigmatize heavy drinkers as being deliberately degenerate, other people believed that the 'inebriate' was not responsible for his condition. For example, in 1841, in Boston, Massachusetts, a home was even created for their treatment and by 1874 eleven such non-profit-making homes for inebriates had been set up. Europeans also used the term 'inebriate' to refer to someone who could not stop drinking, along with other terms such as 'habitual drunkard' and 'dipsomaniac'. The term 'alcoholism' was first coined by a Swedish doctor, Magnus Huss, in 1849 (Huss 1849).

The last quarter of the nineteenth century in both Europe and America saw much commentary on the disease nature of drunkenness and alcoholism and also the founding of societies and journals for the study of the subject. In his classic *The Disease Concept of Alcoholism* Jellinek (1960) could devote an appendix to a listing of many nineteenth century papers on the disease nature of alcoholism. Some reformers of the day tended towards a view of the 'drink problem' as a response to socio-cultural conditions, but the more apparently scientific ideas of 'causes' and 'syndromes' were more appealing to the intellectual tenor of the age. However, scientific works on the subject did not hold complete sway. In fact, Keller (1976) notes that in the latter part of the nineteenth century many moralists began to criticise the idea of drunkenness as a disease because it encouraged sympathy for the drunkard and for drink. An essay by Todd (1882), for example, was assertively titled *Drunkenness a Vice, not a Disease*, and this moralist view still probably retained popular support. Obviously then, the competing notions that alcoholism is a disease and that alcoholism is not a disease are in no way twentieth-century products. Both views have a considerable tradition.

Anderson (1967) comments that the taking of sides was probably more pronounced in America, so it is now little wonder that

Americans are anxious, confused, ambivalent, and guilt ridden in their attitudes towards beverage alcohol. They are said to be a culture divided amongst the wets, the dries, and the damp deniers of the controversy. We tend to be confused about our reasons for drinking and those for not drinking. We tend to communicate this to our young people, and it is present in our local option laws, legal controls, and cultural inconsistencies and ambivalences . . . Thus despite the fact that beverage alcohol has been noted since the beginning of history, there is little evidence that our contempary attitudes towards its functions and use are consistently reasonable and practical.

Alcoholics Anonymous and the Disease Concept of Alcoholism

It is perhaps significant that it was in America, with its ambivalent mixture of moralistic attitudes and ideas about treatment, that Alcoholics Anonymous developed. AA was the first movement formed specifically to help drinkers which was not sponsored by a religious group. But from the outset AA held the idea that alcoholism was not only a disease, but also a disease which could be arrested by admitting to the need for personal responsibility and for spiritual regeneration. To an extent it synthesized a sympathetic response with a moralist response.

The genesis of Alcoholics Anonymous was in the meeting of a New York stockbroker and an Akron physician. In the early part of 1935, the stockbroker had recovered from his obsession with drink through a sudden spiritual insight. This occurred during a discussion with another alcoholic who had been in contact with the Oxford group, a religious movement popular in America in the 1930s and precursor of Moral Rearmament. The broker came to believe that he could only start to recover from his compulsion to drink by admitting his problem to himself and by accepting that he needed support in trying to abstain from alcohol. The only possible sources of this support were another alcoholic and the higher power of God. At first he was uncertain of his own ability to remain sober because he failed to persuade any other alcoholic to join him in sobriety – until he convinced Dr Bob, the Akron physician. The inauguration of AA is usually taken to date from the first day of Dr Bob's permanent sobriety on 10 June 1935 and the first AA group was begun by the broker in New York later that year.

Like many people who find a personal solution to a problem, they believed that what had happened to them would be universally applicable. In retrospect, they admitted that their first rather over zealous approach was none too successful. By 1939, when the 'Big Book' setting out the AA philosophy was published (Alcoholics Anonymous 1939, 1955), and the name Alcoholics Anonymous formally adopted, the fellowship still comprised less than 100 members. But the Big Book confirmed a shift of emphasis from the earlier over-religious approach towards a form of moral psychology. It propounded that the alcoholic had to accept his permanent inability to handle alcohol like other drinkers. His obsession could only be arrested by lifelong total abstinence. Because alcohol to the alcoholic is a power greater than himself he cannot conquer it alone, but must seek the assistance of another recovered alcoholic and also of God as he understands him. This approach was based on spiritual and philosophical principles outlined in the 'Twelve Steps'.

Although AA as a body began to grow in size, it decided against having any formal organization. It resolved to engage in no enterprises or outside activities or to take sides on any issues like temperance. It decided not to promote any research. It demanded no fees or dues; the only requirement for membership was the honest desire to stop drinking. AA has kept faithfully to these ideals since.

Some people believed at the time, and some still do, that Alcoholics Anonymous 'discovered' that alcoholism was an illness, but as Jellinek has pointed out, it was not a new approach but rather a 'renewed approach' (Jellinek 1960). In fact before AA began, the American Medical Association recognized alcoholism in its nomenclature of Disease (Logie 1933). It was the publicity afforded the AA Big Book which really highlighted the idea of alcoholism as a disease and made it appear to be a new approach. Articles on AA and the disease concept of alcoholism were published in influential newspapers and magazines, and leading AA members were invited to the White House. By 1940, AA membership was 2,000; by 1941 it was 8,000. With this massive increase in interest, the early 1940s also saw the development of the American National Council on Alcoholism. This was a voluntary body of interested persons who wanted to promote education, research and treatment. Eventually many states, districts, and cities set up their own councils affiliated to the national body. At the same time, a multi-disciplinary centre of alcohol studies was established in Rutgers University in New York to research into all aspects of drinking problems. AA was introduced to Europe in Ireland through an Irish-American alcoholic in 1947. But national councils were relatively slow to develop, only being established in England in 1962 and in Ireland in 1966.

Why did the disease concept of alcoholism suddenly become so much more accepted in America in the early 1940s? First, the end of prohibition was accompanied by a rapid rise in drinking problems of various sorts. Second, the taking of sides on the prohibition question made it necessary to distinguish interest in dealing with alcohol problems from interest in prohibition and temperance movements. It was crucial to remove some of the stigma of intemperance and immorality from the drinker. Public health action on drinking problems had become impossible because it did not appear medical or scientific, but moralistic and associated with prohibition. The League of Nations Health Committee had considered undertaking an active programme against drinking problems in 1928 but was prevented by the complete lack of any body of medical and scientific opinion. The WHO (1951) has noted in retrospect that there was at that time no differentiation between a medical and scientific outlook on the one hand and the approach of lay reform groups on the other. Action against alcoholism was confused with political and social action against alcohol. It is probable that at that stage any attempt on the part of physicians and public health workers to prevent and treat alcoholism failed largely because the public could not differentiate between the two approaches.

The stage was therefore set for a movement which could distinguish its response to drinking problems from moralistic action against alcohol. The AA philosophy not only allowed this differentiation, but also managed to achieve it without blaming the individual drinker either. By promoting the idea that a particular group of drinkers were unable to cope with alcohol, and by labelling their inability an illness, AA appeared to allow a response to drinking problems which blamed neither alcohol itself nor the drinker as a person. This latter implication must have been particularly valuable in wartime America when drinkers could easily have been stigmatized as irresponsible indulgent hedonists. When the drinker was perceived as ill, it elicited more sympathetic responses from his family and from those dealing with him. When society formally classified his condition as an illness he could even benefit from health care and social security systems. For example, certain societies specify that alcoholics hospitalized for treatment cannot be dismissed from their jobs for a certain period. Thus the 'major advantage of defining alcoholism as an illness is social' (Pattison 1969). It gets 'a better deal for the alcoholic' (Room 1972). Perhaps alcoholism became accepted as a disease more because of the advantageous implications of the idea than because of the epistemology of the idea itself.

Even the translation of the disease concept into a scientific context was channelled through political considerations. The academic and medical rationale for the disease concept of alcoholism was largely formulated by E.M. Jellinek. If the AA Big Book takes prime responsibility for publicizing the idea that there was a disease condition called alcoholism, then Jellinek probably takes equal responsibility for the exact form in which this idea was propagated in a medical and scientific context, and how it was applied. In his paper 'Phases of Alcohol Addiction' Jellinek (1952) suggested that there was no single form of alcoholism, but alcoholisms – different sorts of obsession with drink as in fact the Big Book had noted. However, Jellinek argued that only some of these types of alcoholism should be considered illnesses,

namely those characterised by compulsive drinking. He maintained that
the label of illness should not apply to excessive drinking *per se*, but
'solely to the loss of control which occurs in only a group of alcoholics,
and then only after many years excessive drinking'.

What is this 'loss of control' which became emphasized as so central
to the disease concept of alcoholism? Essentially, it implies that the
sick alcoholic has no power of choice over how much he consumes.
This inability to control his consumption can take two forms. First, he
may be unable to abstain from drinking. Jellinek called this the 'Delta'
form of alcoholism, and it occurred particularly in societies like France,
where people tended to drink very frequently. Second, the drinker may
be unable to control his consumption on an individual drinking occasion. This was the defining characteristic of 'Gamma' alcoholism.
Following the AA theory, Jellinek postulated that alcoholics who suffer
from this form of loss of control have an irresistible urge to go on
drinking even when they have not chosen to do so; once they have had
a drink, this sets off an overpowering compulsion to drink more and
more. It is asserted that a single drink taken either intentionally or
unintentionally by an alcoholic will inevitably trigger off a psychobiological need for more alcohol. This compulsive drinking is seen as quite
different from drinking to relieve withdrawal symptoms, and indeed
the concept has really no corollary in ideas about consuming any other
drug. The concept of loss of control is the crux of the disease concept
of alcoholism: it is because of his loss of control that the alcoholic is
thought unable to return to normal drinking. He must always abstain
from alcohol, or else one drink = one drunk = one relapsed alcoholic.

In 1952, Jellinek claimed it was 'unwarranted' to define any drinkers
as sick if they were not experiencing loss of control. He thought that
misapplying the label of disease to other sorts of heavy drinkers would
mean that 'the nature of alcoholism' would show 'marked differences
throughout the world'. But, as we have seen, it was believed that
labelling people as 'alcoholics' got them a 'better deal'. So whilst
Jellinek at first deemed it conceptually inappropriate to expand the
disease concept of alcoholism, this soon became politically expedient.
He therefore changed his position considerably and came to define
alcoholism as 'any use of alcoholic beverage that causes any damage to
the individual or to society'. From this wide ranging definition, we
should 'single out species of alcoholism' (Jellinek 1960). As Robinson
has pointed out, 'while such a strategy might have helped to solve some
of Jellinek's problems in "international communication", it tended to
cloud rather than illuminate other relevant issues' (Robinson 1972).

For at the same time he clung onto the idea that loss of control was probably due to a 'physiological or biochemical anomaly'.

Jellinek's distinctions between the different types of alcoholism, of which only some counted as diseases, were never popularly accepted. In the real world it was unworkable to classify some alcoholics as ill and others as not ill. In practice, anyone who became labelled an alcoholic also came to be considered as ill and needing medical treatment. And whatever their drinking pattern, it was assumed that they had the 'physiological or biochemical anomaly' – which no one had actually proved to exist – but which would explain, if it did exist, the alcoholic's 'loss of control'.

In many respects, Jellinek concurred with the AA view. His work imparted scientific respectability to the disease concept; it further distinguished the response to alcoholism from the temperance movement or from any other overtones of moral censure; it legitimized more help for the alcoholic and best of all it seemed to explain a condition which on the surface was mysterious and baffling.

The disease concept of alcoholism was also appealing to other groups for different reasons. Those who drank heavily but considered themselves 'normal' drinkers were reassured they were not becoming alcoholics, since they were not physiologically or biochemically anomalous. They could 'give it up if they really wanted to'. To some brewers and distillers, the concept was even more attractive, since it implied that the majority of drinkers were not alcoholics and that they could drink as much as they liked without losing control. Therefore it could be argued that restrictions on alcohol sales for health reasons were unreasonable. After all, why should the pleasure of the majority be spoiled just because there were a few alcoholics whom science had shown to have an odd disease by which they could not keep control over their drinking?

So general agreement was reached on the image of the alcoholic as a sick person, who had some defect which meant he could not control his drinking. This anomaly made him different from all other drinkers.

So although, as we saw in Chapter 1, the effects of alcohol lie on continua and are mediated by very many factors, AA suggested that a single factor created a 'difference' between the alcoholic and the non-alcoholic, and its literature has been largely concerned with promoting the idea that alcoholism and excessive drinking are not matters of degree, but completely different states. AA believes there is a line between the alcoholic and the non-alcoholic, even if it is 'invisible': 'the alcoholic who crosses the invisible line is – and will remain – an

alcoholic all his life. And there is no such thing as a partial alcoholic;
either you are one or you are not' (Morse and Gordon). Although the
Big Book described various types of alcoholic, and their different
reasons for becoming alcoholics, it concluded that

> All these, and many others have one symptom in common . . . they
> cannot start drinking without developing the phenomenon of
> craving. This phenomenon, as we have suggested, may be the mani-
> festation of an allergy which differentiates these people, and sets
> them apart as a distinct entity. It has never been by any treatment
> with which we are familiar, permanently irradicated. The only relief
> we have to suggest is entire abstinence . . . The phenomenon of
> craving is limited to this class and never occurs in the average
> temperate drinker. These allergic types can never safely use alcohol
> in any form at all.

Mann's (1952) famous *Primer on Alcoholism* points out that 'choice'
is 'the vital difference' between the true alcoholic and the heavy
drinker or occasional drunk,

> The alcoholic, who is aptly known as a 'compulsive drinker' does not
> choose. He has lost the power of choice in the matter of drinking,
> that is precisely the nature of his disease, alcoholism. Usually they
> wish to simply enjoy a few drinks, 'like other people'. This, they
> find . . . does not seem possible for them; with alcoholics, choice is
> no longer possible, either to drink or not to drink, or of the amount
> consumed, or the effects of that amount upon them, or the occa-
> sions upon which drunkenness occurs.

The argument is completely internally consistent. Alcoholics are
different because they cannot control their drinking, and it is their loss
of control which distinguishes them from normal drinkers. Yet it seems
almost bizarre that this theory, generally accepted in scientific and
medical circles for many years, had no direct evidence whatsoever for
its important assumption: that the cause of alcoholism was an abnormality which rendered alcoholics unable to control their drinking. As
Roizen (1977) has pointed out,

> From a purely intellectual stand point the theory is surprisingly
> vacuous; it seems only to assert that alcoholics are different without
> anything more than speculation regarding the source or even the

evidence for that difference. What is important to recognise, however, is that the theory is ideal from a utilitarian stand point, and thus provides social managers of alcoholism with a seeming intellectual basis for carrying out their mission.

In the 1950s, this concept was in its full flower and the intellectual basis went uncriticized. The AA approach, based on the idea that recovery could only be achieved via total abstinence seemed to be the most successful response to the mysterious allergy. This implied that the AA theory must be correct. It was also borne out by Jellinek's work, the major scientific account of alcoholism. Medical treatment had been legitimized and moral censure reduced. In 1951, the World Health Organization (1951) remarked, 'the first essential of the work of the alcoholic dispensary lies in a medical approach, namely the approach to an individual's problems by the physician who offers aid without any implications of moral setting'. In 1956, the American Medical Association resolved to urge hospitals to admit patients diagnosed as having alcoholism equally with other patients. The medical response was basically the same as the AA response, aiming to educate the drinker into accepting that he was an alcoholic and must become totally abstinent. Any other goals were merely peripheral, sidetracking the major problem. The 'real' problem was the drinker's inability to handle alcohol — not the effects of alcohol or the circumstances surrounding the drinking. This implied a rather narrow role for treatment, since the social, psychological and economic circumstances of the drinker seemed of little relevance to the etiology or prognosis of the condition. His illness was the focus of treatment, and the unquestioned goal of this treatment was total abstinence.

Criticism of the Disease Concept

A mere two years after the publication of Jellinek's *Disease Concept of Alcoholism* — the culmination of the concepts outlined so far — another publication disturbed this monolithic view. D.L. Davies (1962) reported that out of a sample of 93 alcoholics, 7 had returned to drinking quite normally after a short period of abstinence in hospital. In itself this might not seem the most startling of results, but it implied the heresy that in some cases, alcoholism might be a transitory condition. To have found just one person who seemed to have recovered from the supposedly incurable allergy would have been sufficient to question the whole corpus of the strict disease model. The paper was not merely a challenge to the belief that alcoholism could only be arrested by total abstinence, rather it was a challenge to the whole *Gestalt* of how alcoholism was conceptualized. Reports with similar findings can be traced from as early as 1944 (Litman 1977) but they were not written by alcohologists of such status as Davies. When he challenged the prevailing theory (albeit without advocating moderate drinking as a treatment goal), those who believed in a strict interpretation of the disease concept were obliged to react. Some of them made the rationalization that the patients who appeared to have recovered could never have been *really* alcoholics in the first place. But the bulk of the criticism generated against this paper was based on genuine fears that it might induce abstinent alcoholics to return to drinking in the forlorn belief that they might not necessarily revert to uncontrolled alcoholism. They believed this would undermine the existing response, which aimed to influence drinkers to accept the identity of being an alcoholic and to accept that this meant their only hope of recovery lay in lifelong total abstinence. To people who genuinely held this view, a slogan like 'don't tell me I'm not an alcoholic' was not meant facetiously and the publication of reports purporting to show that some alcoholics could return to normal drinking only seemed to make their task of education and treatment more difficult than it was already. Those who did not believe a true alcoholic could ever regain control over his drinking became all the more vehement in their claims that the alcoholic had a permanent illness for which there was no cure. 'An alcoholic who has not touched liquor for 20 years is just as much an alcoholic as he ever was. To tell such a person that he does not have an incurable and fatal disease is absolute madness' (Morse and Gordon).

Yet despite this outcry, criticism of the disease concept continued to grow.

From a historical viewpoint, we can see this was really no surprise for it had happened before. Whilst the well-publicized upsurge of Alcoholics Anonymous made it appear an entirely new approach based on the 'discovery' of the disease nature of alcoholism, we have seen that this particular interpretation of alcohol abuse had a history that was much more long-standing. And just as before, the increased currency of the disease concept was soon accompanied by growing opposition. But whereas the nineteenth century opposition had been moralistic, the opposition in the 1960s and 70s developed from a more rational critique. This critique has pursued two major issues. First, doubts grew about the validity of the characteristics typically attributed to alcoholics and these have been subjected to scientific examination. Second, doubts grew as to whether the response based on the disease concept was as therapeutically successful or as socially beneficial to the drinker as had been supposed. Two questions therefore became asked of the disease theory of alcoholism — was it valid? — and was it useful?

(1) *Was the Disease Theory of Alcoholism Valid?*

The disease theory was based on two prime assumptions. First, the alcoholic was perceived as being inherently different from other types of drinker — 'either you are one or you are not'. (Morse and Gordon). Second, the alcoholic's inability to control his consumption was a permanent inability which meant his only hope of recovery lay in life-long total abstinence; he could never return to normal drinking.

(i) *Were there Distinct Differences between the Alcoholic and the Non-alcoholic?* When samples of people diagnosed as alcoholics were compared with samples of people not diagnosed as alcoholics, there was only equivocal evidence of inherent differences between the two. Compared to other drinkers, diagnosed alcoholics tend to display a higher prevalence of social and psychiatric pathology, a different style of drinking behaviour and a higher baseline of average consumption. But as Chapter 1 noted, excessive drinking is in any case likely to be associated with vitamin deficiency, increased tolerance to alcohol, more severe withdrawal symptoms, increased guilt, increased social problems and so on. The bad effects of alcohol, which develop as consumption increases, cannot be interpreted as 'proof' that all excessive drinkers have some peculiar personality or physiological makeup in the first place. Studies purporting to demonstrate the distinguishing physiological characteristics of alcoholics have been further questioned (Lester 1966) because most of the studies have had no control groups, and even when they had, these groups were not usually matched on such variables as diet, weight and age, which as Chapter 1 demonstrated, considerably determine the physiological and psychological effects of alcohol. Some supporters of the theory of a metabolic allergy to alcohol have even gone as far as claiming alcoholism might be hereditary, on the grounds that many diagnosed alcoholics have alcoholic parents. But this is a rather dubious 'proof'. We have seen that children of excessive drinkers are exposed to many factors which make them a vulnerable group — emotional disturbance, possible damage through being assaulted by parents, poor diet, poor health through financial difficulties and so forth. Using alcohol as a response to these difficulties might also be learned rather than inherited from parents, just as the spouses of excessive drinkers sometimes begin to drink heavily themselves. So whilst an individual's risk of developing drinking problems must be partly determined by genetic factors, such as liver characteristics and factors effecting the bodily metabolism of alcohol, there is no good evidence to show that the genetic characteristics of diagnosed alcoholics constitute a hereditary allergy or any specific metabolic abnormality.

There have also been equally exhaustive and equally unsuccessful searches to discover evidence of a 'pre-alcoholic personality' — a psychopathic predisposition to become an alcoholic. Such predispositions have sometimes been linked with repressed homosexuality, fixation at the oral stage of development, 'inadequate personality' and various other personality traits. Again, these factors may be important in individual cases, but there is no conclusive evidence that any specific personality traits differentiate alcoholics from other types of drinker.

Thus, the initial hypothesis of a distinct difference between alcoholics and non-alcoholics has tended to mellow into a more sophisticated view of a continuum of alcohol abuse. This trend was encouraged in the 1960s and 70s by survey data which supported the idea that the characteristics of persons diagnosed as alcoholics were at the extreme end of a continuum rather than distinctly different. For general population surveys began to discover people with drinking problems who did not seem to fit the picture of the alcoholic built up by AA and by clinical studies.

Room (1977) characterized this discrepancy as 'the two worlds of alcohol problems — the world of the highly damaged alcoholic who came up in the early research, and the world of the people in general population surveys who did not seem to be 'real' alcoholics but who nevertheless seemed to have significant problems. It was suggested that perhaps most of the work done before the 1960s had been conducted on a rather exclusive category of drinker. For virtually all the authoritative books and papers which had outlined the concepts of alcoholism, its characteristics and its phases of development, had been written by members of AA or by psychiatrists. As soon as other disciplines began to investigate the condition, anomalies in the picture started to appear. Was it that the alcoholism syndrome described by AA and by psychiatrists was a description only of some chronically damaged drinkers? Perhaps this was why the phases and symptoms which these respondents reported were not directly replicated when a cross-section of drinkers was studied.

There was further suspicion that the earlier data were based on samples which were not even representative of all chronically-damaged drinkers. Descriptions of alcoholism had been based on populations such as AA members and inmates of prisons and hospitals. Their experiences were possibly atypical. Even that part of Jellinek's work which defined much that was thought about diagnostic patterns was only based on retrospective questionnaires from Alcoholics Anonymous members. Since many other respondents did not return their question-naires, it was quite possible that this information was unrepresentative even of Alcoholics Anonymous members, let alone of all drinkers with problems.

(ii) *Was the Concept of Loss of Control Valid?* The most literal inter-pretation of the notion of 'one drink, one drunk' would be that if an alcoholic had a single drink it would trigger off a compulsive urge to drink more. However, Parades *et al*. (1969) found that in an experi-mental situation, a single drink did not necessarily make alcoholic patients feel a compulsive need for more alcohol. Neither have experi-ments supported the view that when alcoholics start drinking, they will always try to rapidly achieve a state of stupefied oblivion. The work of Mello and Mendelson (1965, 1966, 1970) indicated rather that alcoholic patients drank until they had achieved a high blood alcohol concentration, where upon they titrated further consumption to main-tain that level. This would suggest excessive drinkers do not so much 'lose control' as drink large amounts to overcome their tolerance to alcohol, as explained in Chapter 1.

Mello and Mendelson concluded that there was little clinical or scientific utility in the concept of 'loss of control'. Even experts who have supported the disease concept have come to admit that the idea of loss of control has a 'hazy borderline' (Glatt 1973). Others have rejected the idea altogether (Merry 1966) and criticized it for drawing attention away from the complex questions of why and when the alcoholic drank, or felt a pressure to drink. By itself, the idea of 'loss of control' could not account for variations in the intensity of craving. It did not explain why 'dedicated clinicians find themselves betrayed by seemingly sincere alcoholics, who while hospitalized, professed resolu-tions of abstinence but who, upon discharge immediately fall off the wagon' (Ludwig and Wihler 1974). It has been hypothesized that per-haps craving is put off by the hospital setting but returns when the drinker is re-exposed to the settings and cues associated with reinforce-ments to drink. Upon returning to his usual environment, alcohol immediately resumes its symbolic power and triggers 'uncontrollable' reactions. Perhaps also the social expectations, difficulties and worries related to drinking behaviour and motivations for drinking are temporarily suspended in hospital. But if these factors are important in the drinker's sense of control over his consumption, then the phenomenon is not simply explicable in terms of traits internal to the drinker. This has been emphasized by the other side of the coin – that when return to the environment is accompanied by improvements in life style, such as marriage and changed occupation, then some patients seem able to resume a pattern of moderate drinking. This has been demonstrated in a five-year follow-up programme in Canada (Levinson 1975) and indeed the idea was implicit in Davies (1962). There was nothing distinctive about the characteristics of his patients who returned to social drinking except that significant social changes had occurred after discharge.

Subsequent to his paper, various studies have shown that between 5 per cent and 15 per cent of diagnosed alcoholics revert to normal drinking. By the 1970s the Sobells could compile a list of over 70 scientific papers which reported normal drinking in recovered alcoholics (Levinson 1977). In the epidemiological field, Drew (1968) concurred that the diagnosis of alcoholism seemed to disappear with increasing age. Again not a new idea – the man who invented the word 'alcoholic' once remarked himself that 'it is a rare exception to meet an alcoholic who is over 60 years of age' (Drew 1968). Although this can be partly attributable to mortality and morbidity, there may be other reasons for reduction in consumption, such as the lesser financial resources of elderly people.

In conclusion, then, there is no good evidence to support a strict disease theory of alcoholism. Extensive research has failed to find an all or nothing distinction between alcoholics and others, or any biochemical or personality defect which makes some people unable to control their drinking. The evidence of 'loss of control' is equivocal, whilst there is growing evidence that a proportion of people diagnosed as alcoholics can revert to more moderate drinking behaviour.

(2) *Is the Disease Theory of Alcoholism useful?*

Although the disease theory cannot be proven scientifically, some believe that it should still be retained because of its pragmatic utility. After all, as Hore (1977) has remarked, the onus is still on those attacking the use of the disease concept to prove there is an alternative approach – 'it will require convincing data to be produced to show in practical terms in relation to the physically addicted subject that the experience of the last thirty years should be abandoned and treatment aims altered'. Because the alternatives have not been proved sufficiently, a major debate has arisen over the therapeutic and social implications of defining alcoholism as an illness. It has been recognized that the disease label has certain clinical and political advantages; that it seems to explain, it seems more sympathetic to call a person ill than to censure him as immoral or weak willed, it seems more appropriate to deal with him in a hospital than in courts and prisons, it seems to get him more sympathy from his family and associates. But it has also been pointed out that there may be an even greater catalogue of disadvantages.

First, there are disadvantages for the therapeutic response. The disease model gives the false impression that alcoholism has an agreed etiology and an appropriate treatment for each stage of severity. Doctors can be misled by the semantic inference and slip into responding to alcoholism as if it were a somatic condition, especially as 'medical education is still heavily biased . . . by emphasis on demonstrable change, so that the approach to alcoholism is through pharmacology and pathology, thus by-passing the psychological and sociological effects of what is essentially a socio-medical problem' (Davies 1973).

Conceptualizing alcoholism as a biochemical anomaly assumes its pathology can be irradicated simply in terms of abstinence. Pattison's review has shown that even total abstinence over a period of years is not in itself proof of improvement in the patient's general health and functioning (Pattison 1966). Nothing may have been done to help the patient deal with the conditions which first caused him to drink excessively. The impact of these causative factors may re-emerge in other forms such as psychiatric complaints, or heavy smoking and gambling, but more frequently, into a relapse back into drinking. The disease model's assumption that the only causes of alcoholism lie within the drinker averts attention from the circumstances surrounding his drinking and precludes both comprehensive treatment and adequate support during rehabilitation.

The impression that alcoholism is a disease with an agreed-on medical response not only misleads those making the response. Patients informed that they have been diagnosed as alcoholics sometimes expect to be 'cured' by some straight-forward treatment or even by a course of tablets. Others find the idea that their condition is incurable to be really rather attractive, since it provides an alibi for not altering their behaviour. The disease model can become a self-fulfilling prophecy in which the drinker who is told he has no control over his drinking then uses it as an excuse to go on drinking. He can deny responsibility for his condition and rationalize his continued drinking on the grounds that he

'can't help it'. If a drinker is repeatedly informed he will feel compelled
to drink to oblivion after one drink, he is already half way to com-
plying with that belief. Some alcoholics identify so completely with
their label that they interpret all their experiences as evidence of their
alcoholism. Engle and Williams (1972) for example gave a strongly
flavoured drink containing alcohol to two groups of alcoholics. One
group who were told that it contained alcohol reported greater craving
for more of the drink than the other group who were not told it
contained alcohol. Jellinek himself noted that when AA members were
asked as to whether they experienced certain symptoms classically
associated with alcoholism, a proportion gave falsely positive answers.
It was almost as though they felt obliged that they should have experienced shakes, blackouts and the other traditional symptoms.

Alcoholism – a Stigmatized Illness

On the other hand, some people who have problems with their drinking
find the idea of having an uncontrollable disease so unacceptable that
they do not seek or receive help for their problems. Such unwillingness
to assume the alcoholic identity is usually interpreted as 'denial'. Yet
unwillingness is only to be expected when it is also stressed that the
alcoholic is a very sick person with a strange compulsion to drink,
which makes him completely different from other drinkers. This idea
makes it easy for many excessive drinkers to dissociate themselves from
the idea that they have any problems from their drinking. To quote one
of the author's patients – 'I used to drink two bottles of vodka a day,
but I was never an alcoholic because an alcoholic can't give up.'

The respondents in our 1974 general population survey, and indeed
many of the doctors, social workers and probation officers in the 1974
agency survey used the term 'alcoholic' to refer to a person who was
exceptionally physically, psychologically and socially deteriorated –
someone who was a member of a deviant minority group completely
different from themselves. Respondents thought that alcoholism was
an esoteric condition which the average person would not contract.
People with drinking problems share this common conception, and
therefore are unlikely to accept that they may be a member of an odd
group with the disease of alcoholism. For the label of alcoholic says
something about one's essence, rather than one's experience. It implies
an abnormal physiological or personal make-up. Even in our 1974
hospital patient study only 28 per cent of attenders at an alcoholism
out-patient clinic were prepared to actually call themselves alcoholics.
The view of AA and of many psychiatrists is that nothing can be done

for a drinker unless he accepts that he is an alcoholic, and that he can only arrest his condition by becoming totally abstinent. Others have begun to wonder if this philosophy, even though it certainly helps drinkers who do accept this interpretation, might possibly keep away from help a larger number of drinkers who cannot accept being labelled an alcoholic. This reluctance to accept the label suggests that defining alcoholism as an illness does not preclude a moral stigma. Although it took some commentators quite a while to realise that the disease theory of alcoholism does not necessarily ensure a sympathetic response to a person labelled as an alcoholic, AA recognized from the start that the alcoholic was actually rarely accepted as blameless, and the Big Book explained why:

> An illness of this sort — and we have come to believe it an illness — involves those about us in a way no other human sickness can. If a person has cancer all are sorry for him and no one is angry or hurt. But not so with the alcoholic illness, for with it there goes annihilation of all the things worthwhile in life. It engulfs all whose lives touch the sufferers. It brings misunderstanding, fears, resentment, financial insecurity, disgusted friends and employers, warped lives of blameless children, sad wives and parents — anyone can increase the list. (Alcoholics Anonymous, 1939, 1955).

One alcoholic recalls this personally — 'I remember very well the reaction among some of my closest friends. It was almost violent . . . derision, denial, anger, endless proof that I could not be an alcoholic' (Morse and Gordon).

When our 1974 population sample were asked whether they agreed or not with a series of attitude statements about alcoholics and alcoholism, 73 per cent agreed that 'alcoholism is a disease', but 32 per cent also agreed that 'alcoholics are degenerate'. Thus some of the people who thought alcoholics were sick also thought they were degenerate. In our 1974 agency survey, GPs were less likely than either probation officers or social workers to disagree with the statement that 'alcoholics are degenerate', but they were the most likely to see alcoholism as a disease.

The AA observation that the label of alcoholism denotes a sickness but that it also provokes resentment and disgust has been accentuated by the development of a stereotypical image developed by public slang about the 'wino' and the 'alkie', and by the prejudices emphasized by mass media. Films like the *Lost Weekend* and *Days of Wine and Roses*

have depicted the alcoholic indulging in outrageous behaviour. On
television, documentaries and plays have tended to concentrate particularly on the vagrant alcoholic, such as the BBC's *Edna the Inebriate
Woman*. Newspaper articles, in line with their continual portrayal of
mental illness within a context of 'shock' and 'sin', have usually over-
played the more melodramatic aspects of alcohol abuse, with stories
such as 'Horror of the Teenage Alcoholic'.*

In the view of many alcohol specialists, these images give people
with no first-hand experience of drinkers a totally inaccurate view. For
example, vagrant alcoholics, at least in Britain, do not comprise even as
much as 5 per cent of all the people who have been diagnosed by
doctors as alcoholics. In the experience of one of Britain's largest
counselling services 'the crude spirit-drinking alcoholic forms only 2 per
cent of those suffering from alcoholism who have come under the
(Council's) notice over a period of nine years', and the Council's
Director has noted that 'because of the false image and the stigma that
attaches to the very word "alcoholic", there is a reluctance by those
affected to come forward and a natural tendency to conceal the illness'.
(Kenyon 1972). Therefore the very word 'alcoholic', because of its
connotations, can actually prevent people getting help. The drinker's
behaviour must be gross and his condition debased before the label of
alcoholic can be applied or accepted. Because drinking is considered
normal and many of its effects, like mood change, tranquillization, and
euphoria are expected and valued, its potential bad effects have been
by and large discounted. So people are only defined as being harmed
by drinking when its bad effects are exceptionally obvious and the
damage is of a very developed and severe nature.

This has a corollary with other sociological and psychological studies
of peoples' attitudes to deviance. For example, Cumming and
Cumming's (1955) study of attitudes to the mentally ill in a Canadian
prairie town noted that 'the existance of abnormal behaviour is denied
as long as possible; when denial is no longer feasible, the degree of
abnormality is exaggerated and the ill person is isolated socially and
conceptually'. Exaggerated abnormality leading to conceptual isolation
recurs particularly in mass media. Films and newspapers usually stigmatize the person who has once been in a mental hospital as retaining an
underlying atavism of their illness which renders them unpredictable
and prone to sudden outbursts of erratic behaviour. Writers and readers
of newspapers do not seem to believe that a murderer defined at one

* *News of the World*, 8 August 1971.

time as having been insane could ever actually fully regain his self-control. The general public tend to take the view that such people should be permanently imprisoned as 'you never know' when they will lose control of themselves again. The corollary is obvious between the popular ideas that 'once mad, always mad', and 'once an alcoholic, always an alcoholic'. And 45 per cent of our 1974 population sample said they believed that 'alcoholics are more dangerous than other people'.

Alcoholism Stigmatized – Alcohol Excused

If people have problems from their drinking, their image of alcoholics as down-and-outs or compulsive drinkers may prevent them seeking help from services labelled as being for alcoholics. So other labels have been invented to describe people on the way to becoming alcoholics, or having problems of a less severe type. These terms include 'excessive drinkers', 'heavy drinkers', 'problem drinkers', 'alcoholic addicts', and so on. We have seen that none of them could ever really have any set criteria to define their area of behaviour and effects; and in fact none of them have ever really gained much popular credence because the stereotype of the alcoholic had already been too well established. For it is precisely the supposed attributes of the alcoholic – his loss of control, his preoccupation with drink, his likely degenerate appearance, his incurability, which strongly dissociates him in the public mind from other sorts of drinker who might get into trouble. So, for example, the person who repeatedly gets convicted of drunken driving is not usually defined as having 'a drink problem'. Indeed, he will probably receive sympathy from many of his friends and associates because of his 'bad luck' in getting caught. He is not defined as a problem drinker; he is not even defined by many people as a criminal; indeed his behaviour will not even be usually defined as, for example, selfish – although this could be one interpretation made of pleasure seeking which puts other people at risk.

The place of alcohol in much social ritual, its cultural traditions, its strong reinforcements from social groups and mass media and advertising, combined with the lack of education and knowledge about its actual effects, all conspire to ensure people do not define problems like drunken driving as a manifestation of 'alcohol abuse' or as having anything to do with 'alcoholism'. These attitudes will not be easily changed. People get worked up in their opposition to Britain's 'ridiculous' licensing laws, yet will remain completely apathetic to statistics which show, for example, that one fatal automobile accident in three involves alcohol. Somehow to say that in any one year 30,000 Americans are killed on the road because of alcohol seems unreal; it does not mean anything; it has nothing to do with alcohol as we know and use it — a relaxant which creates and enhances pleasurable situations. Most educational pamphlets on the dangers of alcohol demonstrate lists of shock figures showing the extent of the bad effects of alcohol on society. They may show that the annual cost to British industry is £30 million. They may list drunkenness offences or deaths from cirrhosis of the liver. But these facts confront very long-standing endorsements of alcohol too strongly inculcated to allow any easy or rapid change — and certainly not by educational pamphlets and lists of statistics. Alcohol is so much part of our personal and social milieu, our business life and economic structure, and our rituals and ceremonies, that the concept of alcohol as a drug with bad effects seems inappropriate and unrealistic. Accounts of vast amounts of damage it is supposed to cause seem incongruent with what everyone else says and does about drink.

Professional agents share these attitudes too. When dealing with drinkers who present histories of family friction, rent arrears, poor unemployment records, and heavy drinking, the drinking is rarely considered as a potential cause of the other problems.

The Ambiguity in Attitudes to Alcohol Use and Abuse

Yet there remains the ambiguity that some effects of alcohol and certain types of drinking behaviour are not considered acceptable. In our 1974 general population survey, only 5 per cent disapproved of people having a drink, but 78 per cent disapproved of drunkenness, (even though 24 per cent had been drunk at least once in the 12 months prior to interview).

People do not wish to be associated in any way with alcohol abuse. The drinker who 'can take it' is all right; the drinker who 'doesn't know when he's had enough' is an object of scorn and disgust. Our survey also showed such attitudes were related to personal drinking behaviour. The more heavily people reported drinking, then the more likely they were to agree with the statement that abstainers are 'missing out' and are 'unsociable', that 'alcoholics are degenerate', and that 'alcoholism is a disease'. In our 1973 Summer School study, agents were asked what level of consumption they thought would cause problems. Although their estimates varied widely, the higher the amount they reported drinking regularly themselves, the higher the level above which they considered alcohol would cause harm. A doctor who does not drink is more likely to diagnose his patients as alcoholics than a doctor who drinks regularly. One GP on a training course given by the authors was worried if his patients drank two pints of bitter a day. On the other hand, a man asking his GP if it is safe to drink four pints a day might get the reply, 'well, look at me, I drink six pints a day and I'm perfectly all right'. Perhaps it is not just a joke to say that an alcoholic can be defined as someone who drinks more than his doctor. Aware of this difficulty in definition and of even so much as implying a client might have problems from drink, many agents find it undesirable to bring up the topic of drinking. As we shall see in Chapter 6 many feel they are likely to antagonize and embarrass clients by asking them about drinking. Some agents were very blunt about their trepidation — 'There are some people I don't ask or else you get into trouble'.

This reflects a general embarrassment about drinking, a vague unease which makes it something of a taboo subject, or at least a subject hastily passed over. Discussing drinking formally seems as discomforting to some people as discussing sexual topics used to be. The 'facts of life' about sex are now widely known and discussed relatively easily in the home and on the media, but the 'facts of life' about alcohol have undergone no such period of enlightenment. When our 1974 general population sample were asked about their drinking and drinking problems, many felt uneasy, some were plainly embarrassed, and a few refused point blank to be interviewed. In our studies, both lay and professional people said they believed that drinking behaviour was a personal matter subject to the rules of privacy. People can be very defensive about their drinking habits and upon examination will often proffer quotes like 'I only like a couple of drinks' or 'I'm just a social drinker'. Some respondents in our 1974 general population survey defined themselves as 'nondrinkers' and then later in the interview reported having drunk in the seven days prior to interview. Partly this may have been their reaction to a survey which they knew had 'something to do with alcoholism'. They were anxious in case anything they said might implicate them as having problems. After all, they were not sure where the interviewer would draw the line between normal and abnormal drinking or what he would think constituted a 'problem'.

The Agents' Concepts of Alcohol Abuse

The 1974 general community agents' study showed that many agents shared the general public's difficulties in conceptualizing alcohol abuse. Their definitions of alcoholism were no more precise: 'If he smells of alcohol in the surgery he is an alcoholic.' 'He is not an alcoholic if he can give up for a week or two.'

Other agents maintained they would never call a client an alcoholic as 'a matter of principle'. Each general practitioner, social worker and probation officer was asked to distinguish in open-ended fashion between an 'alcoholic' and a 'problem-drinker', and to respond to a series of attitude statements on alcohol problems. Half of the general practitioners defined an 'alcoholic' in terms of 'dependence on alcohol' and 'losing control'. The 'alcoholic ' was 'somebody who must have a drink', who 'couldn't exist without it'. Two-thirds of the general practitioners thought that 'once an alcoholic has taken a drink he cannot stop drinking on that occasion' compared to only one third of probation officers and of local authority social workers. Two-thirds of the general practitioners also believed that 'lifelong abstinence is the only goal in treating alcoholics', compared to half of the probation officers and only a fifth of the local authority social workers. Three-quarters of the general practitioners agreed with the statement that 'alcoholism is a disease' and some believed it was hereditary, though the majority tended to perceive 'alcoholism' as a 'disease' in the sense of either a physical addiction or a mental illness. Only one disagreed with the statement that 'alcoholics drink in order to cope with difficult life situations'.

Only two probation officers felt unable to distinguish an 'alcoholic' from a 'problem drinker' although several believed these may be points on a continuum. Probation officers perceived that 'the real alcoholic has lost all hold of the controls he should have', whilst the 'problem drinker' was seen as being disrupted in function, but still basically 'relating to the world'. Probation officers tended to stress the circumstances affecting the 'alcoholic' and the 'problem drinker'. Virtually all agreed that 'alcoholics drink in order to cope with difficult life situations' and were uncertain about notions of a disease process. Probation officers were less likely to see 'alcoholism' as a problem internal to the 'alcoholic' himself. They were much less likely than general practitioners to agree with such statements as 'the alcoholic continues drinking because alcohol is rewarding' or that 'alcoholics are weak-willed' or 'degenerate'. Probation officers tended to see 'alcoholics' as 'isolated' and 'rejected' and consequently put much more stress than the other agents on the need for therapeutic support.

Local authority social workers were slightly less inclined to relate 'alcoholism' to 'dependence' and made less distinction between 'alcoholics' and 'problem drinkers', although some did feel that the label of 'alcoholic' was more critical and damning than that of 'problem drinker'. Local authority social workers did not tend to agree with the

disease model. Unlike general practitioners, or indeed the general population sample, a third of social workers disagreed that 'alcoholism' was
either a 'disease' or that 'only addicts were alcoholics'. Instead, social
workers thought 'alcoholics' should be defined in terms of their effect
on others. The typical social worker was as concerned with helping
those whom 'alcoholics' affected as with helping 'alcoholics' themselves. Nearly all agreed with the statement that 'the drinking of an
alcoholic can often be understood in terms of the effect it has on other
people'.

The Redundancy of the Concept of Alcoholism

In conclusion, then, the concept of alcoholism can be traced histori-
cally as an idea which became accepted during particular periods
because of its apparent validity and because of the advantages accrued
from labelling it a disease. Some retain the philosophy that there is a
distinct entity called alcoholism which is not simply the very end of a
continuum, but a distinctly different condition from that of other
drinkers. Others have become unsure about the validity of this concept but believe that criticism of it may undermine the response to
drinking problems without furnishing a proven alternative.

From a scientific viewpoint, the disease theory of alcoholism has
begun to seem less and less tenable. We are coming to realize that there
are actually many factors involved in why a person comes to be harmed
by his drinking. It is not good enough scientifically to attribute it to a
personality defect or a biochemical freak, which thousands of pounds'
worth of experimental and clinical research have failed to find. If we
consider all the effects alcohol may have and all the factors which conspire to produce an effect at a particular time, it will be obvious why
the search to find the 'cause' and the wonder 'cure' is futile. It is naive
to look for a single cause when there are really a complex cluster of
causes and it is pointless to enforce a distinction when there are really
degrees and types of harm.

Neither can the advantages of using the concept of alcoholism be
shown to outweigh the disadvantages. It is dubious how far its supposed
advantages actually apply in practice. The concept of alcoholism has
become associated with a stigmatized image which prevents people with
drinking problems seeking or receiving help. It disenfranchises the
potential of non-specialist personnel to respond to drinking problems.
These points are two sides of the same coin. The more esoteric and
mystified are concepts of alcohol abuse, the more damaged drinkers
will have to be before either themselves or agents responding to them

will recognize their problems as being caused by alcohol. The bad effects of alcohol — be they neglect of children, withdrawal effects, becoming overweight or whatever — are not all-or-nothing phenomena; they lie upon continua. Up to now these effects have only been defined as caused by alcohol, and requiring a response, if they were at the extreme ends of the continua. Many problems caused by drinking have been excused or ignored. Neither has the disease concept of alcoholism allowed much opportunity to conceptualize the development of drinking problems or to examine possible means of prevention. Of course, it is still accepted that in certain situations, and with certain drinkers, the notions of alcoholism and lifelong abstinence can be powerful explanatory and therapeutic tools. Many agents will continue to use this approach and at times it will be fatal for the drinker not to comply with a goal of total abstinence. But we need to avoid the dogmatic tendency of previous concepts of alcohol abuse to presume that one explanation or one treatment applies to every case. The balance between the good and bad effects should be discussed rationally in a dispassionate way. For this to happen there is a pressing need for basic information about alcohol and its effects. Without knowledge, people cannot come to their own conclusions. But information given to either public and professionals should not be provided in a manner incongruent with their prior knowledge and preconceptions. These preconceptions will be largely an appreciation of the good effects of alcohol: the euphoria, the conviviality, the taste, and the relief from stress. In the public mind, alcohol is probably associated with more good effects pharmacologically, psychologically and socially than any other drug, or perhaps any other substance of any kind. Alcohol makes it easier for you to talk; it gives you confidence, relaxes you, stops you getting bored; it is associated with camaraderie and good times. Is it any wonder that drinkers instructed to abstain often appear 'poorly motivated' and that it is exceptionally difficult for a drinker to become totally abstinent in a society where the good effects are highly reinforced and the bad effects are largely unknown. But whereas in the case of say, cigarette smoking, the public have at least been duly warned of the effects and given their choice, this same level of knowledge does not apply to alcohol. In France, for instance, the drinking pattern produces a very high rate of alcohol-related liver damage. But in one survey there, three quarters of respondents said they believed alcohol was good for their health and a quarter thought it was 'indispensable' (Bastide 1954).

Much popular belief about the effects of alcohol is quite erroneous, but this should not be rectified by any scare campaign. Moreover, the analogy between education about smoking and drinking is only tenuous. Drinking alcohol has a much more extensive tradition of acceptance and approval. The required change in attitude is immense. Education about the possible range of the good and bad effects of alcohol will be hampered by two further factors.

First, interpreting alcohol use and abuse in terms of multifactorial cause and effect is complex to conceptualize and difficult to explain succinctly. The description of the effects of alcohol comprising various types and degrees of severity can appear less definite than the relatively concise view of alcoholism as an all-or-nothing condition with distinguishing characteristics. It is unfortunate, but people often prefer to deal with standardized categorizations and convenient labels rather than consider problems in their real complexity.

Second, there is still widespread belief in the idea that alcohol abuse is qualitatively different from alcohol use, and should be considered as an illness. By the second half of the 1970s this belief had diversified into three versions. First, there was still much popular acceptance of the strict disease theory that alcoholics were distinguished by a permanent psychological or genetic 'loss of control', which meant their only means of recovery lay in total abstinence. The fervent conviction with which many people in America still maintained this view was demonstrated in 1976 by the reaction to the publication of the Rand Report (Armor *et al.* 1976). Its inclusion of some data on persons diagnosed as alcoholics who had reverted back towards a pattern of less excessive drinking provoked a wave of vehement opposition decrying the report as misleading, irresponsible and dangerous. A second and somewhat less intractable form of the disease theory developed in the 1970s amongst those who did accept the growing evidence that some persons diagnosed at one time as alcoholics might return to normal drinking. They also recognized that the supposedly distinctive characteristics of alcoholism could not be sharply defined. Nevertheless, they still considered that the most common trait amongst people with serious drinking problems was an inability to control alcohol intake and that the basic treatment goal of total abstinence should be retained, since no firm prediction could be made as to which patients might be able to return to normal drinking. This watered-down version of the disease theory has tended to devolve still further into a third view of alcohol abuse as an illness, based on the concept of 'dependence' on alcohol. Since the influential figures in this movement have been almost exclusively members of the medical profession, one could perhaps interpret this trend as an attempt to maintain an essentially medically-oriented explanation of drinking problems whilst seeming to disown the more contentious aspects of the disease theory.

The Concept of Dependence on Alcohol

At one time, the notion of dependence on alcohol tended to be restricted to the idea of psychological dependence, involving such concepts as 'compulsion', 'craving' and the pathological 'need' to drink. Dependence tended to be distinguished from the physiological aspects which were referred to as 'addiction'. However, the concept of dependence has gradually broadened its scope, encompassing physiological, psychological and even social dimensions. The increased coinage of the term 'dependence' was confirmed in 1972 when the Criteria Committee of the American National Council on Alcoholism 'was unanimous in defining the disease of alcoholism as a pathological dependence on ethanol' (National Council on Alcoholism 1972), and advanced in 1976 when the World Health Organization (WHO) discarded the concept of alcoholism in favour of the idea of the 'alcohol dependence syndrome'. Although definitions of dependence have varied as widely as definitions of alcoholism, the WHO classification deserves special consideration since it represents the most concerted attempt to delineate and formally support the use of the term 'dependence' and their terminology will, as noted by one reviewer, 'influence attitudes and services for many years'. (Evans 1977). It is unfortunate, then, that the concept of alcohol dependence retains many of the disadvantages and questionable assumptions intrinsic to the concept of alcoholism which it purports to replace.

First, the 'alcohol dependence syndrome' has been clearly promoted as a disease. It was included in the ninth revision of the International Classification of Diseases approved by the twenty-ninth World Health Assembly in 1976, officially coming into force in January 1979 (World Health Organization 1977). The 'alcohol dependence syndrome' under which 'alcoholism' was listed as an inclusion term, was defined as

> a state, psychic and usually also physical, resulting from taking alcohol, characterised by behavioural and other responses that always include a compulsion to take alcohol on a continuous or periodic basis in order to experience its psychic effects, sometimes to avoid the discomfort of its absence; tolerance may or may not be present.

Thus not only has dependence been officially defined, like alcoholism, as a disease, but also as a disease that 'always' includes a 'compulsion'

to drink. Moreover the last phrase of the definition also suggests that
the phenomenon of tolerance is not a continuum, but rather a feature
which 'may or may not be present'. Perhaps the definition means to say
that not all 'dependent' persons have a highly developed tolerance to
alcohol, but even so some cut-off point is still implied.

A more thorough attempt to define and justify the concept of the
'alcohol dependence syndrome' was included in the 1977 WHO publication *Alcohol Related Disabilities* (Edwards *et al.* 1977). When compared with 1951 Reports which led to the oft-quoted WHO 1952 definition of alcoholism (World Health Organization 1952), *Alcohol
Related Disabilities* demonstrated how concepts of alcohol abuse had
shifted over those 25 years. The earlier reports had discussed drinking
problems almost entirely by reference to the classic symptoms of
alcoholism such as 'craving' and 'loss of control', and any other alcohol-
related problems had all been included together in a single page en-
titled 'Borderline Problems'. By 1977, the scope and importance of
social and health problems caused by alcohol were seen as much wider
and as requiring a response whether persons experiencing them were
categorized as 'dependent' or not. Nevertheless, the core alcohol-
related disability was still perceived as being the alcohol-dependence
syndrome 'related to what has sometimes been understood by the term
alcoholism or, more closely "alcohol addiction".'

The document argued that the new classification incorporated two
major improvements upon the former concept of alcoholism. First, it
was asserted that the concept of dependence was supported by scientific
evidence; second, that the idea of a syndrome allowed for the conceptualization of phenomena as existing in clusters and degrees.

The Scientific Evidence of Dependence

The syndrome was conceived as a triad of 'altered psycho-biological
state', 'altered behavioural state' and 'altered subjective state'. The
altered psycho-biological state basically referred to the phenomena of
tolerance, withdrawal and reinstatement after abstinence which we have
already described in Chapter 1. The altered behavioural state generally
referred to the changing pattern of drinking behaviour, also described in
Chapter 1, which gradually develops as tolerance increases and withdrawal symptoms become more noticeable. However, the altered subjective state referred to the ambiguous concepts discussed in this
present chapter, namely: (i) 'loss of control' – the classic symptom of
alcoholism, (ii) 'craving' and (iii) 'drink centredness'. So although
dependence was presumed to comprise three types of 'altered state' the

key concept of the disease theory of alcoholism — 'loss of control' — was retained as the key concept of the alcohol dependence syndrome. It was stated that the syndrome 'might be defined simply as a disability marked by impaired capacity to control alcohol intake', and that the 'leading symptom' of the syndrome was an 'impaired control of intake of the drug ethyl alcohol'.

Since the reader has seen that the evidence for the distinct existence of 'loss of control' is equivocal and that some experts have declared the concept to be of little scientific or clinical utility, he may begin to wonder how impaired control can be touted as the 'leading symptom' of the alcohol dependence syndrome and how it can be claimed that 'the reality and significance of the syndrome seem to be well supported by a review of present evidence'. This claim presumably referred largely to Gross's review of research (Gross 1977), which was indeed a most thorough and careful account — but only of the altered physiological states of levels of tolerance and withdrawal, and reinstatement of these levels after abstinence. In effect, the evidence about these phenomena was inferred to be a validation of the alcohol-dependence syndrome *en bloc*. Thus any rejection of the other concepts included in the alcohol dependence syndrome, such as 'loss of control' would come to appear as a rejection of evidence of the processes of tolerance and withdrawal. It was stated, for example, that 'the alcohol-dependence syndrome is a psycho-biological reality, not an arbitrary social label'. But while it is perfectly reasonable to claim that tolerance, withdrawal and reinstatement of these after abstinence are a 'psycho-biological reality' — no one would seriously argue otherwise — it is much less justifiable to claim that 'a diminished variability in the individual's drinking behaviour' or 'drinking . . . no longer in accord with cultural expectations' are also psycho-biological realities whose definitions involve no element of arbitrariness. As for the evidence of the altered subjective state, the document admitted 'it is often difficult to relate this material satisfactorily to the biological level of explanation or to translate it into formal psycho-logical concepts'. It was not considered that this may be because concepts such as 'loss of control' are not in themselves so much existent phenomena as rather interpretations of experience.

An Alternative Interpretation of Impaired Control
Drinkers may come to believe they have lost control over their drinking because their increasing tolerance and increasing withdrawal effects compound their original (often subconscious) motives for drinking. For example, a woman might sense she is competing with her husband's job

for his time and attention. On occasions she may confront his indifference or force him to attend to her by getting drunk. In reaction to this he may become embarrassed and repelled and avoid her even more or stop taking her out. In consequence she may begin to get drunk with increasing regularity. Simultaneously, the regularity and heaviness of the drinking will increase her tolerance to alcohol and in order to become drunk she will gradually have to consume more and more alcohol. Additionally, she may begin to suffer more severe withdrawal symptoms and the desire to ward off or to relieve some of these symptoms may become a further motivation for increased consumption. At this point, according to the WHO criteria she could be classified as suffering from the alcohol-dependence syndrome, but this would be little explanation of how or why she had got herself into this position, and presuming her 'impaired control' of alcohol to be her 'leading symptom' might well confuse the issue. Of course, if she were not intellectually conscious of her real reasons for continually getting drunk, then because her increasing tolerance and experience of increasingly severe withdrawal effects would gradually mean she had to consume more and more to become drunk or to ward off withdrawal, it might indeed appear to her that she was beginning to become unable to 'control' her amount of intake. Even if she managed to abstain for a while, upon drinking again her high tolerance level and severe withdrawal effects would be rapidly reinstated, thus forcing her very quickly after resuming drinking to return to a very high consumption level. She might appear again to have 'lost control', 'proving' that 'alcoholics' or those suffering from the 'alcohol-dependence syndrome' cannot manage to drink normally for any length of time. But this interpretation would mystify the development of her drinking problems. It would prevent a more thorough investigation into the dynamics of the marital relationship, the place of drinking within it, the level of her tolerance and the severity of her withdrawal symptoms.

Alternative interpretations might also be made of the woman's subjective feelings of a 'compulsion' to drink. Her feelings of subjective dependency would be taken by the theories of alcoholism or of the alcohol dependence syndrome to be an explanation in itself for her drinking behaviour and to be the cause of her high consumption. An alternative interpretation might be that her sense of being compelled to drink was rather her experience of having to drink increasingly more because of her marital situation and her increasing tolerance and withdrawal, when simultaneously she was intellectually aware of the bad effects of alcohol and felt that it might be better for her if she did not

drink or at least drank less. For it is only possible to experience a
'compulsion' to do something if at the same time there is a feeling one
ought not to do it. To consider her 'compulsion to drink' or her 'loss of
control' as an explanation in itself is possibly interpreting a symptom
to be a cause. On the other hand, to say that she was at a certain level
of tolerance, experiencing a certain severity of withdrawal and that these
developed interactively with certain dynamics within her reasons for
drinking, would begin to make some scientific and therapeutic sense.
Merely adding on the classification of whether or not she was 'dependent' would be unnecessary in a thorough interpretation.

Even if one encompassing word were required for pragmatic convenience, 'dependence' would be an unfortunate choice. It imparts a
misleading semantic emphasis to the development of the tolerance and
withdrawal. For in a commonsense way, to say someone is 'dependent'
on something implies that they rely on it, that they use it as a crutch
to cope with the stresses of life. But this is only one of many reasons
why a person may use alcohol. To subsume all possible reasons under
the umbrella of dependence implies that all persons who develop a
high tolerance and experience severe withdrawal do so because they
have some 'need' for alcohol to cope. This is conceptually inappropriate.
Drinking to achieve some good effect of alcohol is conceptually distinct
from being tolerant to alcohol so that more alcohol is needed to achieve
and maintain these desired good effects. In assessment, motivation for
drinking should be distinguished from increasing tolerance and increasing withdrawal, which are both effects of alcohol consumption, although
simultaneously factors leading to increasing consumption.

It is difficult then to accept the WHO's opinion that 'there can be
little doubt that scientifically the most apt designation of the basic
condition under discussion is alcohol dependence', not just because the
document tells us on the same page that 'science is in no position to
classify alcohol dependence as a condition of known etiology, established pathology and determined natural history', but because the concept of dependence presumes subjective experiences to be the 'leading
symptom' and the focus of assessment and treatment, rather than the
dynamic process which led to the drinker experiencing a sense of loss
of control.

Is Dependence Conceptualized as a Continuum?

The second claimed advantage of the alcohol-dependence syndrome
over the parent concept of alcoholism was that the notion of a syndrome disowns that the characteristics of the dependent drinker are an

all-or-nothing phenomenon. Rather, it was suggested that the different elements of dependency exist in clusters and degrees and types of severity. It was claimed that the term syndrome 'has the advantage of emphasizing the openness of the position that has been taken . . . it is implicit only that a number of phenomena tend to cluster with sufficient frequency to constitute a recognizable occurrence'. 'We are dealing with gradients rather than all or none alterations'. Yet other statements in the document contradicted this assertion and ambiguously implied that the alcohol-dependence syndrome was an all or none phenomenon. For 'the complete description of an individual's alcohol-related pathology comprises . . . a statement as to whether *he is* or *is not* suffering from the dependence syndrome (with added description of degree of dependence and any modification of the picture)' and 'the alcohol-related disabilities of any individual are susceptible to the same multifactorial analysis whether that person *is* or *is not* alcohol dependent'. The WHO stated (quite rightly) that terms and labels such as 'problem drinker' were of only 'spurious concreteness','but they did not perceive a statement as to whether a person was or was not dependent to be of equally spurious concreteness. Alcohol-related disabilities, it seemed, required multi-factorial analysis, but when it came to being dependent, the drinker must be classified as all or nothing, dependent or not. How could we say whether or not a person was or was not dependent? What, for example, constitutes the cut-off point at which a psycho-biological state can be defined as 'altered'? Any amount of alcohol consumption will have some kind of withdrawal effect. Anyone who drinks fairly regularly might increase his tolerance to some degree. Is a symptom such as 'craving' a category of feeling which people either experience or do not experience? It may be that most people crave for alcohol at some time and under certain circumstances. Some people crave alcohol a little and rarely, others crave a lot and often, whilst the majority are distributed somewhere in between.

How then did the WHO propose it was possible to determine whether or not a person was dependent? Their solution was never made formally explicit, but was nevertheless inferred throughout the document — and this inference most clearly exposed the association between the theory of the alcohol-dependence syndrome and the disease theory of alcoholism. Both implied that the assessment and response to a drinking problem came primarily under medical jurisdiction. Like alcoholism, the alcohol-dependence syndrome was something from which one 'suffers'; it was 'diagnosed' and required 'treatment'. So while alcohol-related disabilities — including social problems, marital dis-

harmony, and so forth, were deemed amenable to classification, it was
assumed that the decision as to whether a person was dependent or not
was not so amenable, and the decision about categorization had to be
left to 'intuitive', 'clinical judgement'.

The document stated that,

> There may be something of a contradiction between the needs of
> administrative convenience (the setting up of simple rules and
> classifications), and the habitual manner in which clinicians approach
> the individual case in terms of an intuitive interactive analysis . . . It
> seems premature to propose cut-off points and more reasonable to
> suggest that a clinical judgement be made. The physician should also
> make the assessment of a possible prodromal condition.

Although it was accepted that the description and classification of disabilities related to alcohol consumption should include 'what might be
termed social diagnosis', the diagnosis of the alcohol-dependence syndrome itself — 'a profound and central disability' was considered the
preserve of clinical judgement. In effect the concept of the alcohol-
dependence syndrome discriminated against the ability of non-medical
agents to recognize and understand the effects of alcohol described in
Chapter 1, viz, the development of tolerance to alcohol, withdrawal from
alcohol, reinstatement of tolerance and withdrawal after abstinence,
associated patterns of drinking behaviour and physiological, psychological and social effects of increasing tolerance and withdrawal. Yet
surely agents such as social workers, counsellors or community nurses,
given appropriate training and experience could be perfectly capable of
recognizing that a client had a high tolerance to alcohol and was
experiencing severe withdrawal symptoms and that these phenomena
were altering his drinking behaviour and his 'subjective state'. Indeed,
in the hypothetical case of the woman described above, a community
agent such as a social worker might well be in a more advantageous
position than, say, a hospital psychiatrist, to also observe and understand the marital dynamics which interactively contributed to the
woman's drinking problems. Factors such as marital problems, which
may lead to the development of drinking problems, are obscured and
neglected because the 'leading symptom' of dependence, as of alcoholism, is considered to be 'impaired control'. The preoccupation with
'impaired control' mystifies the interactive process which leads to this
subjective feeling being experienced. It diverts attention away from the
causes and development of drinking problems and concentrates treat-

ment efforts upon the experience of impaired control rather than upon the reasons why such impairment came to be experienced.

This is not to deny that some drinkers feel 'compelled' to drink or believe they have 'lost control' over their drinking, but the concern should be to discover why they experience these sensations, rather than to accept these feelings as explanations in themselves of why the drinker consumes alcohol in the way he does. Neither would a more interpretative view of 'impaired control' necessarily mean that all drinkers would be able to regain a feeling of 'control' over their drinking. If the drinking behaviour of the woman in the example above was so channelled by the dynamics of her marriage that she perceived getting drunk to be the major good effect of alcohol, and if her tolerance was so high that to achieve this desired state of drunkenness would mean consuming very large quantities on most drinking occasions, then it would be unlikely that this woman could be helped to return to more moderate drinking since this would not satisfy her motivation for drinking. Consuming any less than the high amount she required to become drunk would not achieve the good effect she sought. In this case, it might well be advisable to suggest she became totally abstinent. But this treatment goal of abstinence would then be based upon an interpretation of the woman's motivation for drinking and the effects of alcohol upon her, not upon the arcane conception that her 'loss of control', her 'alcoholism' or her 'dependence on alcohol' inevitably implied that total abstinence was the only possible road to recovery. Neither should abstinence be seen as a goal in itself, for a more comprehensive understanding of the development of her drinking problems would focus on the need to discuss the difficulties within her marriage. Without attention to the problems in the marriage she would be unlikely to remain abstinent for long, or if she did, her marital problems might be translated into some other activity as harmful as excessive drinking. For example, she might escalate her use of other forms of tranquillizer. But if some marital therapy reduced her motivation to become drunk, then her reasons for consuming alcohol might change. She might no longer drink in order to become drunk. If this were so, then it might become possible for her to drink again at lower levels of consumption without experiencing any subjective feelings of wanting to escalate. If her motivation for drinking (not necessarily overt motivation) changed, her subjective experiences of these motivations might also change; she might no longer feel 'compelled' to drink until drunk. An actual example of such a change in subjective experience associated with changing circumstances and reasons for drinking is provided in

Chapter 12. Chapter 3 following develops the argument that responding to drinking problems cannot evolve effectively around concepts such as 'alcoholism' and 'alcohol dependence', and demonstrates how attempts to determine the prevalence of 'alcoholism' have led to similar conclusions about the importance of considering drinking problems on continua, and have also shed more light on the reasons why drinking problems develop. For as this present chapter has suggested, little is explained and much may be ignored by classifying clients as 'alcoholics' or 'dependent on alcohol'. By concentrating primarily on the concept of 'impaired control', we neglect the process leading to the subjective experience of 'impaired control'. When these concepts are challenged and the subjective experiences interpreted as manifestations of a conflict between the good and bad effects of alcohol, it then appears that a more complex but more worthwhile approach would not be to ask, 'Is this client an alcoholic?' and 'Does he suffer from impaired control?', but rather to ask, 'Why does this client drink so much so regularly?', 'How high is his level of tolerance and how severe are his withdrawal symptoms?', 'How are these effects of alcohol exacerbating other problems he may have, which may also be interactively causing him to drink excessively?' and perhaps most important of all, 'What do these assessments suggest would be the most appropriate response to this client?'

PART TWO   DRINKING PROBLEMS: EPIDEMIOLOGY
          AND ETIOLOGY

3 THE PREVALENCE AND CAUSES OF DRINKING PROBLEMS

The previous chapter began by looking at attempts to categorize drinkers into 'types' such as 'normal drinkers' and 'problem drinkers'. This chapter begins by discussing attempts to estimate how many drinkers were in each of these categories. Since we have seen that there have been many different categorizations of types of drinker, none of which have had firmly established criteria, it is not surprising that estimates of the number of drinkers of each 'type' have been equally variable and overlapping. As the WHO noted in 1977 'the extent of problems related to alcohol consumption is difficult to gauge, partly because assessments are often hinged on the term 'alcoholism' whose definition varies widely'. (Edwards *et al.* 1977). In fact, most attempts to estimate the prevalence of drinking problems have just been attempts to estimate the number of 'alcoholics' in the population. But the magnitude of this number has simply depended upon whichever definition of alcoholism was chosen. This was amply illustrated in a survey of a population sample in San Francisco by Clark (1966) who demonstrated how different definitions of alcoholism created all sorts of prevalence rates. A very tight definition of alcoholism produced a rate of 3 per 1,000 but using a variety of indices of alcoholism made the prevalence estimates increase to 62 per 1,000 adults. If all criteria were employed, including indications of drinking problems past or present, moderate or severe, then the prevalence reached an extraordinary 272 per 1,000. Which rate would be the most appropriate measure? A low rate might reflect a limited view of the problem; a high rate might be an exaggeration. The basic difficulty is that there is no distinct point at which alcohol 'use' ends and alcohol 'abuse' begins. The only certainty is that the wider the defining criteria of the problem, the more cases will fit the definition.

This makes it quite difficult to gain some perspective of the size of the problem. In 1975, for instance, the Department of Health and Social Security concluded that 'different surveys indicate that about 400,000 persons in England and Wales (about 11 in every 1,000 of the adult population) have a serious drink problem' (Department of Health and Social Security 1975). In the same year, less than 14,000 persons were admitted into mental hospitals in England and Wales with a primary or secondary diagnosis of alcoholism or alcoholic psychosis. In part, this discrepancy has been created because surveys of general population samples usually determine whether respondents are 'alcoholics' or not by asking them if they have experienced any of a list of a dozen or so problems associated with drinking, such as getting into fights after drinking or having shaky hands the morning after drinking. Some number of these problems is then arbitrarily declared the cut-off point between alcoholics and non-alcoholics so that any respondent who reports having experienced, say, 5 or more of these problems is defined as an 'alcoholic' whilst anyone reporting less than five is 'normal'. It is doubtful how far people defined as 'alcoholics' by such a method are comparable to people admitted to mental hospitals for alcoholism treatment, since the latter often have a longish history of many severe interrelated problems from drinking. Although some overlap probably occurs, it would be almost certainly alarmist to project results of survey prevalences as evidence that there is some enormous hidden population that resembles people in treatment for alcoholism in every way except for their not being in treatment. Rather, the discrepancy between the size of the survey-defined alcoholic population and the clinically-defined alcoholic population showed that throughout Britain there were probably many thousands of people experiencing various alcohol-related problems who were not recognized by doctors or other agencies as having alcohol-related problems and who were not counted in numbers of 'alcoholics'.

The inconsistency and confusion in assessments of the prevalence of drinking problems put epidemiologists — scientists who specialize in assessing the prevalence of diseases — into a rather delicate position. The different measures of the number of alcoholics were widely discrepant and research failed to find any precise distinctions between the different categories of drinker. Yet there remained the practical necessity of estimating the extent of problems of alcohol abuse in order to design a proper and adequate response. This dilemma attracted some epidemiologists to an alternative perspective which appeared to override the inconsistencies in definition and the limitations imposed by arbitrary categorizations. For a body of information and analysis began to suggest that whatever the inconsistencies in definition, a very noticeable consistency could be found between the level of alcohol consumption and the extent of alcohol-related problems as indicated particularly by hospital admissions for alcoholism, drunkenness arrests and deaths from liver cirrhosis. Over the years, this relationship has gradually appeared to tie in more and more with the scientific erosion of the theory that the causes of drinking problems lay in physiological or psychological predisposition. Epidemiology began to compile evidence which seemed to suggest that the cause of alcoholism lay not in the drinker but in the drink.

Consumption and Problems

The level of alcohol consumption in a society is usually expressed in terms of per capita consumption – the amount drunk by the average person. Firstly, the total consumption of a society as indicated by production and sales figures is translated into an equivalent volume of absolute alcohol, as explained in Chapter 1. Per capita consumption is then simply derived by dividing the total national consumption of absolute alcohol by the number of people in the adult population.

The relationship between the level of per capita consumption and the prevalence of alcohol related problems was first noticed in periods when the availability of alcohol was suddenly reduced. Per capita consumption dropped markedly and so did all the rates of alcohol-related problems. This pattern was well illustrated in Britain during the First World War, when the availability of alcohol was reduced by licensing hours. The consequent reduction in consumption was associated with such a noticeable decline in alcoholic mortality and drunkenness that the Registrar General commented that 'it is difficult to avoid associating the two phenomena (consumption and mortality) as cause and effect' (Wilson 1939). When Mapother (1928) considered the five years following World War I in comparison with the five years which had preceded it, he noted that when consumption was lower between 1918 and 1923, so was the prevalence of alcoholism as indicated by mental hospital admissions and so was the prevalence of polyneuropathy as indicated by general hospital out-patient records. Since 'human nature cannot have changed then other factors, boost, availability and cost must be responsible'. Exactly the same phenomenon was observed in the USA during the Prohibition era when rates of liver cirrhosis were drastically reduced. This received little attention at the time, since the disease concept of alcoholism began to flourish soon after the Prohibition era and Alcoholics Anonymous tried to dissociate themselves from the temperance movement for the reasons discussed in Chapter 2. The general acceptance of the AA view diverted attention from the possibility of prevention and reducing alcohol-related problems by reducing consumption, because AA presumed that the causes of alcohol problems did not lie within consumption but within the biochemistry and personality of individual drinkers. The idea that

overall consumption determined the number of mental hospital admissions for alcoholism did not seem to comply with the popular view
that alcoholism was a permanent affliction. The disease theory could
not accept that the number of alcoholics was affected by national
trends in consumption and certainly not by licensing hours and the
price of alcohol.

After the Second World War, however, the discrepancy between the
disease theory and the epidemiological evidence began to grow wider.
Whereas previously the relationship between consumption and problems had been noticeable when they decreased together, the relationship was noticed after the war because per capita consumption rose in
most post-war societies and invariably this was accompanied by increases in the prevalence of alcohol-related problems.

A particularly strong tradition grew up within French epidemiology
in the 1950s and 60s which related the level of consumption in various
societies to the prevalence of various alcohol-related pathologies such as
pancreatitis, carcinoma of the aesophagus and alcoholic psychosis itself. The higher the amount drunk by the average drinker in a society,
the higher seemed to be the prevalence of these alcohol-related pathologies.

During the 1960s, but more especially the early 1970s, alcohol
consumption and alcohol-related problems accelerated so much in
England and Wales that some commentators talked of an 'alcoholism
explosion' (Merseyside C.A. 1975). Per capita consumption had been
rising markedly throughout the 1960s, increasing 23 per cent between
1960 and 1969. It then took a dramatic upswing, rising 40 per cent
between 1969 and 1974, when it seemed to level off on a new high
plateau. This pattern of increase was thought to be related to falls in
the real price of alcohol as a proportion of disposable income and to
changes in the availability and distribution of alcohol. The number of
public houses actually dropped 2 per cent between 1962 and 1975
(from 65,645 to 64,261), while off licences, including many within
supermarkets, increased 28 per cent (from 24,644 to 31,644) in the
same period – a process begun partly by the 1961 Licensing Act and
accelerated by the ending of price maintenance at the end of the 1960s.

Changes in the prevalence of alcohol-related problems closely
mirrored these trends in the pattern of availability and consumption.
Convictions for drunkenness rose 11 per cent between 1960 and 1969,
then accelerated through a 27 per cent increase between 1969 and
1974. Hospital admissions of persons diagnosed as alcoholics rose 48
per cent in the five years before 1969, but 63 per cent in the five years

following. As consumption stabilized from 1974 onwards, the increases in rates of alcohol-related problems correspondingly decelerated. The number of persons found guilty of drinking and driving had increased an average of 23 per cent annually between 1969 and 1974 (from 23,721 to 56,153) but only increased another 4 per cent (to 58,145) in 1975. Since 1974, convictions for drunkenness itself have remained virtually static at around 21 per cent per 10,000 of the population.

So despite all the vagaries in definition and difficulties in measurement, a clear pattern can be discerned. Both the consumption of alcohol and the prevalence of alcohol-related problems in England and Wales grew steadily throughout the 1960s, increased markedly between 1969 and 1974 and then remained at their newly elevated level. The years in which alcohol consumption increased the most were the same years in which the prevalence of alcohol-related problems increased the most.

Why should this relationship hold so strongly? The French epidemiologist Ledermann (1964) had tried to explain it by a statistical and mathematical theorem which claimed that a population's consumption would always be distributed in the same way with the majority drinking relatively small amounts and successively less and less drinkers consuming larger and larger amounts. Ledermann therefore asserted that an increase in per capita consumption must always represent a general movement of drinkers throughout the population towards heavier drinking. He believed it was this shift to generally heavier drinking which accounted for the observed fact that societies with a higher per capita consumption also had a higher rate of alcohol-related pathologies such as liver cirrhosis. He claimed therefore that a movement of a society to a higher overall consumption must inevitably lead to a higher rate of alcohol-related problems within that society. De Lint and Schmidt (1971) compiled much more evidence to support this theory and concluded that 'the prevalence of alcoholism is invariably determined by the overall level of consumption in the population'. The evidence they collected suggested that the number of people diagnosed as suffering from alcoholism − conceptualized by some as a permanent affliction − actually rose and fell with the amount of alcohol consumed in the society. This suggested that the size of the problem should not be conceived in terms of the number of people who were in some way pathologically inclined to become alcoholics. If there was a relationship between national consumption, individual consumption and problems then we were all, in a way, at risk. De Lint and Schmidt realized that focusing on continua in this way represented a critique of the disease perspective. De Lint (1977) has remarked, for instance, that 'the gradual transition from moderate to excessive consumption agrees very well with the failure thus far to discover real differences in the personality and physiology of the so-called social drinker and the so-called "alcoholic" '. Since De Lint and Schmidt have also indicated that per capita consumption was in turn inversely related to the price and availability of alcohol, it has been hypothesized that a reduction in the availability of alcohol would always reduce per capita consumption and thus reduce the risk of people experiencing alcohol-related problems. This view was supported in 1975 by a review of Public Health Aspects of Alcohol Control Policy prepared by a group of international experts, who concluded that 'our main argument is well substantiated; changes in the overall consumption of alcoholic beverages have a bearing on the health of people in any society'. (Bruun *et al.* 1975). Their version of Ledermann's argument was that alcohol-related health problems were concentrated amongst heavier drinkers and that the greater the average consumption the greater the number of heavy drinkers. They too suggested that the number of heavy drinkers and consequently the number of alcohol-related problems could both be reduced by restricting the availability of alcohol.

It is not particularly surprising that there should be staunch opposition to these theories, most notably from brewers and distillers. They were naturally disinclined to accept the implication that the more alcohol drunk (and the more profits they made) then the more problems alcohol was causing. Brewers and distillers felt more vindicated by the view that there were a deviant group of alcoholics who could not control their drinking and that it was unfair to restrict the drinking of the rest of the population to protect these few. Then there have been other critics without any vested interests. In the mid 1970s statisticians (Miller and Agnew 1974) began to re-examine the mathematical and statistical principles on which the above theories were based and found the underlying assumptions to be rather dubious. Furthermore, when Duffy (1977) examined the distributions of consumption amongst some general population samples, he found they did not comply with the distributions predicted by the Ledermann-based theories. Others have criticized the premise of an inexorable relationship between consumption and problems because of the sheer intuitive unacceptability of a theory which maintained that such a complex matter as the prevalence of alcohol-related problems was really all determined by a single factor, the level of per capita consumption. It did not seem to allow for the individual circumstances of each drinker and for idiosyncratic risks and vulnerabilities.

Despite these criticisms, there remains a wealth of evidence showing a very strong relationship between consumption and problems. If the mathematically and statistically based theories are not valid explanations of the strength of this relationship, there is a need to consider other possible mechanisms operating behind overall national trends. The main shortcoming of the epidemiological approach is that it relies on national statistics without examining the underlying patterns. National trends might be made up of quite different patterns amongst different groups and individuals. Without studying general population samples, we cannot find out, for example, if consumption increased in England and Wales because heavy drinkers started to drink even more or because the number of abstainers decreased. National statistics do not tell us if the rise in alcohol-related problems was a general increase throughout the population or just concentrated in certain social groups. Although there is plenty of evidence to trace the relationship nationally, there is an almost complete lack of data tracing the relationship over time between consumption and problems within particular groups and individuals.

Fortunately, some indications of why alcohol-related problems increased in England and Wales in the 1960s and 1970s can be gleaned from an analysis of consumption and problems in our 1974 general population survey compared with similar measures made in the same London suburb in 1965 (Edwards *et al.* 1972). In both surveys, each respondent was asked what type of alcoholic beverage they had drunk on each of the seven days prior to the interview, and how many drinks of what size they had consumed of each type. Each drink was translated into its equivalent volume of absolute alcohol, as explained in Chapter 1, assuming that half a pint of beer, a glass of wine, a small sherry or a single tot of spirit each contained one centilitre of absolute alcohol.

Between 1965 and 1974 the national per capita consumption of absolute alcohol rose 48 per cent. The surveys conducted in these same years registered an increased per capita consumption of 46 per cent amongst the population of the London suburb, so there was good reason to believe the changes in the suburb were representative of national changes in drinking patterns.

The increase in per capita consumption in the suburb represented a general move towards heavier drinking throughout the drinking population; there being relatively few overall changes in drinking patterns. The percentage of abstainers in the population remained constant at 11 per cent, and despite the increased consumption, people did not drink on any more days of the week in 1974 than in 1965. Rather the major change was that on a drinking day in 1974, 'average drinkers' consumed 56 per cent more alcohol than they would have done in 1965.

These results fitted in with suggestions from research in Scandinavia that increases in per capita consumption did not usually create new drinking patterns, but rather added new elements to existing patterns. Mäkelä (1975) has supported this 'addition hypothesis' with examples from Finland and Sulkunen (1976) has stated that similar observations could be made in other countries. He pointed out that these additions to the existing drinking patterns comprised new consumer groups, new drinking situations and new ways of drinking. Examples of these three dimensions within the changing drinking patterns in Britain might be that young women became an important consumer group; they became more likely to go into public houses unaccompanied by men and they tended to experiment with a wider range of drinks than previously. Yet apart from such innovations the major elements in the drinking patterns remained stable. For example, the majority of the alcohol consumed in England and Wales continued to be consumed in the form of beer.

How did these measurements of consumption patterns relate to the prevalence of alcohol-related problems? In both London surveys, each individual drinker was asked:

In the last 12 months have you
1. Ever found that your hands were shaky in the morning after drinking?
2. Ever had a drink first thing in the morning to steady your nerves?
3. Ever found you did not remember the night before after drinking?
4. Been criticized for your drinking?
5. On any occasion been unable to stop drinking?

There was no special significance in this choice of questions. Because the 1974 survey was not a systematic attempt to replicate the 1965 survey, they just happened to be the only questions which were asked in a similar form of both samples. Even so the direct longitudinal measure of these same questions at two points in time avoided possible changes in diagnostic and administrative procedures which always cast doubt on how far national statistics of changes in alcohol-related problems represent real changes in prevalence. Nevertheless it should be noted that over the nine-year period, the number of residents of the suburb receiving psychiatric treatment for alcoholism increased 87 per cent.

There was a consistent correlation between consumption and the five measured problems within each sample and within the two samples combined. The same relationship held — the respondents who consumed more alcohol were also likely to report more alcohol-related problems. The figure below demonstrates the strength of the relationship. Drinkers in both samples were classified into consumption categories according to how many centilitres of absolute alcohol they reported having consumed during the seven days prior to interview. The group of drinkers in each successively higher category of consumption reported a successively higher average number of problems. When represented graphically as below, the relationship between consumption and problems was virtually a straight line.

Figure 3.1 Mean Problems reported by Groups of Drinkers in Successively Higher Consumption Categories

Mean number of
alcohol-related
problems reported

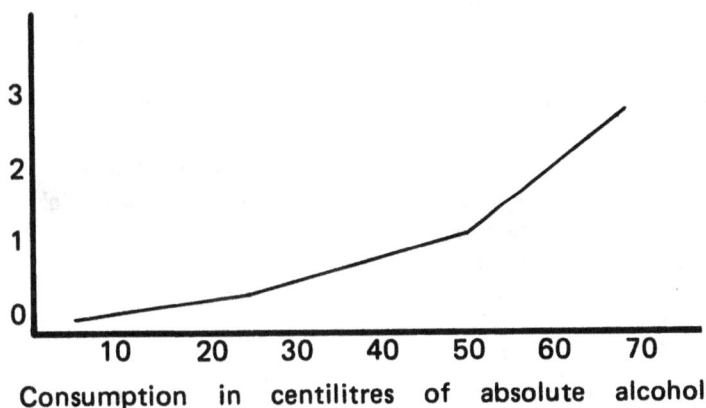

Consumption   in   centilitres   of   absolute   alcohol

Yet beneath this consistent overall correlation between consumption
and problems which matched the studies of national statistics, there lay
considerable variation between different demographic groups. Demographic groups who reported a similar level of consumption did not
necessarily report a similar average number of alcohol-related problems.
For example, as a group, middle-class males aged 18 to 34 drank the
same amount in a week as upper-class males aged over 55. Yet the
younger males reported an average of three times more problems than
the older males. Closer investigation of these differences showed that
whilst there was a consistent relationship overall between consumption
and alcohol-related problems, in the individual case this relationship
appeared to be mediated by two major factors (1) the individual's
drinking pattern and (2) demographic characteristics.

(1) *The Relationship between Drinking Patterns and Drinking Problems*

The consumption of the middle-class young males was concentrated on
fewer days of the week than that of the upper-class older males. And
whenever two demographic groups in the samples drank the same
amount, the group who consumed more *per drinking day* reported a
higher average number of problems. Perhaps these problems were more
frequently associated with a drinking pattern which produced higher
blood alcohol concentration. Although this finding might suggest that
spreading consumption over more days of the week implied less risk of
experiencing the particular problems which happened to be measured in
the London surveys, this may not be true of other alcohol-related
problems. For example, other studies have shown that high frequency
moderate consumption is more likely than occasional heavy drinking to
cause liver cirrhosis (Rankin *et al.* 1975). Each set of data however
suggests that there are probably relationships between types of drinking
patterns and the development of specific alcohol-related problems. This
undoubtedly deserves much closer attention in the future.

(2) *The Relationship between Demographic Characteristics and Drinking Problems*

There was a second factor mediating between the level of consumption
and the prevalence of problems resulting. For when people at the same
consumption levels were compared, there were still differences in the
numbers of problems reported by different demographic groups. There
was no significant difference between the problems experienced by men
as compared to women at any consumption level, but persons aged
below 35 seemed more vulnerable to experiencing the problems than

did persons aged 35 and over, and occupational status groups III, IV and V seemed more vulerable than the upper status groups. Indeed, status groups I and II appeared to be the most protected of all the demographic groups against experiencing the five problems. Again it must be stated that this protective effect might not apply to all alcohol-related problems. But whatever the precise relationships, the data suggested that the number of alcohol-related problems an individual experienced from a given level of consumption seemed to be determined by some form of interaction between demographic variables and drinking patterns.

Sociological Theories of the Development of Drinking Problems

The results of our survey analysis further undermined the plausibility of those theories which have tried to explain the prevalence and etiology of alcohol-related problems just in terms of the drinker, like the theories of genetic or biochemical predisposition to 'alcoholism', or just in terms of the drink, like the epidemiological theories which linked prevalence just to the availability of alcohol and the amount consumed. The survey results tended to give further credence to those theories which have tried instead to explain the prevalence and etiology of alcohol-related problems in terms of both the drinker and the drink by considering their socio-cultural context.

In their review of theories and data about the etiology of drinking problems, Roebuck and Kessler (1972) noted that the lack of general acceptance of the 'constitutional' (i.e. genetic and bio-chemical) theories and the failure of psychological research to find a 'unique personality type associated with alcoholism' had led to what they referred to in 1972 as 'the current pre-eminence of the sociological approach to alcoholism and to problem drinking'. Since the authorities they mentioned in this section included people such as Jellinek and since some of the data referred also to physiological and psychological factors, it was possibly a little misleading to label the socio-cultural theories as just being limited to a sociological account. Rather these theories have adopted a sociological perspective which nevertheless has incorporated other dimensions. Take, for instance, the classic example cited by Roebuck and Kessler of a socio-cultural explanation of the prevalence of alcohol-related problems, namely the explanation of the disparity between the prevalence of alcohol-related problems in France and Italy. The analysis made by various authors of this disparity has fitted closely with the findings of the London general population surveys. The socio-cultural analysis has attributed a major causal role to the different level of consumption in the two countries, but has also pointed out that the effects of this consumption were mediated by drinking patterns and by demographic variables — in this case the demographic variable being nationality. It is worth considering this example here since the analysis of the different level of drinking problems in France and Italy provides some indications to why the London surveys found that demographic variables and drinking patterns affected the number of alcohol-related problems associated with particular levels of consumption.

Alcohol Use and Abuse in France and Italy

On the surface, France and Italy seem relatively similar cultural environments, both with a common penchant for wine drinking. In 1975 the per capita consumption of wine in each population was almost identical. The average French drinker consumed 182.5 pints of wine, while his Italian counterpart consumed 189.2 pints. However, the rate of liver cirrhosis mortality and the proportion of persons diagnosed as alcoholics have usually been about five times greater in France than in Italy. Why? First, the French consume much more beer and spirits than do the Italians, so the total per capita consumption is higher in France than in Italy. Second, the French drinking pattern is more likely to cause alcohol-related problems. The London surveys recorded more risk of problems amongst those groups who drank more alcohol per drinking day, and in general the French probably drink more per drinking day than do the Italians. For in Italy wine is considered a food and consumed almost exclusively with meals, while in France alcohol is drunk not only with meals, but also at various other times. This also suggests that the French may be more likely to experience greater physiological and psychological effects of alcohol. For as explained in Chapter 1, the faster alcohol is metabolized, the more effect it has on the body's organs and on the central nervous system. The Italian pattern of consuming alcohol mostly with meals will tend to prevent rapid metabolism. The French pattern of sometimes consuming alcohol apart from meals will mean they experience generally more instances of faster metabolism and hence both greater physiological harm and more acute intoxification. Thus drunkenness is more common amongst the French. Third, this is compounded because the demographic variable of being French as opposed to being Italian implies a certain difference in attitudes to alcohol use and abuse. Italians tend to be introduced to alcohol in a domestic and culinary setting, drinking moderate amounts within a family group. The French are more liable to experience rigid parental attitudes strongly in favour or strongly against childhood drinking. Amongst adults, the French tend to be more accepting of drunkenness, which Italians are more inclined to regard as something of a personal and family disgrace. There is in general much greater social pressure to drink amongst the French, particularly amongst French males who tend to view heavy drinking as a symbol of virility and manhood.

In conclusion then, these explanations of why the French experience more alcohol-related problems than Italians have been suggesting lines of thought which appeared to be vindicated to an extent by the London surveys. The prevalence of alcohol-related problems is higher in France than in Italy because the level of consumption in France is higher and the effect of this higher consumption is aggravated by drinking patterns and norms about alcohol use and abuse which make the French more vulnerable than Italians to experiencing alcohol-related problems even if their consumption had been the same.

The Relationship between Ethnicity, Immigration and Drinking Problems

Somewhat similar explanations have been proffered to account for different prevalences of alcohol-related problems amongst different ethnic groups within a single society. For example, American Italians and American Jews have been much less susceptible to problems caused by drinking than have American Irish (Pittman and Snyder 1962).

In England, patients of Irish and Scottish ethnicity comprise an exceptionally high proportion of the number of persons receiving hospital treatment for alcoholism. In our 1974 survey of the London suburb, quite a number of the heaviest drinkers had originally come from Ireland and Scotland. Again, their higher per capita consumption can be linked with a combination of drinking patterns and culturally channelled ideas about the good and bad effects of alcohol which make the Irish and Scots more liable to develop drinking problems. In their case this can be compounded by their experience of being immigrants. The social setting of drinking in public houses patronized by large proportions of Irish and Scotch may be one of the major links with their previous culture. Their possible separation from normal sexual relationships, from a domestic environment and from family constraints have all been thought conducive to the development of heavy drinking amongst immigrant males in various societies.

The Relationship between Occupational Factors and Drinking Problems

Probably the area of most current research and analysis into the high risk of alcohol-related problems amongst certain social groups is the study of occupational groups prone to developing drinking problems.

The occupational groups amongst whom the prevalence of alcohol-related problems is highest are those involved in the production, distribution and selling of alcohol, those in the hotel and catering trades, members of the armed services, seamen of various sorts, entertainers, journalists, company directors, commercial travellers, customs officials and medical practitioners. The most obvious reason why these should be the occupational groups who have the highest risk of developing alcohol-related problems is that people in these occupations are more likely to consume a greater amount of alcohol than people in other occupational groups. There appears to be two major overlapping reasons for their greater likelihood of high consumption. First, alcohol is highly available to them and second, there are pressures on them to drink either from the demands or logistics of their occupation or from the ethos of those engaged in it.

(i) *Occupations with High Availability of Alcohol*

High availability may take various forms. Alcohol may be free or cheap to many of the occupations at risk. This may be legal in the case of brewery workers or company directors, but may be illegal in the case of tippling cooks or barmen who drink the profits. Availability may simply be a case of alcoholic beverages being closer to hand than other alternative drinks, as to draymen for example. As noted by Murray (1975), the availability of alcohol during working hours may take the more subtle dimension of lack of supervision, as in the case of rural family doctors, which might not only allow workers to drink throughout the day but also allow their consumption and its effects to go largely unnoticed by others. In some cases, it may be that people with an overt or covert desire to drink heavily might be attracted to these occupations with high availability of alcohol.

(ii) *Occupations involving Pressures to Drink*

Pressures in the occupational situation towards heavy consumption may be because of the demands or the logistics of the job. For example, a journalist has to buy people drinks or often interview them in pubs in the same way that company directors and commercial travellers may have to entertain potential customers. The occupational situation may simply make drinking more probable: commercial travellers, for example, are often likely to have meals in licensed premises. Alternatively, the pressures to drink may come more from the habits and value system of the occupational group, such as in the cases of seamen and servicemen. Occupational groups who place much positive stress on heavy drinking are typically male-dominated and deprived of sexual relationships and domestic comforts. Since they are also typically deprived of many other forms of alternative activities and enjoyment, the good effects of alcohol become highly valued within the group ethos.

In conclusion, the study of occupational factors reiterates the implications of the epidemiological studies of whole societies. The most important variable in the development of drinking problems is the level of consumption which, in turn, is highly determined by the availability of alcohol. Moreover, the study of drinking problems in different occupations also reasserts that sociological and psychological factors influence both the drinking pattern itself and the individual's interpretation and valuation of the effects of alcohol. Thus 'pressures to drink' such as deprivation of sexual relationships and stresses induced by job demands and responsibilities can both motivate the individual to drink excessively and also influence him to perceive the good effects of alcohol as very valuable.

The Development of Drinking Problems amongst Members of the Same Family

The group of persons who seem most vulnerable of all to developing drinking problems are the relations of other people with drinking problems. Amark (1951), for example, computed from studies of family histories of several large samples of Swedes diagnosed as alcoholics that the likelihood of drinking problems amongst brothers of diagnosed alcoholics was 21 per cent and amongst fathers 26 per cent. Relations of people with drinking problems are probably at such high risk because of the same factors which affected their relative and because these factors are likely to comprise every type of risk factor; risky drinking patterns and availability, social, psychological and physiological factors. If alcohol is free, cheap or otherwise highly available to one family member, it may be equally available to others. Relations such as brothers may well adopt the same style of drinking pattern. Family members may share similar social and psychological pressures to drink such as poor and overcrowded housing, frequent domestic fights and arguments. Turning to alcohol in reaction to such pressures may be a response learned from the drinking habits of other relations from whom they may also pick up highly ambivalent or pro-drinking attitudes. For children whose parents have drinking problems, this may be aggravated by a generally disturbed and deprived upbringing.

There have of course been attempts to explain the vulnerability of relations of persons diagnosed as alcoholics in terms of bio-chemical, genetic and hereditary factors. As explained in Chapter 2, such theories fitted in well in the past with the disease model, but no good scientific evidence has ever been produced to show that drinking problems were purely genetically transmitted. Most obviously, they could not explain why the spouses of diagnosed alcoholics often developed drinking problems themselves. The major limitation of most attempts to demonstrate genetic causes of alcohol related problems have been their concern to 'prove' the disease theory and to refuse to consider the other factors of availability, and sociological and psychological influences. To explain the development of alcohol-related problems purely in terms of transmitted genes has been as unsuccessful as trying to explain the prevalence of alcohol-related problems purely in epidemiological terms of the level of per capita consumption, purely in psychological terms of a predisposing personality or purely in sociological terms of group tendencies towards heavy drinking. The conclusion of this chapter must surely be that all of these factors must be considered to play a part in the prevalence and etiology of alcohol-related problems. In the past, theories of the causes of drinking problems have too often been seen as competing rather than complementary. What we need now, as Robinson (1976) has stated are 'studies which will enable statements to be made about the *relative weight* of genetic as opposed to environmental influences. Workers in other disciplines have tended to assume that the factors or parameters in which they were interested were of *exclusive* importance.'

Such comments are not to be directed just at these workers who have tried to completely explain drinking problems via bio-chemical and genetic factors. Sociologists and psychologists have often equally refused to accept the possibility of any causal role at all for genetic factors. Thus when assessing the different etiological perpsectives, Roebuck and Kessler (1972) felt obliged to include a section on 'behavioural science bias against the constitutional approach'. Although it has obviously been simplistic and unverifiable to claim that 'alcoholism is hereditary', this should not obscure the likelihood that hereditary factors are important in creating individual differences in brain structure, taste and other traits which may, for example, influence a person's tolerance to alcohol and affect the way they metabolize alcohol.

Neither do the physiological and psychological factors involved have to
be necessarily attributable to heredity. Therefore in our enthusiasm for
epidemiological and sociological studies, and in our rejection of
attempts to prove the abnormal bio-chemical or psychological predispositions of people with drinking problems, let us not forget that the
turning of a risk into a problem in the individual case must involve
physiological and psychological components as well as social factors
and availability factors. Just as there are patterns of social groups who
seem to be relatively vulnerable to alcohol abuse, so there may be
groups with particular physiological and psychological traits who are
more at risk. For example, a longitudinal study of males followed from
childhood to their early thirties (McCord *et al*. 1960) showed that the
personality development of boys who later became diagnosed as alcoholics was marked by inconsistent relationships with parents, particularly mothers, who alternated between giving them affection and
rejecting them. The boys tended to promote a façade of masculinity
and aggression. As adults, their feelings and attitudes were characterized
by hedonism, inconsistent relationships with their own sons, a sense of
being victimized by society and by alternating feelings of grandiosity
and low self-esteem. This unique study thus indicated that certain
personality traits related to patterns of upbringing might make some people
more vulnerable than others to the development of drinking problems
in later life. Perhaps it has just been easier so far to pick out the large-
scale social and demographic patterns which shape the prevalence of
drinking problems. It is much more difficult to trace individual variations within these groups since differences of upbringing, emotional
feelings, and psychological reactions to alcohol are very contentious
to demarcate.

However, some lines of thought on this subject can be drawn from
the perspective developed in this book so far. We have seen that our
survey and most other epidemiological research pointed to the level of
consumption as the major determinant of the severity of drinking problems, although some drinkers were more vulnerable than others to
suffer particular problems from given levels of consumption. This
suggests that other factors which might help explain how drinking problems develop, such as individual variations in attitudes and feelings
about alcohol and its effects, should be considered as both factors
which may lead people to drink excessively and factors which may
render some drinkers more vulnerable to developing problems from
that consumption level. But in effect, these factors can all be considered as reasons why certain drinkers find social, emotional, psycho-

logical and physiological effects of alcohol to be particularly valuable.

People to whom the Effects of Alcohol are Particularly Valuable

It would be logical at this point to review the research into individual motivations for drinking, but unfortunately such research is conspicuous only by its absence.

There have been clinical studies of motivation amongst populations of diagnosed alcoholics, usually trying to measure the equivocal constructs of 'compulsions' and 'craving', but more straightforward investigation in non-labelled populations has comprised little more than a few questions asked in general population surveys, which have not produced particularly discriminating results. However, the information and perspective developed in Chapter 1 allows us to at least consider why some people might be particularly motivated to consume alcohol regularly and possibly heavily and to develop drinking problems as a result. These reasons following are speculative to an extent, and are certainly not meant to be mutually exclusive factors.

For the purposes of conceptualization, individual motivations which lead to the development of excessive drinking and drinking problems can be classified into two major areas. First, there are factors intrinsic to the effects of alcohol upon the individual, and second, there are symbolic factors, which apply when the drinker is not directly seeking the effects of alcohol *per se*, but rather uses the symbolic meaning of alcohol and its effects to attain some other goal.

1. *Intrinsic Factors*

The most prevalent intrinsic factors involved in the development of excessive drinking and drinking problems are the psychotropic, i.e. mood-altering effects of alcohol described in Chapter 1. These in turn can be classified mostly into two interconnected categories: tranquillizing effects and intoxicating effects.

(i) Tranquillizing Effects. Particularly valuable to people troubled by tension and anxieties. These may be largely internalized personal emotions or may be related more to stressful life circumstances such as poor housing conditions or difficulties coping with children. The reduction of anxiety brought about by alcohol may also be related to the act of consumption itself: reducing tension by the oral stimulation of sucking and swallowing. Sometimes the tranquillizing effects of alcohol are used for purposes of disinhibition in order to improve the performance of anxiety-provoking tasks.

The sedative effects of alcohol can sometimes be used to counteract the bad effects of other psychotropic substances, to offset the effects of stimulants or to offset the effects of withdrawal from tranquillizers, including withdrawal from alcohol itself.

(ii) Intoxicating Effects. Drinking to achieve the effects associated with intoxication can vary from the purely hedonistic pursuit of pleasurable sensations to seeking a release from a socially-deprived or otherwise painful existence. Thus intoxicating effects may be sought for their own sake or in reaction to other circumstances. Intoxication may blot out feelings of guilt, shame, depression, meaninglessness, boredom and frustration, or may help the drinker to assert himself by achieving a state in which no-one can influence or control him. Whatever motivations apply, the degree of intoxication sought may vary from a mild state to total oblivion.

(iii) Other Intrinsic Factors. These are probably less likely to lead to excessive drinking and drinking problems, but may be important in certain individual cases. The anaesthetic effect of alcohol, for example, might be highly valued by people who drink to numb persistent pain or discomfort. It is generally unlikely that a drinker's taste or thirst alone could account for him drinking excessively, but in certain situations, it is possible. For instance, workers operating in conditions of intense heat such as in iron foundries or glass factories might drink very large amounts daily purely out of thirst and this might cause them physical harm.

2. Symbolic Factors

Some individuals drink excessively and develop drinking problems because they use alcohol to achieve certain goals. It is the psychosocial symbolism surrounding alcohol and its effects which motivates them to drink. The act of drinking itself can help individuals feel a sense of identification with social groups and activities or with certain elements of the social imagery of drinking such as sophistication, manliness or maturity. In other cases, the value in the act of drinking may be related more to specific underlying motivations. Heavy drinking may be used by sexually inadequate men or butch lesbians alike as a symbol of their desired self-image of masculinity and aggression. Even the identity of being an 'alcoholic' or a 'problem drinker' can be attractive to some people and influence their drinking behaviour.

In other cases, the drinking behaviour may be related specifically to

the symbolic interaction between the drinker and other people. Alcohol
and its effects can be used to evade responsibilities or to avoid otherwise painful situations and can be used in interpersonal transactions to
legitimize certain feelings and types of behaviour. Drunkenness, for
instance, can legitimize the emotional expression of underlying frustrations with other people, and often an individual's drinking problems
are only understandable in the context of his relationships with those
close to him. Steiner (1969) presented, in a perhaps somewhat frivolous
fashion, a series of cameos of drinkers whose behaviour was bound up
in transactional symbolism. Some men, for example, indulge in overtly
unacceptable behaviour when drunk to incite their wives to nag and
criticize them, which they can then interpret as justifications for their
feelings of being persecuted and seeing the wife in the role of persecu-
tor. The drunken behaviour becomes a guilt-free expression of hostility.
In the hypothetical case described in Chapter 2, the wife's drinking
began primarily as a means of seeking attention from her husband,
which again could be interpreted as internalized frustrations which the
drinker felt unable to express in any other way.

3. *Intrinsic and Symbolic Motivations amplified by the Phenomena of Tolerance and Withdrawal*

As we described in this latter case, the woman's drinking problems
gradually developed as other motivations for drinking came into play.
Drinkers' reasons for drinking heavily sometimes change completely,
although more commonly the drinking pattern becomes self-reinfor-
cing such that the original motivations may become obscured, matched
or amplified. The drinking and its effects may be reinforced because
they achieve the drinker's goal. Other people may give the drinker more
attention or accept him into the social group to whose membership he
had aspired. But as explained in Part I, the reinforcement can come
directly from the effects of alcohol itself. If the drinker's main motivation for drinking was to relieve anxieties, then the phenomena of
increasing tolerance would pressurize him to drink successively more
to keep on attaining this relief. The original anxieties may be worsened
by increasingly severe periods of withdrawal and the drinker may
become forced to drink to relieve this. The drinker may also have
learned to associate alcohol consumption so strongly with relief from
anxiety that he may begin to drink in the absence or just in anticipation
of former cues. The drinker may thus drink regularly and heavily even
when the initial precipitating causes of his anxieties have mostly passed.

Vulnerability Factors

Besides the factors above which may amplify or compound the individual's motivation for drinking excessively, there are other factors which may amplify or compound the resultant problems. For just as the good effects of alcohol can be relatively more valuable for some people than others, so the bad effects of alcohol can be relatively more harmful to certain groups of drinkers. These may be persons, for instance, whose socialization has created intense feelings of guilt about their drinking or whose parents were abstainers and therefore transmitted no advice or rules about how to handle alcohol. Straus and Bacon's (1953) study of American college students, for example, found a relatively high incidence of heavy drinking and intoxication amongst students from a Mormon background with its emotionally charged anti-drinking attitudes. Some drinkers may be more physiologically vulnerable than others to the toxic effects of alcohol. Indeed, we saw in Chapter 1 that the good and bad effects of alcohol were subject to various physiological and psychological mechanisms internal to the individual. It would simply be common sense to assume that there must be many physical, social and psychological factors which would explain why one person was more likely than another to experience more problems from the same level of consumption consumed in the same way. An individual's vulnerability to the experience of alcohol-related problems must depend on a variety of factors – whether he has a family or not, whether he can drive or not, what weight he is, whether he has any physical vulnerability to certain illnesses, what his diet is like and what has been his previous drinking behaviour. Some drinkers will obviously be much more vulnerable than others to experiencing financial problems from their drinking. Others will be vulnerable to the effects of alcohol because of their physiological or psychological condition. Those who drive more will have a higher statistical chance of experiencing the alcohol-related problem of a conviction for drunken driving. Besides the greater vulnerability to objectively suffer a problem like a conviction for drunken driving, there is another dimension to vulnerability which relates to the differential effect of an alcohol related problem on different people. To a wealthy person, a fine for drunken driving would be less of a problem than to an impecunious drinker, while a person convicted for drunken driving who earned his living from driving would obviously experience this same objective problem as having infinitely more severe repercussions.

The Etiology of Drinking Problems

This chapter has attempted to draw together many strands of etiological thinking into a comprehensive perspective of the prevalence and causes of drinking problems. Much work clearly remains to be done in this area, but certain important advances can be drawn out.

The traditional AA theory of alcoholism had no etiological theory. The Big Book almost deliberately set out a bewildering variety of members with different personalities, in different sorts of jobs and different sorts of social situations, as if to demonstrate that 'alcoholism' could strike anybody, at any time. The only common trait it was envisaged there could be amongst such disparate types was some core biochemical or personality defect. Much costly research failed to 'find' this defect.

The epidemiological and sociological approaches adopted the alternative perspective that the prevalence of alcohol-related problems was not determined merely by individual idiosyncracies, but could be seen instead as a multi-factorial pattern largely determined by the level of consumption. The evidence compiled in this book so far clearly demonstrates that the prevalence of drinking problems does relate to the level of consumption. For many years this relationship has been shown to hold consistently at a national level and the London surveys demonstrated that this relationship held within groups as well, although mediated by drinking patterns and demographic variables. We cannot say that a person drinking a specific amount will experience specific problems, but we are able to say that the more a person drinks, the greater risk he runs of experiencing alcohol-related problems. We can also say that his risk of experiencing particular problems will be probably greater if he drinks in a certain pattern, and if he is particularly vulnerable to certain types of alcohol-related problem. Both motivations for drinking and vulnerability factors are determined by a whole series of availability, physiological, psychological and social factors. It will often be the case that the same factors which precipitated excessive drinking, such as an emotionally disturbed and deprived childhood, would be the same factors which made the drinker less able to cope with the effects of excessive drinking.

In summary then, the reconceptualized view of the etiology of drinking problems could be represented diagramatically thus:

Physiological,
psychological
social and
availability
factors

Drinking ← Vulnerability ← Consumption
problems factors patterns

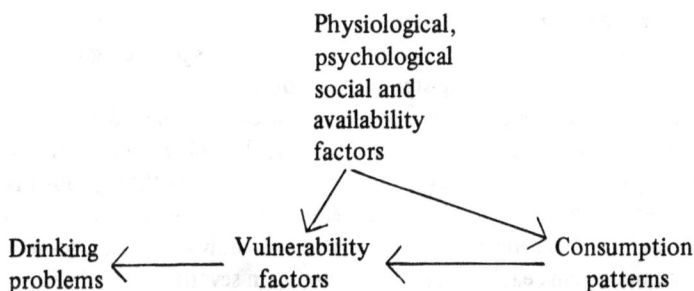

D.L. Davies (1977) has recognized that such a theory implies it
would be more rational to treat people with drinking problems in terms
of the factors which led them to drinking excessively, and in terms of
risk associated with their particular drinking pattern and their personal
vulnerability. The question would then become not 'is this man an
alcoholic or not?', but rather, 'what factors operated in his case which
made him drink so much and therefore what can I do to help him in the
future to deal with those particular factors?'

Thus the epidemiological challenge to traditional concepts of
alcoholism is developing into a rationale for alternative approaches to
conceptualization and in turn, therefore, for treatment. To realize the
potential of this new direction, there is a need for much closer investigation of the relationships between an individual's motivations for
drinking, his consumption pattern, his vulnerability and the development of alcohol-related problems.

The same conclusions apply also at a national level to alcohol
control policy. The data presented in this chapter still reaffirm the basic
principle that reducing alcohol availability is likely to decrease per
capita consumption and hence the overall prevalence of alcohol-related
problems. However a more sophisticated task for future epidemiology
will be to outline a detailed strategy for prevention by determining *in
which ways* and *to what extent* alcohol could be controlled to produce
what size of a reduction *in which* particular alcohol related problems.

The Prevalence of Drinking Problems

As for the prevalence of drinking problems the pattern seems clear
enough. As an individual's or a society's consumption of alcohol fluc-
tuates, so will an individual's or a society's level of alcohol-related
problems. Therefore it is meaningless to conceive of 'problem drinkers'

and 'normal drinkers' as though these were qualitatively different and
static groups or to perceive the size of the problem as just being the
number of people with a long-standing combination of very heavy
drinking and many severe problems who are probably labelled as
'alcoholics' by someone at some time. Rather, alcohol-related problems
of varying severity affect a larger number of people, and these problems
range over a wide spectrum. In our general population sample, problems
were found to occur in various combinations in individual cases, sometimes compounding each other and increasing in severity, sometimes
receding as new situations presented themselves. Alcohol-related problems range from falling behind with the rent to dropping out of
education, from personal neglect to neglect of the family, from accidents to anxiety, from poor sleep patterns to depression, from getting
involved in arguments to getting the sack. There are undoubtedly a
great number of people who experience one or some of such problems
as a result of alcohol at some time.

Neither do drinking problems just affect drinkers themselves.
Families of heavy drinkers frequently suffer before the drinker himself,
who may be disturbing children, creating marital problems and wasting
the family budget. The drunken driver is a danger to others besides
himself, as is the person drinking at work and likely to cause accidents,
and the drunken doctor who cannot treat his patients properly.
Drinking problems also make heavy demands on medical and social
services. Doctors, social workers, nurses, and many sorts of agents,
both professional and voluntary, have to cope with various personal,
medical, social, legal, occupational and financial problems caused and
compounded by alcohol consumption. The police, probation service,
and prison service deal with a range of alcohol-related crimes; not only
the more obvious and frequently quoted crimes such as public drunkenness, but numerous others often committed under the influence of
drink, including hooliganism, vandalism, rape, burglary, and murders
and suicides, both attempted and 'successful'. As for the economy at
large, a large number of man-hours are lost due to the effects of
drinking, combined with a general inefficiency in some cases and
accidents and mistakes in others.

It is only when all these areas are perceived in combination that the
cost to individuals and to society of alcohol related-problems begins
to become apparent. The number of people labelled as 'alcoholics' is
relatively few; if a comprehensive view is taken, the size of the problem
appears very extensive and beside it all other drug problems are mole-
hills in comparison.

PART THREE   THE EXISTING RESPONSE

4 CONCEPTS OF THE RESPONSE

The nature and extent of the response to a problem is determined by how the problem is perceived and how prevalent it is estimated to be. As we have seen, the immediate post-war years were characterized by a fairly strict disease-model of alcoholism which advocated a specialist response consisting of Alcoholics Anonymous and Psychiatric Alcoholism Services, both primarily aimed at achieving a treatment goal of total abstinence. Gradually concepts of alcohol abuse widened out to perspectives which conceived drinking problems to be much more diverse in nature than the concept of 'alcoholism'. Problems came to be seen as multi-factorial in both cause and effect. Over the same period, studies of both national statistics and general population surveys showed that the prevalence of drinking problems was much more extensive than previously thought. Moreover, much concern was expressed in the 1960s and 70s about the seemingly accelerating growth in the prevalence of alcohol-related problems. These shifts in perspective were not simply challenges to the disease theory, they were also fundamental challenges to the whole rationale of treatment for drinking problems and the ways in which treatment services were organized. Accordingly, there were considerable changes in thinking about the nature and extent of the necessary response.

These changes can be traced, for example, in a series of statements made by English health policy documents between 1962 and 1975. These documents represented a major shift of emphasis from specialist psychiatric in-patient alcoholism services and AA towards community services involving a variety of professional and voluntary agents.

The concepts of alcohol abuse described in a 1962 Memorandum (Ministry of Health 1962) were highly influenced by the disease theory and particularly the ideas of Jellinek. The concepts of treatment stressed the importance of a group setting, as recommended by AA. Therefore the document recommended the establishment of specialist in-patient units, comprising twelve beds — the number considered optimal for the type of group therapy thought necessary for 'alcoholics'.

In 1968 (Ministry of Health 1968) alcoholism was still being described as a 'chronic relapsing disease' but by then treatment was thought to be directed particularly against 'alcohol dependence'. The paper also mentioned that alcoholism 'destroys personal relationships and leads to social decline.'

The requisite response to this disease was still presumed to be
fundamentally a medical response, comprising treatment for both the
illnesses caused by excessive alcohol consumption (seen largely as the
responsibility of GPs) and treatment of 'alcohol dependence' itself
within specialist psychiatric units:

> Illness associated with or caused by excessive drinking will call for
> treatment in its own right which can be best carried out by the
> general practitioner . . . treatment for alcohol dependence as such
> would take a different form . . . treatment will frequently involve
> an initial admission to hospital as an in-patient; more than one
> admission into hospital may be necessary because of relapse. In-
> patient treatment can best be undertaken in small specialised hospi-
> tal units as recommended in H.M. (62)43, which should provide
> out-patient services including help in emergency as well as planned
> support.

Between 1962 and 1973, 19 regional treatment units were brought into
operation based upon the model advocated in the departmental circulars. However, confidence in their capacity to deal with drinking problems was soon compromised; first, by a growing realisation that such
highly specialist services could only cope with a minority of their
target population, and second, by growing doubts about the efficacy of
the treatment provided even for the minority to whom the specialist
services could respond. These doubts, combined with changes in the
conceptualization of alcohol abuse, produced a new policy more in
line with the general shift of emphasis away from hospital psychiatry
towards the goal of a community-based response. In the first place, the
regional treatment units were too small to deal with all the people
admitted to mental illness hospitals in England and Wales with a diagnosis of alcoholism or alcoholic psychosis. Over 60 per cent had still to
be treated by general psychiatric services. Yet this was nothing compared with the discrepancy between the numbers treated by all psychiatric services compared to prevalence estimates of the target population.

This point was demonstrated by our 1975 report (Cartwright *et al.*
1975) comparing the number of people with drinking problems in an
English health district with the number of people treated. This particular district had an Alcohol Treatment Unit which fulfilled most of the
requirements of the 1962 circular. Furthermore, the District also con-

tained AA and Al-Anon groups, a local council on alcoholism and hostels and specialist voluntary organizations dealing with many vagrants with drinking problems.

Each respondent in our sample of 286 local residents was asked whether they felt that drinking caused them problems, either at the time of interview, or during a period in the past. 0.7 per cent felt they had current problems and 2.4 per cent reported having had problems from drinking in the past. There was some indication that of those who admitted only a past problem period, about half were still probably experiencing some significant problems at the time of interview. When asked about their drinking habits, 2.1 per cent of the sample reported having consumed at least 70 cl of absolute alcohol in the seven days prior to interview.

However, during the same year as the general population study, only 0.16 per cent of the adult population of the district were treated for alcoholism by a psychiatric service of *any* kind in any area. Of these people who did attend a psychiatric service and who were diagnosed as alcoholics, only a minority were treated by the specialist alcoholism services. At that same time, the local Alcoholics Anonymous group was reporting an attendance of about 20 persons per meeting and approximately three or four new members per month. There was clearly, then, a sizeable discrepancy between the number of people with drinking problems as suggested by our survey and the number treated by specialist services. Although both AA and the specialist alcoholism services were probably dealing with a particularly damaged group of people with drinking problems, it would appear quite clear that they had only minimal impact upon the total pool of problems within the community. Yet services in this particular district were almost certainly more developed than in many other areas. There was probably a greater opportunity for residents to receive psychiatric care than in other districts. So the discrepancy found between the numbers of persons whom the general population survey indicated might have problems from drinking and the number treated in the hospital services was probably much greater in other areas with less-developed services. Although the district we have considered is known to have a large proportion of homeless drinkers passing through its boundaries, this factor should not be allowed to confuse the argument, for the survey was entirely based upon people who were resident in the district. The specialist response was almost certainly less adequate in many other areas. Indeed, this was partially confirmed by our findings that a high proportion of those treated by the local psychiatric services were residents of other districts

who had presented or who had been referred in default of adequate
services in their own locality.

It might appear initially that if there is a discrepancy between the
numbers of people with problems and the numbers being helped by
specialists, then the solution must be to create more specialists. However, even the most cursory consideration of the logistics of expanding
a specialized response to drinking problems would reveal that, whether
desirable or not, the designing of services based on more specialized
hospital facilities and more medical personnel would be utterly impractical. Even the most conservative estimates of prevalence which could
be made from our own and other current research indicate that if all
the people experiencing drinking problems presented to specialist medical services, these services would be completely swamped. In the whole
of England and Wales, there are little more than 1,000 consultant
psychiatrists. If the survey projections were correct, each psychiatrist
would be responsible for dealing with at least 300 to 400 patients with
drinking problems apart from their other patients! A massive expansion
of the fellowship of Alcoholics Anonymous would be an equally unrealistic expectation. It has been estimated that AA reaches not more
than 5 per cent of all the alcoholics in Canada and the United States
(Kellermann 1974). In England and Wales there are an estimated 300
groups comprising only about 3,000 active members. AA groups vary
in size and orientation from place to place and country to country, and
it is obviously difficult to assess the active and passive membership of
a fellowship which keeps no records. Nevertheless, it was generally
believed that in the first half of the 1970s there were about 16,000
AA groups throughout the world, with about 450,000 active members.
If the 1975 estimate that 400,000 people in England and Wales had a
serious drinking problem were correct, then the total active membership of AA throughout the world would be only 50,000 greater than
the number of people with drinking problems in England and Wales
alone.

This is only to be expected of an organization which does not
actively seek out members or engage in any publicity or promotional
campaigns. AA believes that drinkers must come to them with the
honest desire to stop drinking. It is not designed to persuade people to
develop this desire in the first place; it does not believe that this is
realistic. Neither will it accept outside financial contributions and has
clung to the principle that it 'should remain forever non-professional'.
Given these ideals, it is only natural that Alcoholics Anonymous cannot
make a thoroughgoing active response to all people with problems from

drinking.

Moreover, AA is not always an attractive organization even to those drinkers who find it even when they do want to stop drinking. For some people it is too religious or too middle-class, its concepts may be untenable or they cannot get on with other members. It is well known to everyone actively engaged in the field that the AA programme of recovery is simply not acceptable or attractive to the majority of people suffering problems from drinking.

It is not surprising then that the English Department of Health and Social Security came to realize that no long term design for responding to alcohol abuse could be based on specialist psychiatric hospitals and Alcoholics Anonymous, although these will of course continue to make valuable contributions within the overall response.

Given the logistics of the situation, these services could never be sufficiently expanded to respond to the size of the problem. To do so would only produce an enormous bill for hospital in-patient units and make demands on hospital services which are already over-stretched.

Nevertheless, there would probably have been an attempt to at least expand specialist services as far as possible, if it had been shown that they were making an effective response to the fortunate few who received their treatment.

But when the efficacy of the specialist units was evaluated, they did not appear to respond any better than other forms of service. Willems *et al.* (1973) showed that client improvement was unrelated to the length of time spent in such a unit. Studies by Edwards and Guthrie (1967) and Ritson (1968) indicated that clients treated in out-patient clinics were as likely to improve as those treated within in-patient units. It was not that the specialist in-patient treatment itself was ineffective, but rather that in-patient treatment showed no appreciable gains over out-patient treatment. Given a reasonably stable group of clients, each approach has appeared to bring about some degree of improvement in about 60 per cent of cases.

This was a further economic argument against the expansion of specialist in-patient services since they were obviously more expensive to provide than out-patient services. Besides the actual physical hardware of the unit, there is the wastage of the time and skill of staff in performing routine tasks which would be fulfilled by the patients themselves were they outside the hospital. Other arguments against in-patient treatment reflected more the generally negative opinion of much hospital psychiatric care which developed in the 1960s. It was realized that the units were sometimes remote in position from the community they served and while separating clients from their environment might be temporarily useful, it often snapped their social contacts. They became isolated upon returning to the community. It was generally conceded that if clients needed temporary physical and mental convalescence and protection from outside pressures they did not necessarily require psychiatric treatment or a hospital environment. Ideally, hospitals should not have to provide custodial or convalescent services in default of appropriate community services.

These factors alone might have brought about a shift in treatment policy away from the in-patient to the out-patient situation; from hospital services to community services. But the changes in policy that occurred between 1962 and 1975 represented more than a shift in the means of delivery of care. The changing concept of what constituted an appropriate response reflected more a complete change of emphasis in the concept of what was being treated. The shifting stress in policy from hospital to community services accompanied the changing concepts of alcohol abuse away from the idea of alcoholism as a fairly specific disease syndrome to a more comprehensive view of drinking problems as a wide-ranging and varying cluster of social and medical problems.

Official support for this conceptual development appeared particularly in two documents issued in 1973. The pamphlet *Alcoholism* (Department of Health and Social Security 1973a), issued primarily for the information of general practitioners, stressed the growing size and severity of problems of alcohol abuse in Britain. The pamphlet used not only the terms 'chronic alcoholics' and 'alcohol addicts', but also the term 'excessive drinkers with problems'. This latter group were also stated to be the concern of doctors, for 'they are starting to be alcoholics'. The pamphlet stated that 'alcoholism is difficult to describe and difficult to detect, yet its effects on the sufferer, on his family and on society are so serious that it is worth attempting to do so'.

The assumption that alcoholism was a disease had evaporated and a much more flexible concept propounded:

It would appear indeed, that there is no one cause for alcoholism —
social, cultural, personality and physical factors may all contribute.
Alcoholism appears to be a medical-social problem in its origins and
in its manifestations, and as such, it is probably best tackled by a
medical-social approach.

There was much less stress upon 'alcohol dependence' as the core problem requiring a response:

> Some people are excessive drinkers, they drink more than most other people, more often, or more on occasions when they drink. This may not cause much in the way of problems with either their health or social relationships. If not, they do not concern us, but excessive drinkers with problems do. Their social functioning, work, friendships, social relationships may be affected by their drinking.

The reconceptualization of alcohol abuse was accompanied by changes in ideas about the necessary response:

> The general aims of treatment are straightforward. First, to reverse as far as possible the damage done in the physical, mental and social life of the alcoholic and then to deal with such underlying addiction as is present. In this latter connection special measures are called for based on an assessment of which of those factors specially relevant in the individual cases are susceptible to modification. Clearly, ethnic and personality factors are not in this category. The type of work, recreational interest, domestic and social stresses may well be.

This new view altered the required roles and areas of responsibility of various agents. Only five years before in 1968, the roles of non-specialist personnel in responding to alcohol abuse *per se* had been mentioned in the vaguest terms, appearing merely to pay lip service to the new model of a community response outlined in the Mental Health Act of that same year. Whilst general practitioners were clearly expected to treat the illnesses caused by alcohol problems, the involvement of non-medical personnel had been treated with great caution: 'It is important to obtain the patient's full consent and co-operation before enlisting the help of local authority and other supportive services and his own family'.

Non-medical personnel were excluded from recommendations about appropriate training. 'Training is required especially for doctors and nurses in the treatment of alcoholism and the provision of such training should be recognized as one of the roles for the specialist units'.

By 1973 the perspective had changed dramatically. Perhaps this was partially due to the growing professional status of non-medical personnel, but it probably reflected more the redefinition of the nature and extent of drinking problems.

In 1973, a circular to local authorities (Department of Health and Social Security 1973b) used a wide range of concepts of alcohol abuse, implied the idea of a continuum in the development of problems, and advocated the necessity of a wide range of support. The circular used the term 'problem drinkers' whose 'dependence on alcohol is developing'. And this 'developing' process was believed to take place over a 'relatively long time'. Correspondingly, the document emphasized that the services should be complemented by a wide range of community services including prevention, social work support for the drinkers and their families, rehabilitation and residential care. Financial inducements were offered to voluntary bodies to sustain the growth of community services. The co-ordination of these various services and facilities were deemed essential for the development of a comprehensive response network. 'Treatment involves not only the efforts of the doctor but also the participation of other professionals such as social workers, clinical psychologists and nurses . . . The community health and personal social services needed range across a broad front.' Social workers in particular were believed to have an important new role to play:

> The social problems the alcoholic creates within his or her family are already familiar to those social workers, health visitors and others working in the community, but specific social work with alcoholics and with their families has until now been largely undertaken by hospital social workers in the alcoholism treatment units, where they exist, probation officers and workers in the voluntary organizations. It is suggested that Local Authority social workers and others who may become aware of an alcoholic in the course of their work with families should consciously endeavour to motivate him towards treatment. The alcoholic and his family may need a great deal of help before they can accept the need for treatment. Social work support will need to continue during treatment and may be necessary for a considerable time while the client and his family work through other problems and readjust to altered patterns of living.

This point was reinforced in the 1975 White Paper *Better Services for the Mentally Ill* (Department of Health and Social Security 1975), 'Local authority social workers should recognize the needs of alcoholics and their families and should not, as sometimes happens now, shrink away from the attempt to help them, either personally or by referring them to other agencies.' While the earlier documents had made no mention of the training of social workers in responding to drinking problems, the later statements became very concerned about this omission:

> It cannot be taken for granted that social workers will have any theoretical instructions on alcoholism in their basic training. The training officers of social service departments should be allied to the need to help social workers as part of the staff development programmes, to gain greater understanding of the nature of dependence whether on alcohol or other habit forming substance, some skill in recognizing alcoholism in its early stages and more knowledge of the scope of the social work techniques and the contribution of specialized treatment in the support facilities for alcoholics.

Thus departmental policy in England and Wales changed considerably from the goal of a highly specialized psychiatric service towards the goal of an integrated community service, with particular emphasis on social work.

These new policies had suddenly brought the response to drinking problems within the area of responsibility of most agents working in the community. Yet no directions were given as to how community agents should go about fulfilling this role for which it was recognized they might not have been trained.

There was a suggestion that they would carry out their role with some form of connection with regional treatment units, who would also possibly be responsible for their training: 'the regional treatment units were not developed to replace the facilities offered by the existing psychiatric services, but so they might serve as a local focus of expertise, training and research for all services concerned with alcoholics in their region'. Again there was little guidance as to how exactly the units might become 'a local focus on expertise, training and research'. How were they to relate to community agents? By which mechanisms would 'all the services concerned with alcoholics' work together? Most important of all, why did the DHSS have to rebuke social workers gently for 'shrinking away' from the attempt to help alcoholics?

It indicated doubts as to whether general community agents such as social workers would be happy to accept their new responsibility and comments about their lack of training in this area also cast doubt on their competence for the task. Thus the shift of emphasis to a community response was something of a leap in the dark. While much research had been conducted on the orientation and efficacy of specialist hospital treatment, very little was known about the existing range of responses to drinking problems within the community. It was therefore one of the prime objectives of our studies of the general population and of general community agents to investigate the experiences of drinkers being treated in the community and to consider the difficult situation now confronting general community agents, who were being increasingly directed to respond to drinkers, but who were given little guidance as to how to respond, and seemed by inclination to prefer to 'shrink away'.

5 SEEKING, REFUSING OR HIDING FROM HELP

We have seen that specialist services cope with only a small proportion of people with drinking problems. In their present forms, Alcoholics Anonymous and the specialist psychiatric alcoholism services are neither logistically capable of dealing with more than a minority, nor are they seen as acceptable or approachable to many drinkers with problems. Counselling services are still embryonic, and non-existent in many areas. Services responding specifically to drinkers of no fixed abode are aimed at less than 5 per cent of all the people with problems from drinking.

What happens then to all the rest — the vast majority of people with problems from drinking who appear neither to seek nor receive help from specialist services? The most conservative estimate of the situation in England and Wales, for example, in the mid 1970s would have been that at least 300,000 people with a serious drinking problem made no contact with services making a specialist response to drinking problems. Did such people receive any help at all? And if so, where?

Consider a person experiencing problems with his drinking or worried about his drinking. Where is the first place he could turn? It might be thought that the first obvious source of advice, help or support would be his own family and friends. After all, various medical sociologists have shown that when there is a discrepancy between the overall prevalence of some problem and the numbers treated for that problem by formal agencies, this can often be explained by the existence of a lay helping network — a process operating within the community to provide informal, non-professional help. Such lay helping networks have been traced, for example, in the cases of pregnancy and child care by McKinlay (1973), who found that under-utilizers of natal services had tightly-knit social networks of kin and friends within close reach, while those who had their kin and friends more differentiated and geographically scattered were more likely to use the professional services. Satin (1971) concurred that the majority of symptom presenters at a psychiatric out-patient clinic had psycho-social problems particularly linked with isolation. Help seekers included significantly higher proportions of those living alone and those unmarried, separated or divorced. Kreitman and Chowdury (1973) found that nearly a half

of Samaritan clients were living alone, and a quarter of them could not
name one friend.

These studies suggest that the more family and kin are available, then
the less need there is for formal help. The fewer family and friends a
person has, the more likely he is to present problems at formal agencies.
Yet the indications from our own and other research appeared to show
that in the case of seeking help for drinking problems, exactly the
opposite applied.

In our 1974 general population survey, we tried to pick up evidence
of any lay helping network through a variety of questions designed to
elicit its possible existence and form. We particularly concentrated on
two groups within the sample who might have been expected to have
been involved in the giving or seeking of help because of problems
caused by drinking. These groups were (i) 'self-labelled' people with
problems from drinking: 10 respondents who answered affirmatively
when asked if they had problems from drinking either at the time of
interview or in the past and (ii) 36 respondents who answered
affirmatively when asked if anyone they knew well personally had
problems from drinking. The persons they talked about are referred to
as 'other-labelled' drinkers.

(i) *'Self-labelled' People with Drinking Problems*

Data on two of these 10 respondents was lost due to interviewer error.
The other 8 respondents were all asked if they had ever thought of
seeking lay help and if not why not, whether they had approached
anyone, or had been approached, to discuss their drinking problems
and if any help had ensued.

Only one respondent reported having ever approached any relative,
friend or workmate about her drinking problems. Even this only constituted asking her husband for help when she had a hangover, to
which he had responded by bringing her a Guinness, which she had
then duly consumed. No further 'help' had ensued. As for the remaining
seven, only one reported ever considering seeking help, but he had not
actually done so.

Four respondents thought that some of their friends, relatives or
contacts at work were aware of the effects from drinking, but only
one reported that another person had approached him about his
drinking. A fellow teacher at his school had suggested that he contact
Alcoholics Anonymous, but the respondent had considered this
unnecessary.

So these respondents neither tended to seek help for their drinking problems from their family, friends or workmates, nor did their personal contacts tend to approach them.

(ii) *'Other-labelled' People with Drinking Problems*

The 36 respondents who identified a person whom they knew well as having problems from drinking were asked whether they had ever discussed or had ever thought of discussing the person's drinking, either with the person concerned, or with other people. If problems had been discussed, respondents were then asked if any help had ensued.

Twenty respondents had never discussed the subject with the drinker they identified. Ten said that it was 'none of their business to interfere'. Four others felt it would be pointless and another four felt threatened by possible consequences. They clearly felt it was the place of only the closest relatives to approach drinkers about their problems: 'It's not my place', 'there were other members of the family nearer to her'. There were only four of these 36 respondents who were very close relatives of the drinker they knew, i.e. in a marital or parent/child relationship. All these four had discussed drinking problems with their relative.

Eight respondents had approached the drinkers by pointing out adverse consequences or advising them to 'pack it in' or 'ease up'. Nothing appeared to have come of these criticisms. A further three respondents reported having tried to reason with the drinker, but two got involved in rows whilst the other one had just been ignored. Another respondent said he had unsuccessfully tried 'gentle persuasion'.

Nineteen had spoken about the drinker's problems to persons other than the drinkers themselves. Fourteen of these cases involved just general conversation with no particular active approach in mind. Three respondents had attempted slightly more positive steps. One had warned off a girl from getting involved with the drinker in question; one made sure that the drinker's sister restricted the drinker to only one glass of wine when friends called; and the other respondent had offered help to the drinker, but he had 'started getting stroppy'.

In only three cases did the respondent know that the drinker he had identified had discussed drinking problems with anyone else. Two knew that the drinker's condition had been improved, one by a psychiatrist and one by a friend. The third respondent, who had identified her husband as having problems from drinking, reported that a friend of her husband's had offered him financial incentive not to drink: 'He bet my husband £10 he wouldn't drink till August . . . but the next night he was in the pub'.

In conclusion then, the response to both the 'self-labelled' people and 'other-labelled' people with drinking problems was not so much inadequate as virtually non-existent. There appeared to be no informal lay helping process at the disposal of these people. It appeared quite certain then that people with problems from drinking did not reject or postpone help from formal agencies because lay help was available to them.

Difficulties in initiating Responses to Drinkers

Most respondents in our general population sample perceived that drinking could cause a wide range of problems. Yet the survey also showed that on the whole respondents had not succeeded in helping drinkers who experienced these problems. It must be suspected then that there were considerable difficulties inherent in the process of responding to people with drinking problems. Two major areas of difficulty recurrently presented themselves throughout the data, the delicate nature of discussing drinking problems and the different perceptions of the situation held by the drinker and by those attempting to intervene.

The respondents who knew a drinker with problems obviously experienced great difficulty in trying to raise and discuss the subject with the drinker, and the survey mostly showed that the general population tended to consider drinking and drinking problems to be a matter of personal privacy. Any intervention was something considered best left to very close relatives, the family doctor or to a specialist in the field.

Not only was the topic of drinking and problems a delicate one to raise, but the validity of whatever comment was made would invariably be questioned or disregarded by the person inferred to drink heavily or to have problems. Almost everyone in the general population considered themselves to be average drinkers and would have been insulted to be told that they were drinking excessively or had problems from their drinking. Most persons considered themselves 'normal' drinkers and normal drinking was approved. An analysis of respondents who reported that they had been 'criticized' for their drinking or had been 'advised to cut down', showed that they were no more likely than other respondents to define themselves as having 'drinking problems' or to have sought help for drinking problems.

Each respondent was asked if they had suffered any of a list of 15 specific problems caused by drinking in the 12 months prior to interview, including the five problems referred to in Part 2. Ten respondents reported having experienced five or more of the problems and nine of these reported having been 'criticized' and eight being 'advised to cut down'. None of this, at least at the time of the interview, seemed to have had much bearing on their self-definition. None of them considered themselves to be 'problem drinkers' or 'alcoholics' or overtly wanted help. Indeed, whatever categorization one extracted from the general population, be it persons defining themselves as having problems, persons reporting experiencing alcohol related problems or persons reporting a consumption level way above average, none of these persons saw themselves as 'alcoholics' and only a minority of 4 defined themselves even as 'heavy' drinkers. It is hardly surprising then that respondents who identified persons they knew as having problems from drinking made little impression on the drinker by either persuasion or outright criticism. The data also added further support to our impression that persuasion and criticism had little effect if it did not come from someone close to the drinker. The respondent who reported the most alcohol-related problems — 12 out of the possible 15 — had been both 'advised to cut down' and 'criticized' for his drinking, but probably not by persons able to influence him strongly. He was single and did not live with his family. He had not sought, and seemed unlikely to seek treatment, despite the catalogue of problems from his drinking. Perhaps for him, at the time of interview at least, the benefits and enjoyment of his drinking outweighed the bad effects. This was encapsulated in his statement: 'It's nice to get completely and utterly inebriated. It's better than suicide'.

Unlike isolated people with other kinds of psycho-social problems, the socially-isolated person with problems from drinking tends to be unlikely to seek help. In this respect, the effects of alcohol itself may prevent help-seeking. The drinker's solution to his isolation and his alcohol related problems may be more alcohol. The drinker can become enmeshed in a vicious circle in which his drinking and problems will interactively accelerate, but neither are likely to be directly presented to a helping agent until a drinker is in a very damaged condition.

Reasons for seeking Help for Problems from Drinking

Since we found that most people perceived that drinking could cause a wide range of problems but they found it difficult to respond to them, either in themselves or in other people, it might be expected that

people to whom a response was made must have been (i) forced or
pressurized to accept help without necessarily wanting it or else (ii) the
bad effects had become so pronounced that they wanted help to reduce
the harm.

A small pilot survey was conducted of 18 patients at a specialist
psychiatric out-patient alcoholism clinic to discover if any preliminary
validation could be garnered for these speculations, though of course
the findings would have to be properly tested by more rigorous future
research. Nevertheless, these pilot interviews strongly suggested that
persons entered treatment when either they had been more or less
forced to come, or when a change in their experience of the effects
of alcohol made them reinterpret the bad effects as starting to outweigh
the good effects.

(i) *'Forced' and 'Pressurized' Help-seekers*

Twelve out of the sample of 18 hospital respondents had help thrust
upon them. Three were 'forced' to come by medico-legal referral and
nine were 'pressurized', in the sense that either (a) the contact had been
arranged for them by someone else or (b) another person had
threatened undesirable consequences if the person did not seek help.
Usually, the person applying the pressure had been the drinker's spouse.
In most of the cases, the spouse had threatened to leave the drinker if
they did not seek help. Out of the ten married respondents in the
sample, spouses had been instrumental in the help-seeking of nine of
them. The impact of the marital relationship upon help-seeking was also
a corollary of the fact that only very close relatives were likely to be
able to discuss the problems with the drinker in the first place.

There was no guarantee that a person 'forced' or 'pressurized' to
accept treatment wanted help or was prepared to change their definition of themselves. Some still defined themselves as 'normal' drinkers.
Yet an interesting reaction was that the only five persons in the hospital sample to define themselves as 'alcoholics' were all amongst those
respondents defined as 'pressurized' to accept help. It may have been
that they were using this label as a self defence for their own lack of
responsibility, and defining themselves as being in this situation because
they 'couldn't help it'.

(ii) *'Voluntary' Help-seekers*

The other six respondents in the sample had sought help more or less
voluntarily. This had not been directly due to the criticism or advice
of others, but rather because the drinkers themselves had come to

perceive the effects of alcohol as beginning to cause 'problems' which required assistance. In most of the cases, this re-interpretation had been triggered by the sudden onset of physiological or psychological effects after drinking which had frightened the drinker. To an extent the revised perception of the effects of drinking also acted as a validation of the criticism and advice of others which up to that point had been denied or ignored.

Drinkers and General Community Agents

If drinkers only arrived at specialist services when their problems had become so pronounced, how did they cope with the bad effects of alcohol up to this point? We have seen that there was little informal lay help available in the community, yet there would be many drinkers suffering considerable problems who had not been compelled or frightened into accepting specialist help. For instance, heavy drinkers would be very likely to experience harmful physiological effects, but they may not have connected their physical problems with their drinking or accepted the idea that drink may be harming them physically. This would still leave them with the physical problems, so perhaps these were presented to a helper working in the community such as a family doctor.

However, general community agents did not tend to believe they helped many people with drinking problems. As Davies (1974) noted, 'one of the unsolved mysteries of alcoholism has been the reports from surveys carried out by general practitioners of how few alcoholics they see, and the generally accepted findings of epidemiologists who stress how many there are'. So it would seem that the discrepancy between the prevalence of people known to have drinking problems and the small proportion receiving treatment was not just peculiar to specialist services, but seemed to apply equally to doctors working in the community. Indeed, when we asked our samples of general practitioners, social workers and probation officers to discuss a client they had seen in the last 3 months prior to interview whom they considered to have a drinking problem, some of the agents could not think of a single client who came into this category. Although 30 of the 31 GPs could select such a case, only 17 (74 per cent) of the 23 probation officers who worked in the district could think of one client of theirs with a drinking problem, whilst merely 8 (29 per cent) of the 28 social workers reported dealing with such a client in the 3 months prior to interview, although another 7 said they dealt with a family who included a person with a drinking problem.

Did this match up with the reports of contacts with general community agents made by drinkers with problems in our general population sample of the same district?

(i) 'Self-labelled' People with Drinking Problems

The 8 'self-labelled' people who felt they had problems from drinking were shown a list of all sorts of potential helpers whom they might have contacted, covering medical personnel, the social services, clergymen, Alcoholics Anonymous and so on. The respondents were asked if they had had any contact with any of these agents for any reason at all, and if so, whether the agents had become aware of their drinking problems.

It transpired that only one of the 8 had been helped directly for drinking problems by any of these agencies. He had been referred by his general practitioner to a psychiatric hospital and had also been sent by the hospital to Alcoholics Anonymous, which he had 'disliked intensely'.

The other 7 respondents had neither discussed drinking with any agent nor even so much as considered ever bringing up the question of their drinking.

(ii) 'Other-labelled' People with Drinking Problems

The 36 respondents who had reported that someone whom they knew well had problems from drinking were shown a similar list of potential helping agents whom the person they had identified might have contacted.

Eight of the 36 respondents knew that the drinker had been in contact with their general practitioner because of drinking or its effects. Three of these had been referred to psychiatrists and one had been admitted into a hospital.

Respondents mentioned a few other contacts, two with social workers, two with Catholic priests, one with Alcoholics Anonymous and one who had been sent to a rehabilitation centre, but they reported that either nothing had come of these contacts or else they were uncertain of the outcome.

No respondent knew of any contacts at all with Samaritans, Citizens Advice Bureaux, Alcohol Advice Centres, Marriage Guidance Councils or with any other helping organizations.

Because these respondents were not reporting their own contacts, but those of other people, it was not possible to make definitive statements about the response towards these 'other-labelled' people with problems from drinking. Nevertheless, it would appear that on the whole these drinkers had not received much help from formal helping agencies.

(iii) *The 'Research-labelled' People with Drinking Problems*

This group comprised 16 (5.6 per cent) respondents who either reported drinking more than 70 cl of absolute alcohol in the 7 days prior to interview or reported at least 5 out of the list of 15 alcohol-related problems. Although these cut-off points were of course arbitrary, the essential point for the present discussion is that this group were the respondents who reported the most consumption or the most problems — or both. It was only appropriate to ask two 'research-labelled' respondents who felt they had problems from drinking at the time of interview if they had contacted agencies about these problems. However, the other 14, like all respondents in the general population sample, were asked about their contacts with agents for any sort of problem.

Most of the 16 respondents had been in contact with their general practitioner. All but three had seen their general practitioner during the 12 months prior to interview and some had made multiple visits. Respondents mentioned other contacts, including four who had seen social workers. Five of them had been in contact with psychiatrists at some time and all five contacts could have been related to problems caused by drinking. Three had seen a psychiatrist about their own mental condition and the other two had seen a psychiatrist about a close relative. One had seen an educational psychologist about his son and the other had contacted a psychiatrist about his wife's nervous breakdown. Drinking problems might well have contributed to the unstable condition of these close relatives.

Yet again, it would seem that none of these drinkers had received very much help directly for their drinking problems from any of the agencies. But note an important fact: although in most cases they had neither directly sought nor received help specifically for their drinking, they had nevertheless been making a considerable number of contacts with formal agencies for one reason or another. In fact, when their rate of contacts with formal agencies was compared with that of the rest of the general population sample, it transpired that, on average, these respondents who reported the heaviest consumption and the most problems from drinking had a rate of contact with professional helpers *three times higher* than the rest of the sample and yet as far as could be detected, *none* of them had received any help specifically for their drinking problems.

Part of 'the mystery of the hidden alcoholics' was thus solved. It was not the drinkers who were hidden or the problems caused by their drinking; what did remain hidden was the drinking which caused the problems they presented to general community agents. It would therefore be no explanation of why GPs reported seeing 'so few alcoholics' to say that such people never visited their surgeries. They obviously did, three times more than the average patient. Why was it then that they received no direct help? Most obviously, it must have been because the subject of drinking was never brought up by the client and was never recognized by the agent.

Why did clients not present their problems as being due to drinking? First, there was the prevailing ignorance about the effects of alcohol. A person was simply unlikely to realize that his stomach troubles, his depression, his accidents or his poor sleep might be caused by too much drinking. It was also possible that agents responding to these problems might not have realized that drinking could be causing them. The question of drinking might never arise when people seek help for what are actually the bad effects of alcohol.

Second, the attitudes towards help amongst people with problems from drinking created something of a 'Catch 22' situation. They saw specialist services as unacceptable and unapproachable and yet at the same time they tended to think that only specialists could help. For the most part, the respondents in the general population sample did not think that non-specialist agents, with the possible exception of the family doctor, would have the knowledge or ability to deal with drinking problems. The table below shows which of a list of 10 agencies respondents thought would be 'the most or the second most helpful for people whose drinking is causing them problems' and also which agencies they thought would be the least or next to least helpful.

Obviously the family doctor was the only non-specialist agent whom a significant proportion of people considered to be the most helpful for people whose drinking was causing them problems. When asked their reasons for making this choice, a quarter replied that of the agents listed, the GP would know the most about the patient and his family, whilst another quarter said he could give 'good advice'. Yet the most popular reason for choosing the GP from the list was that he could refer on to the experts. Moreover, even many of the people who thought the family doctor was the most appropriate and approachable helper, felt that the potential advantages of general practice were not realized in actuality. People expected that the GP would be too short of time. Surgeries were not generally perceived as places where problems could

Table 5.1. Sources of Help for 'People whose Drinking is Causing Them Problems'.

Most or 2nd most helpful	N	%	Least helpful	N	%
1. Alcoholics Anonymous	134	46.9	1. Employer	137	47.9
2. Family doctor	132	46.2	2. Priest/Clergyman	49	17.1
3. Alcoholism Advice centre	93	32.5	3.Probation officer	31	10.8
4. Psychiatrist	47	16.4	4. Social worker	16	5.6
5. Drinking Advice centre	42	14.7	5. Family doctor	11	3.8
6. Social worker	30	10.5	6. Psychiatrist	9	3.1
7. Priest/Clergyman	26	9.1	7. Samaritans	4	1.4
8. Samaritans	26	9.1	8. Drinking Advice centre	4	1.4
9. Probation officer	6	2.1	9. Alcoholism Advice centre	3	1.0
10. Employer	6	2.1	10. Alcoholics Anonymous	1	0.3
Don't know	30	10.5	Don't know	21	7.3
Total	286		Total	286	

be discussed at length. Instead, respondents felt they were 'like factories'. More importantly, these same feelings were mirrored by the opinions of those people who had problems from drinking and who had contacted their family doctor. Of the three 'self-labelled' respondents who went to their GP, one did not want help for his drinking problems from his GP, one said 'it wasn't the doctor's job' whilst the other said his problems were 'not serious enough' to warrant taking up some of the GP's valuable time. Of the 16 'research-labelled' respondents who reported the heaviest consumption and/or the most problems, only five thought that they could discuss personal problems with their GP, and none felt that a doctor could do much to help practically, 'He can only advise, he can't really help'. Only one of these 16 respondents said he had ever considered approaching his GP about family or personal problems, but even he had not actually done so.

If the general public were not sure about the response made by GPs, they were even less convinced about potential help from other non-specialist agents. Many people did not think that agents such as probation officers or social workers had even so much as the right to bring up the topic of drinking or to discuss it with their clients. Whilst nearly all the general population sample thought that the family doctor had the right to ask questions about drinking, only 59 per cent thought social workers had this right. Respondents in all demographic groups believed the family doctor had the right to ask questions about drinking, but men were much less likely than women to believe social workers had any right to investigate drinking; older people were less likely than younger people to accept this right and lower occupational status groups accepted it less than the higher status groups. Of 116 (41 per cent) respondents who believed social workers had no right to discuss drinking, 15 said they were unsure why not, and 29 said that they felt social workers had no general right, but that questioning might be valid if drinking problems were the main reason the social worker was dealing with the case. The remaining 72 respondents thought social workers never had the right to ask questions about drinking. When asked why they believed this, their reasons fell into five major categories:

	Number of respondents
1. The client's drinking is his private concern	23
2. It is not the part of the social worker's function	17
3. A social worker has not got the right or authority	13
4. A social worker is not qualified enough	12
5. A social worker has no medical understanding	7

The most common reason for denying the social worker the right to ask about drinking, that it would intrude upon the privacy of the client, was often contrasted by respondents to the rights of doctors: 'A very personal thing, only the doctor should have the right'; 'Poking into their private affairs. They haven't got the same right as the doctor'. One respondent summed up the attitudes of many respondents: 'In a way nobody has, but a doctor has a certain amount of right'.

In general, respondents did not expect a probation officer would have to ask questions about drinking — 'I shouldn't have thought it was in his line' — unless drinking had something to do with the law breaking, when it was accepted that the probation officer had some right to make a response.

As for the other agencies on the list given to respondents, their potential response tended to be dismissed almost out of hand. Employers were expected to be largely unsympathetic and more likely to make a person with drinking problems redundant than to help him. In the case of priests and clergy, five times as many people considered they would be the least helpful as considered they would be the most helpful. They were expected to be too moralistic and critical and in some cases to be hypocritical, 'some of them drink heavy themselves, so they can't advise you'.

The disinclination to present drinking problems to a general community agent was thus not necessarily always the 'fault' of the drinker
or because he intentionally denied his problems or was afraid or
ashamed to discuss them. He might simply not have realized he could
discuss drinking with a particular agent, he may have felt it was pointless, or he may have been unsure whether he should raise the subject or
not. Not presenting problems to agents has often been interpreted as
conscious or unconscious 'denial' on the client's behalf, perhaps
because of their fear of possible stigmatization of themselves or their
family (Glatt 1961). In a study of clients of information centres, 74 per
cent of male clients admitted trying to 'fool' their general practitioner
about their drinking in the 12 months prior to interview and giving false
reasons for requiring a medical certificate (Edwards *et al.* 1967). The
general practitioners we interviewed frequently said that patients with
drinking problems often lied or denied their problems. But this might
sometimes have been more due to misunderstanding or a difference of
perspective between doctor and patient. When the sample of general
practitioners were asked to categorize the last patient they had seen
whom they considered to have a drinking problem, two thirds defined
them as 'alcoholics', and the rest as 'problem drinkers' or 'heavy drinkers'. When asked how the patients viewed themselves, only 30 per cent
of the doctors thought the patients would consider themselves 'alcoholics' and that only a further 6 per cent would agree that they had
problems from their drinking or even that they drank heavily. About
half the general practitioners said that their patient denied drinking
heavily, that drinking caused them problems or were otherwise unwilling to accept the general practitioner's view of their condition.
When doctor and patient could not agree, at least approximately, on
the nature and severity of a condition, a therapeutic relationship was
precluded with unfortunate results for a condition whose treatment,
especially via abstinence or reduced consumption, usually requires the
patient's active co-operation. Of course, possible apprehension about
being told to be abstinent or to cut down, and thus losing the good
effects of alcohol, may have increased the patient's tendency not to
discuss the bad effects of his drinking. The situation would be even
more confused when the client was unsure whether the agent had any
right or ability to deal with drinking problems.

All these complex factors helped explain why the majority of
people with drinking problems did not get help. Lay help was not
forthcoming and specialist help was not available, acceptable or
approachable. Although people with problems from drinking contacted

a variety of general community agents, three times more than the average person, their confusion, prejudices and uncertainty meant that the drinking itself never received a response. The subject might never have been discussed between client and helper. But so far we have mainly considered this in terms of the client. The general community agents themselves could not go blameless, for to have failed to recognize problems from drinking and to have failed to tackle drinking itself must have indicated some failings on their part.

6 THE ANXIETIES OF GENERAL COMMUNITY AGENTS

The discrepancy between the known prevalence of drinkers with problems and the minimal proportion who receive help has usually been explained in terms of the personality and behaviour of drinkers — that they are unmotivated to seek help and hide and deny their problems. The studies described in this book suggest that a much more rounded perspective is required. 'Hiding' of problems may reflect the prevailing belief throughout the community that drinking is a matter of personal privacy. Drinkers may not want anyone investigating or interfering with their drinking behaviour. The 'denial' of problems may sometimes be more of a misunderstanding between agent and client over definition and interpretation. The lack of 'willpower' and 'motivation' for treatment may be as much a reflection on the unacceptability and unapproachability of specialist treatments as upon the personality of the drinker. Just as alcohol abuse cannot be explained purely in terms of traits internal to drinkers neither can the 'mystery' of 'hidden drinkers' be explained purely in terms of the personality and behaviour of drinkers. The major explanatory factors may not lie within the drinkers themselves, but within the relationship between drinkers and those who respond to them. For we have seen that the difficulties within this relationship prevent informal lay help for drinking problems, whilst simultaneously making a specialist response which labels people as 'alcoholics' unacceptable to most drinkers with problems. Because lay help is precluded and specialist help is inadequate and inappropriate, what tends to happen is that the 'hidden' drinkers actually take their problems to various non-specialist agents within the community, although usually neither client nor agent will recognize or admit that drinking is causing the problems. Drinkers with problems contact general community agents much more regularly than other people, but their drinking rarely receives any recognition or response.

This is the element of the existing response which requires investigation. For we have noted that specialist services, because of their logistics and their approach, could never cope with the majority of drinking problems. On the other hand, it would be a very long term approach to try to create a lay response by public education campaigns attempting to change people's attitudes to discussing and dealing with drinking problems. Therefore the most pressing source of inadequacy in the existing response is the response of non-specialist community agents. Why was it that our survey could show that respondents who were drinking excessively and having problems from drinking made three times as many contacts with general community services as other respondents, and yet none of them had been helped specifically for their drinking?

We hypothesized that the explanation of this inadequate response would be found as much within the attitudes and behaviour of agents as of their clients. As described in the introduction, much of our work became focused on agents. Three major related themes emerged from all these studies. The general community agents failed to recognize and respond to drinking problems because they felt (1) anxieties about role adequacy through not having the information and skills necessary to recognize and respond to drinkers; (2) anxieties about role legitimacy through being uncertain as to whether or how far drinking problems came within their responsibilities; (3) anxieties about role support through having nowhere to turn for help and advice when they were unsure how to or whether to respond.

(1) Anxieties about Role Adequacy

The most obvious reason why many drinkers with problems go un-recognized is that nearly all the agents interviewed and examined by questionnaire lacked the necessary knowledge and skills to recognize symptoms and behaviour which indicated problems from drinking.

The data from our *Alcohol and Alcohol Problems Perception Questionnaire* completed by many geographically-dispersed agents from different professions and working environments revealed that less than 10 per cent of community agents had received any educational training whatsoever in dealing with alcohol and alcohol abuse and that the training of the 'educated' agents had generally been limited to less than one day. General community agents who completed a questionnaire section examining their knowledge of academic and clinical facts about alcohol and alcohol-related problems scored virtually no higher than a sample of intelligent laymen. As social workers commented in our 1974 agency study:

In generic training, very little attention is paid to this sort of thing and there is very little opportunity when working to go on courses to get the specialized knowledge that is needed ... There is no real training or experience in the field which goes against us picking up drinking problems . . . We lack access to knowledge. We have a lack of training facilities.

Not one of the GPs in our 1974 agency study had received any education at all about drinking problems. Even though problems from drinking are probably as extensive amongst the patients of general practitioners as, say, chronic bronchitis and marital difficulties, the medical undergraduate curriculum has in the past made only passing reference to the more esoteric symptoms of 'chronic alcoholism'. Recent developments have gone some way toward redressing this gap, but even when information about alcohol-related problems is included in the education of social and medical professionals it is rarely accompanied by any training in how to acquire the skills necessary to translate this knowledge into practical responses. For example, agents have rarely been trained in the skills necessary to investigate clues to drinking problems.

A Narrow Range of Clues

All the agents in our 1974 study were asked 'what sort of things generally lead you to suspect that a client might have a drinking problem?' The sign most frequently mentioned by GPs was simply the smell of alcohol on the patient's breath. Their other main clues were the various physical symptoms associated with excessive alcohol consumption and a quarter of the doctors also reported having detected drinking problems through the patient's history of accidents and family troubles. But in general GPs mentioned a fairly narrow range of clues. Half mentioned only two clues and most of the rest mentioned either one or three. This compares with a potential list of 64 indicators of drinking problems complied by Wilkins (1974) from the literature and from a study of drinkers in his own group practice. Using this list, 155 patients in this practice were diagnosed as 'alcoholics', of whom only eight had consulted specifically for help with their drinking problems. The disparity between the usual low recognition rate and the high rate achieved by a methodical drink-focused recognition procedure reflects not just the lack of training in recognition but also the fact that virtually every presenting symptom of drinking problems could be caused by factors other than alcohol. Doctors are faced with a most complex differential diagnosis in which they will probably tend to firstly consider possibilities other than drink.

The interviewed probation officers likewise reported that the clue which most frequently alerted them to the possibility of a drink problem was the smell of alcohol on the client's breath, especially when coupled with a dishevelled appearance and reports of family troubles and financial difficulties. Several probation officers also felt that persistent unpunctuality and failure to keep appointments might be significant. But like doctors, probation officers were also aware that many drinking problems went unrecognized. Only two disagreed with the statement that 'alcoholics often pass unnoticed'.

Half the local authority social workers also mentioned the smell of alcohol as a clue in detecting drinking problems, but to them the most significant clue was financial difficulty. They also thought family troubles, accidents and poor work record were often indicative of drinking problems, and some reported having been alerted by indirect evidence of drinking, such as bottles lying around the client's house. Like the other agents, virtually all the social workers agreed that 'alcoholics often pass unnoticed'.

Failure to detect Drinking Problems

Very few of the agents who had dealt with a client with drinking problems in the three months prior to interview had detected the drinking problems of this client by themselves. GPs had usually been informed by members of the patient's family, although in some cases the patient himself had brought up the subject, and in others the problem had been documented in case notes written by another agent. Only a quarter of the GPs had detected the problem by themselves. There was a somewhat different pattern amongst probation officers and local authority social workers. Their contact with clients is usually not as long-standing as between patient and family doctor and clients are often referred to them because of specific problems about which they have been notified in considerable detail before they make any contact with the client. Accordingly, only one probation officer and none of the social workers had detected the client's drinking problems by themselves. In most cases, they had been notified of the client's drinking problems by another agent though in a few cases they had been informed by the client's family.

So the community agents were not aware of many indicators of drinking problems and they did not detect them much by themselves. This is one reason why drinkers with problems in the community can attend surgeries and contact social services without the subject of drinking ever being raised by agents. These clients can make multiple demands on services, especially since the problems caused by their drinking, such as gastritis, neglect of children or crimes committed while intoxicated, will just recur, possibly increase in severity and in turn create other problems. For example, if a social worker does not recognize that a client's financial problems and difficulties looking after her children are both due to heavy drinking, the social worker may increase the client's financial assistance. The client would be likely to spend the extra money on more drink, thus making her even less able to look after her children. The failure of general community agents to properly identify and assess the place of alcohol in the sum of a person's problems reflects a widespread ignorance and underestimation of the bad effects of alcohol, which agents share with the rest of the community, as described in Part One. Because agents have not been trained to appreciate the potential importance of drinking in causing or exacerbating problems, they do not focus on drinking itself even when it is a root cause of many problems. This can waste much of their therapeutic effort. More seriously, the failure to recognize might be potentially dangerous for the client. But it would not really be fair to castigate agents for this failing. They have never been told what clues to look for, what are the important questions to ask or how to interpret the answers. Many of them were aware of their inadequacy in this respect. As one social worker remarked, 'It tends to be a problem which is overlooked. There seems to be a tendency for problems within the family to be dealt with to the exclusion of the actual alcohol problem'.

A Sense of Hopelessness

The overlooking of drinking problems is not just a lack of intellectual awareness. The problems may be overlooked because agents feel they have not been trained to respond and cannot really do anything to help anyway — 'There are no set procedures for doing anything even if one has discovered the problem'. To overworked general community agents there can seem little or no point in recognizing drinking problems. As one doctor said of his colleagues, 'a lot feel it's a waste of time'.

The pervasiveness of this sense of hopelessness in responding to drinking problems was confirmed when the agents were asked what they, as members of their profession, had to offer clients with drinking problems. A quarter of the general practitioners felt that they personally had 'nothing to offer' to people with drinking problems and another quarter were uncertain whether they had anything to offer or not. A sense of helplessness surrounded their views of diagnosis, treatment and referral. As one doctor said, 'I was interested ten years ago, but I failed and gave up'. Not surprisingly then, over half the GPs said that their most important resource was referral and one in five felt referral would be the 'only' thing they had to offer. One doctor remarked 'I can't handle this problem — I don't want to know how to, apart from referral'.

In contrast, probation officers seemed slightly more self-confident about their ability to help drinkers and more optimistic about the efficacy of their intervention. Probation officers tended to perceive drinkers with problems as being isolated, rejected and drinking to cope with difficulties in their life. Probation officers therefore put more positive stress on the value of therapeutic support, especially in overcoming what they saw as the drinker's loss of personal esteem. They felt they might be able to help drinkers recover some of this — 'We try to make them realize they are worth saving.' In this way, as one officer put it 'clients with drinking problems are encouraged to stay within society'. Even so, over half of them perceived referral as their main resource.

Most of the social workers felt they could do more for the families of clients with drinking problems than they could for the drinkers themselves. Assistance for the client's family was the form of help most mentioned by social workers. One in three social workers felt they had 'little or nothing' to offer clients with drinking problems, and many of the rest thought referral was their main resource. They said that they lacked the time and knowledge to do anything themselves.

The three groups of agents were also asked what exactly they had done to help the last client they had dealt with whom they considered to have drinking problems. Half the GPs felt they had done 'nothing at all' and of those who thought they had helped very few appeared to have had any set programme or ideas about treatment. Some said they had given some form of medical help, usually drugs. Others reported having given the patient 'emotional help' or 'general support', while a couple felt they had given the patient insight into the causes of their drinking behaviour, but as one doctor summarized the situation, 'we are swimming around in the dark'.

On the other hand, only two of the probation officers reported feeling they had done nothing to help. The majority said they had given various types of support, particularly 'emotional support', in the sense of acceptance and understanding and help for the client's family, especially over financial matters. Over half felt they had given their client insight into their problems and a third reported giving them legal advice.

Of the social workers who had seen a client with a drinking problem in the three months prior to interview, half said they had done nothing to help their client, whilst the others reported helping with financial and

accommodation problems, and supporting the drinker's spouse. Social
workers reported referring some of these clients to psychiatrists.

Half the GPs reported having referred on the client, mostly to
psychiatrists, though in a couple of cases to AA. Half the probation
officers had referred on their clients, in equal proportions to psychiatrists and to AA. The other clients, who had not been referred by
probation officers and social workers were mostly already in contact
with psychiatrists.

When agents were asked if their intervention had improved either
the client's drinking behaviour or their life in general, about half the
GPs felt there had been an improvement on both these dimensions.
However, the other half reported no change or even a deterioration in
the client's drinking and life in general. Nearly half the probation
officers saw no change or a deterioration in the client's life in general
and only a few perceived any improvement in their drinking behaviour.
On the other hand, half the officers reported some improvement in the
client's life in general. Only one local authority social worker said there
had been any improvement in either the client's drinking behaviour or
life in general.

The sense of having little to offer clients with drinking problems and
the feeling of hopelessness in responding to drinking problems was
probably the keenest indication of the agents' anxieties about role
adequacy. They did not feel they had the information and skills necessary to help people effectively with drinking problems. Only 45 per
cent of the GPs, 39 per cent of the probation officers and 36 per cent of
the social workers disagreed with the statement, 'I have nothing to offer
clients with drinking problems'. Those who felt that they could offer
something predominantly felt that referral was their most appropriate
response.

Many of the interviewed agents were openly concerned about the
inadequacy of their own information and skills and about the feelings
of anxiety which this engendered.

'You feel that you haven't got the expertise and you feel that for
some reason she doesn't take your position seriously.' 'I don't know
if he knows I don't know but I do and that's what makes it so
difficult.' 'She's been drinking and at the time saying she doesn't
drink . . . which completely unnerved me because I didn't know how
to get through that.'

In general, the sense of being inadequately trained was least marked

amongst GPs, although the interview data gave no indication that
general practitioners were any more skilled or knowledgeable than
probation officers or social workers. Indeed, subsequent studies on the
other groups of agents, using the AAPPQ, have shown that non-specialist medical personnel tend to score lower than social workers and
probation officers on measures of therapeutic skill with drinkers.

As we will proceed to demonstrate, the feeling of role adequacy is
not simply a reflection of the amount of information and training
which an agent has received, but also depends on other factors in the
agent's working situation.

(2) Anxieties about Role Legitimacy

Recognizing and responding to drinking problems is not assured even if
an agent feels he had adequate information and skills. Neither does the
mere fact that an agent suspects or detects a drinking problem ensure
any subsequent investigation. A response is still sometimes precluded
because the agent does not feel he has the right to make a response even
when he strongly suspects that drinking may be one of the major causes
of problems.

In particular, the general community agents tended to be uncertain
about whether they had the right to discuss drinking with their clients,
and felt that broaching the subject might ruin their relationship with
clients.

The agents were asked if they felt they had the right to ask a client
how much he drank even if the client himself had not raised the
subject. GPs and probation officers felt in the main that they did have
the right to ask clients about drinking problems, because of their respective medical and legal authority. Yet, only a quarter of the doctors and
probation officers said that they felt 'no reservations' about asking
clients such questions. Most believed that drinking was a delicate question and inquiries had to be made tactfully 'in a round-about way'.
Many reported that they had to 'mix in' questions about drinking with
other questions 'to make it less obvious' and some remarked that 'you
can ask the questions, but you can't expect an honest reply'.

Nearly two thirds of GPs and probation officers reported that clients
whom they considered to have drinking problems denied them when
the agent first raised the issue. But it is not just clients who are sometimes frightened or embarrassed about discussing their drinking; agents
can be equally apprehensive: 'I would be concerned that he would see
me as a hostile figure'; 'One has to tread very delicately, particularly if
they are feeling guilty about it. I would tread warily, they get very bad-

tempered.'

Thus uncertainty over role legitimacy makes the agent feel threatened and therefore disinclined to approach the client with a drinking problem. Even though 90 per cent of the GPs thought they had the right to ask their patients how much they drank, none of the interviewed GPs knew the actual consumption level of the last patient they had seen whom they considered to have a drinking problem. Virtually all the GPs reported some difficulties in asking patients about their drinking. Two specifically mentioned being embarrassed about asking women, two mentioned their fear of violence and one that the patient might leave the practice. GPs were thus aware not only of the reluctance of patients to present and discuss drinking problems, but also of their own reluctance to bring up the subject. If GPs feel threatened by patients with drinking problems and have difficulties discussing the subject, it is not surprising that recognition is not vigilantly carried out.

The social workers did not even agree that they had the right to intervene in principle. Whereas GPs and probation officers saw their role and rights as being ascribed to them and legitimized by medical and legal authority, the local authority social workers perceived their role and rights as being negotiated with each client. Over a third of the social workers disagreed with the statement that 'social workers have the right to ask any client how much they drink and others were 'uncertain'.

Social workers believed that their right to ask questions about drinking depended on their relationship with each individual but in general they feared that inquiries about drinking might wreck the casework relationship. Several said they would only 'do it hesitantly' while others stated that they would prefer the clients themselves to bring up the matter. The social workers' approach seemed to be extremely tentative, 'Very delicate, personally, I won't do it initially. I would take a long time before asking him'.

Accordingly, only a few social workers reported having had clients deny their drinking problems, presumably because social workers tended to raise the subject when the relationship felt right to them and not because they thought they had a medical or legal right to raise the issue regardless of the relationship. However, one could not help but suspect that a number of the interviewed social workers perhaps used their concern for maintaining the relationship as an excuse for never raising the subject of drinking.

Uncertainty over Responsibilities

Agents were not only unsure about how far clients accepted their rights to respond to drinking problems. They were equally unsure about how far either their colleagues and those who set their priorities saw responding to drinking problems as part of their professional responsibilities. Of a sample of 46 in our 1976 probation officer study, 44 felt it was part of their professional responsibility to work with drinkers. But only 38 felt that their colleagues shared this perception of their role, only 33 felt that it was shared by their profession as a whole, and only 27 believed that those who set their professional priorities included responding to drinking problems amongst the responsibilities of the probation service. In sum, 96 per cent felt a responsibility to respond to drinkers, but only 31 per cent believed this was clearly defined and accepted by the probation service.

So although the Department of Health and Social Security had been exhorting general community agents to respond to drinkers, many agents were uncertain and confused about how far this should apply in practice. They sensed a discrepancy between their own priorities and those of the organizations for which they worked. Numerous agents interviewed openly criticized the attitudes and policy of their department towards clients with drinking problems.

In our 1974 study, many probation officers working in the London suburb said drinking problems were seen as a low priority for the probation service and others bemoaned the lack of official procedure for coping with people with drinking problems — 'We don't have a stated policy — each officer is free to do as he likes.'

Over two-thirds of the local authority social workers criticized the way in which their social services department responded to people with drinking problems. Like the other groups of agents, they remarked upon the recurring problems of lack of resources, staff and time and were concerned about a lack of awareness and training amongst social workers. But the most common criticism, mentioned by half of them, was of the confusion surrounding their responsibility for clients with drinking problems.

A majority of social workers interviewed in both our 1974 and 1976 studies accepted some responsibility for working with drinkers, but many felt that 'in reality' they were better dealt with somewhere else, especially as those who set their priorities had not clearly outlined their rights and obligations — 'We are confused by the lack of statutory obligation to help. The problems seem to be pushed under the mat.'

Some social workers denied responsibility for responding to drinking problems on the grounds that they had been deemed a low priority by departmental policy — 'The Department sees alcoholism as a subsidiary problem'. 'The problem is practically not recognized as a problem. Since Seebohm we deal with families'.

The interviewed social workers said that clients with drinking problems were neglected or had insufficient time spent on them because they were not specifically included within the principal mandatory statutory responsibilities of local authority social workers. Social workers in Britain have only 'permissive' obligations to respond to clients with drinking problems. Since they consider themselves a highly overworked scarce resource, they rate people with drinking problems as a low priority within their overall work.

Uncertainty over Boundaries of Competence

The agents' uncertainty about whether they were responsible for responding to drinking problems was compounded by the way drinking problems straddle professional boundaries of expertise. Each group of agents was uneasy about responding to those aspects of drinking problems most distant from their usual sphere of knowledge and responsibility. The 1976 probation officer study revealed them to be least confident in their knowledge of the effects of alcohol in the areas of psychological and clinical aspects. Two-thirds of them felt they lacked sufficient knowledge of the medical effects of alcohol and that they did not know enough about the roles and approaches of other agencies in dealing with these effects. Half felt they did not know enough about the causes and indicators of drinking problems. The probation officers felt most confidence in their knowledge and ability in the area of social problems caused by alcohol — the area of drinking problems for which they had the most clear role-responsibility and related training. Even so, this sense of confidence might not stretch as far as dealing with the underlying drinking itself, especially when it is perceived as lying within the sphere of medical competence into which probation officers, like social workers, are loathe to intrude.

Yet the GPs also felt uncertain whether it was legitimate for them to respond to drinking problems. Many felt it should be the responsibility of a specialist. GPs did not conceptualize 'alcoholism' as a straightforward illness and did not always perceive themselves as clearly obligated to respond.

The agents' anxieties about role legitimacy thus comprised three major themes. They were unsure of their rights and responsibilities as regards individual clients, the policy and approach of their organization and the sphere of their competence in responding to problems with both medical and social facets.

(3) Anxieties about Role Support

The agents' feelings of lacking knowledge, training, and resources, combined with uncertainty over their rights and obligations, created a general sense of ignorance, helplessness and doubts about their competence.

Neither was there any available source of help to assuage their doubts. The feeling of lacking role support was endemic to a working situation in which agents had to respond to drinking problems, felt neither adequate nor legitimate in doing so and had nowhere to turn for information, advice and support.

The agents' expressions of their need for support took two dimensions. Some agents said they would welcome a person with whom they could talk about their difficulties. Others wanted someone who would take over responsibility for clients with drinking problems. In either case, general community agents wanted a specialist. In our 1974 agency study, 84 per cent of GPs, 74 per cent of probation officers and 71 per cent of social workers believed that organizations should have workers with a special responsibility for dealing with clients who have drinking problems.

This concurred with their responses to the statement, 'To effectively help alcoholics requires specialist training' with which 81 per cent of the GPs, 70 per cent of the probation officers and 61 per cent of the social workers agreed.

Yet general community agents did not feel supported by the existing specialist services and so their feelings about the current specialist response were rather ambivalent. Although the GPs referred drinkers to psychiatrists they were openly sceptical of psychiatric treatment, which they believed was 'notoriously ineffective in alcoholism'. Others felt psychiatrists could not be conversant with the patient's family and background and some felt it might be a disadvantage to stigmatize drinkers as 'mentally ill'. One-third of doctors also referred clients to AA, but they were often uncertain about what went on there — 'I am not sure what they do, but it is a very good thing'. Some took a more critical view of AA as being 'lay people dabbling in semi-science'. GPs did not refer drinkers to anyone but psychiatrists or AA and did not tend to incorporate any other agents in their treatment programme. Like GPs, probation officers felt in general that psychiatry did have something else to offer, particularly deeper insight and the advantages of more time and greater detachment. But again several officers criticized the psychiatrist's distance from the actual situation – 'they stand too far back to do anything much'. Probation officers found psychiatrists particularly unhelpful in the feedback process. There was a general feeling that psychiatrists 'could be a little more forthcoming about what they are doing with their clients'. Some expressed stronger attitudes – 'psychiatrists sometimes send back bald statements about clients with no explanation, as if they were handing down a judgement'. Probation officers felt that this belittled their own professionalism and expertise. There was also a strong undercurrent of sceptism amongst social workers about the effectiveness of psychiatric therapy, particularly in the case of clients without much motivation. Their general feeling about AA was that its orientation towards self-help and group support could be useful for a relatively small proportion of drinkers with problems, but that most 'could not stick to it'.

So there was an ambivalent situation in which agents said they believed in a specialist response, but were uncertain about the competence and the effectiveness of the specialist response which existed. A considerable proportion of agents felt they themselves have nothing to offer, but that when it came down to it neither did the supposed experts.

General community agents did not only feel unsupported by specialist services, they also felt unsupported by each other. GPs reported virtually no contact with probation officers in dealing with clients with drinking problems. Half the GPs felt that social workers had something else to offer, especially practical help such as sorting out financial problems. However, it was their potential that they regarded as valuable rather than their actual work. Numerous critical comments were made of the way local authority social workers operated in practice. Several GPs complained that social workers had not fulfilled functions they should have carried out such as making domiciliary visits requested by doctors. One GP commented, 'They are singularly unhelpful. It is difficult to contact them'. Another complained that 'They are rare visitors. Visits are too few and far between'. Others complained of the rapid turnover of social work staff. One GP concluded, 'the DHSS said we should accept them as colleagues but doctors don't tolerate them. They are not a colleague on the same level'.

Probation officers tended to see social workers as having insufficient time and too overburdened a case load to be able to respond properly to drinking problems. Probation officers thought that the GPs' medical knowledge and unique relationship with the client and his family meant his competence and authority was accepted and that this put the GP in an excellent position in which to make early detection of drinking problems, to give appropriate medication and to refer clients. But probation officers considered that in actuality GPs were handicapped by lack of time and by the impersonality of modern general practice. They thought that GPs 'could be crucial people' but that 'they do not perform their function well'. Another felt that 'he would like to say that they could offer expertise – but in practice they don't appear to'. Social workers looked to general practitioners to recognize symptoms at an early stage, to treat them and to make referrals when necessary. But some felt GPs were not sympathetic or interested in helping people with anything other than clearly medical problems, others felt GPs had insufficient time and a few believed that GPs were ignorant of the symptoms of alcohol abuse.

Not surprisingly, then, general community agents seemed disinclined to co-operate with each other in responding to drinking problems.

Over a third of the GPs expressed reservations about passing on information to non-professional and non-medical agencies and to social workers in particular. They said they were reluctant to do this in cases of drinking problems because they were afraid of losing the patient's trust. One GP described social workers as being unaware of the confidentiality of information, and another described them as 'not bound by professional secrets', believing that 'a lot of gossiping went on'. Social workers themselves had little reservation about informing GPs or indeed other professional agencies, but they reported that they sent less information to administrative and lay agencies. Probation officers too said they had little hesitation about passing on information to professional agencies where they felt the ethic of confidentiality would be understood, but some said they had reservations about passing on information to voluntary organizations like AA and to administrative agencies such as employment offices, to whom they reported sending much less fully-documented information. Many of the agents in each profession felt that current communications between them over cases of drinking problems were inadequate, but they tended to attribute this to inefficiency and lack of opportunity to discuss cases rather than to an outright refusal to share information or to share the therapeutic response.

Agents thus felt as though they were operating in a vacuum – responding to drinking problems without any worthwhile assistance from others. This further exacerbated their uncertainty over their obligations to respond and their sphere of competence. They felt forced against their will to become involved with problems which, as they saw them, should have been the responsibility of someone else. For example, a social worker faced with a client undergoing severe withdrawal would be completely unprepared by his training to interpret the client's experiences and behaviour or to advise and support him through the withdrawal period. The social worker's anxiety over his inability to respond will be increased if a GP or psychiatrist cannot or will not inform the social worker about the condition of the client and the best ways to help him. A remark which typified the social worker's feelings was that 'we feel we are being left to carry a lot of things we are not able to manage. We need support.'

This sums up the three major threads running through the subjective feelings of general community agents about their response to drinking problems. First, they were anxious about their role adequacy. They felt unprepared to make a viable response to drinking problems. They had no resources at their disposal, either from their personal training or from their work situation. They did not know enough about alcohol and alcohol abuse, they could not recognize, assess or counsel drinkers and they felt they had little to offer except referral. Second, they were anxious about their role legitimacy in responding to a problem area which required not only skills generic to their own profession, but those of other professions too. Anxieties about role legitimacy centred on the way drinking problems have both medical and social components; agents were unsure of their rights, responsibilities and spheres of competence. They were doubtful whether their view of how they should respond to drinking problems would be shared by their clients, their colleagues or those who set the priorities for their profession. They therefore declined to stray into areas where they felt unable to manage. Third, they were anxious about lacking role support. They felt that those specialists to whom they referred drinkers were little better equipped to respond than themselves, and these specialists did not communicate or co-operate with the referring agent. Neither was there any helpful interaction with other community agents or even their own colleagues. They felt as though they had to 'go it alone'. That is why they said 'we need support'.

7 ROLE INSECURITY AND LOW THERAPEUTIC COMMITMENT

During the phase of the analysis of the data reported in Chapter 6 we adopted an overall theoretical term which would conceptually combine the three interacting components of the inadequacy of the response of general community agents to clients with drinking problems — that they did not know how to respond, they were unsure whether they should respond or not and felt unsupported in making their response. Agents who subjectively experienced these feelings we defined as experiencing 'role insecurity'. They were insecure because they did not know what their role with drinkers should be, how it could be carried out or who could help and advise them.

All three aspects of role insecurity — anxieties about role adequacy, role legitimacy and role support were all basically caused by deficiencies either in the agents' training or in their working situation. They were unprepared to respond to drinking problems either at an intellectual level or by the conditions of their profession. In turn, they also felt *emotionally* unprepared to respond to drinking problems.

Since role insecurity was manifested emotionally, agents were not always able to discuss the components of their role insecurity objectively or dispassionately. Although their sense of inadequacy was due to deficiencies in their training and working situation, feelings of personal inability were not easily tolerable to professional helpers. To feel so uncertain and so incapable represented a considerable threat to professional self-esteem and it was the manifestation of this sense of threat which most strongly characterized the role-insecure agent. Role insecurity was therefore caused initially by agents feeling unprepared *intellectually* and *situationally* to respond, but it was manifested by them being unprepared *emotionally* to respond. Emotionally, they did not want to recognize and respond to drinking problems. We termed this emotional expression of role insecurity *'low therapeutic commitment'*.

Low therapeutic commitment to drinkers was in a sense a safeguarding strategy to protect professional self-esteem, a justification for the agents' inability to respond. The agents were insecure because they felt unable to respond to clients with drinking problems, so they safeguarded themselves by maintaining low commitment to such clients. Low therapeutic commitment was manifested by five overlapping dimensions.

First, as noted by the 1975 White Paper (Department of Health and Social Security 1975), some agents did indeed 'shrink away' and avoided responding to drinking problems. Second, they sometimes tried to get rid of clients with drinking problems. Third, some agents pessimistically interpreted drinking problems as unalterable and so believed that it was useless to respond and fourth, some projected their feelings of threat onto the client and blamed the client for posing the difficulties actually created by the agent's own feelings of inadequacy. Fifth, agents sometimes rationalized not responding to drinking on the grounds that it would be unfair or too demanding on their clients.

1. Avoiding Drinking Problems

Avoidance took various forms but most commonly agents simply denied the existence of drinking problems: 'In this office we don't seem to have clients with drinking problems or people don't seem to talk about them'. Sometimes their existence was recognized, but agents denied their seriousness thus implying they neither required nor merited any response. This was rationalized by the agents in terms of the low priority of drinking problems compared to other matters more pressing on their scarce time and skill. Avoidance behaviour by agents was also indicated by the high prevalence of unrecognized and untreated alcohol-related problems amongst people in the general population sample who had been in contact with general community agents.

General community agents rarely diagnosed any drinking problems by themselves until they had become blatant and when, possibly, some of the damage had become irreversible. To quote one social worker, 'I would only intervene anyway if it was beginning to have obvious effects on themselves or others.' General community agents only felt assured in defining exceptionally physically, psychologically and socially deteriorated clients as 'alcoholics'. The stigmatizing implication of the label, which agents shared with the general public, made them avoid applying it for as long as possible. Moreover they would only tend to refer on a client as an 'alcoholic' or as having a drinking problem when they were sure that a specialist would agree with their diagnosis, for it would reflect badly on their professional competence if the specialist disagreed that the client had a drinking problem. General community agents therefore tended only to 'recognize' clients whose problems of alcohol abuse had reached an advanced stage.

In some cases, the recognition of clients with drinking problems was completely precluded from the outset: 'If our receptionist sees someone for example, middle-aged, male, no family, who looks run down, she would tend to send him on . . . social workers don't get them coming through, though this isn't formal policy.'

2. Getting Rid of Drinkers

In some cases the problem was too obvious for the agent to be able either to avoid it or to deny that it merited a response. In such cases, referring the drinker to another agent, especially a 'specialist', was a way of safeguarding the agent's professional self-esteem. It maintained the veneer of 'having done the right thing', while really achieving the desired effect — getting rid of the client. Amongst the general community agents, referral was the most common form of response they felt they could offer clients with drinking problems, and often it was the only response they felt they could make. Referral was justified on the grounds that the client was not clearly the agent's responsibility or that another agent may be better fitted to deal with the client. Some agents linked this to their belief that 'alcoholism' was an esoteric condition which could only be dealt with by an expert.

Yet the study revealed that nearly all the general community agents who claimed that a specialist response was necessary for drinkers, and who tended to refer them on, also demonstrated in their answers to other questions that they were largely pessimistic about the efficacy and purpose of this specialist treatment, and did not really believe the specialist would be able to respond any better than themselves. Knox (1971) has also noted that referral of drinkers is usually made with a degree of cynicism. Psychiatrists and psychologists working in the community tended to recommend hospital treatment for people with drinking problems although they felt it was unlikely to be effective and were not inclined to take part in that treatment themselves. Numerous agents we interviewed gave equivocal reasons for referring clients with drinking problems and some admitted using referral as a means of avoiding personal responsibility. Agents often discontinued seeing the drinker after referral: 'We have a tendency to opt out of responsibility once the client is being seen by a hospital, even as an out-patient'. For some agents, the cynical nature of their referral of drinkers was quite overt — 'We don't do anything . . . we try to get rid of them.'

3. Regarding Drinking Problems as Unalterable

Some agents justified not responding on the grounds that drinking problems were unalterable, and therefore by implication were not worthy of any responsive effort. This was expressed in two attitudes. Some perceived drinkers as incorrigible clients who would never change their drinking behaviour. Clients with drinking problems tended to be despairingly dismissed as 'hopeless cases', a concept abetted by the idea of the incurability and continual relapsing of 'alcoholics'.

'A bit of me says don't try to do too much because what will happen then? This produces frustrations so you decide to limit yourself and give only a bit of yourself . . . I'm a pessimist as regards drinkers.' 'There is no way of stopping them.'

The assumption that nothing can be done relieves the agent of any anxiety over failing to make any progress with clients with drinking problems.

When agents knew clients drank heavily, but did not consider them to be 'alcoholics' the excessive drinking was still wearyingly accepted as an inevitable part of life. In the words of one social worker who said she had no 'problem drinkers' on her caseload — 'every wife I have complains that her husband drinks too much'. The emotional response of such agents was one of despairing hopelessness.

4. Blaming the Drinker

When agents did not feel knowledgeable or adequate enough in making a response to drinking clients, these clients became a distinct threat to the professional's self-image. But agents did not blame their working situation for their role insecurity; they chose the simpler rationalization of blaming the client. By projecting their feelings of threat onto the client, they also justified to themselves their failure to respond. The client became the scapegoat for the professional's lack of training, support, and clear responsibility. The agents thus explained away their own feelings of inadequacy and therapeutic ineffectiveness. To quote a social worker: 'I don't feel I have any success in working with people with drinking problems. They lack motivation.' Her explanation for her failure to respond was that the drinkers did not allow her to respond: 'They won't co-operate.'

As a probation officer said, 'My attitudes to alcoholics are fairly neutral, but it's the reaction of the client.'

One form of blaming of the client with drinking problems seemed peculiar to the local authority social workers. They were responsible for whole families as compared with a doctor's primary obligation to the individual patient, and a probation officer's usual responsibility for individual clients. In dealing with the family, the social worker some-times perceived the drinker as causing the problems which affected the others, and saw their own role as protecting the rest of the family rather than empathizing with the problems of the drinker: 'We are involved to protect others; we see others suffer from those who do not want help.'

Some social workers spontaneously expressed their feelings of role conflict between their responsibility to the drinker's family and their responsibility to the drinker whom they blamed for causing the family's problems.

5. Reaction Formation

This form of safeguard came to light during the Phase 2 studies which will be described in Part Five. It was the most complex safeguard, being hidden under a veil of empathy with the client. The safeguard was developed by agents who claimed the client was in some way similar to themselves and they were therefore unable to intervene without a sense of guilt. The most apt concept we felt could describe this phenomenon was the psychoanalytic term 'reaction formation', as employed by Moore (1961). 'I feel it's a bit mean . . . I can go out drinking in the evening but you (the client) can't. . . . That's where they all go, where they meet their mates and if their mates drink do you say you shouldn't go to the pub?'

Yet these agents often failed to take account of the very obvious harm that the client's drinking was causing. The reaction formation obscured this from the agents' perception. They were subconsciously jealous or angry over the client's drinking, but could not express their hostility because this conflicted with their self-image of a professional helper as caring and empathatic. Agents who felt anxious that clients might interpret them as being moralistic opted for an indulgent acceptance of clients' drinking. Agents rationalized excessive drinking as 'only to be expected in the circumstances', but this sometimes covered the agents' fear of hostile rejection by the client.

Other Research On Inappropriate Attitudes of Agents Towards Clients with Drinking Problems

These five expressions of low therapeutic commitment described above were not mutually exclusive. Individual agents sometimes adopted various strategies in combination to maintain their self-esteem in the face of their inability to respond to drinking problems. Our studies of agents have not been alone in discovering these forms of emotional reaction.

Robinson and Podnos (1966) distributed a questionnaire to 90 psychiatrists working in the New Orleans area of the USA, asking why they felt psychiatrists were reluctant to treat alcoholic clients. The most common reasons given were that such clients were 'over-demanding', 'likely to act out', 'have a poor prognosis' and 'poor motivation toward treatment'. Robinson was able to link these concepts directly to more emotional experiences on the part of the psychiatrists. For she found a strong correlation between the psychiatrists' reports of feeling 'frustrated', 'angry' and 'inadequate' when working with alcoholic patients, and their reluctance to treat patients with a diagnosis of 'alcoholism'.

Fisher *et al.* (1975) asked general practitioners to rate adjectives describing three concepts: the 'average person', the 'alcoholic' and the 'diabetic'. The doctors considered the 'diabetics' and 'alcoholics' to be 'sicker' and 'feebler' than the 'average person'. But whereas the diabetic was considered similar to the average person in every other respect, 'alcoholics' were perceived to be more 'foolish', 'weak', 'hopeless', and 'dangerous' than the 'average person'. Mackey (1969) used the same adjectives to find how different professional groups perceived the concepts of 'normal' males and females in comparison to 'alcoholic' males and females. Each group of agents differentiated 'alcoholics' from 'normal' people along exactly the same dimensions as those reported by Fisher. In summarizing his findings, Mackey noted that

> Although there was an overall trend to ascribe moderately desirable characteristics to these concepts identified with normality, this trend was reversed in ratings of concepts identified with alcoholism . . . relatively undesirable characteristics were associated with alcoholics . . . or alcoholics are then seen as undesirable to treat by mental health professionals and as a mysterious threat to police officers and guidance counsellors. Although the underlying dynamics may vary, the result of such views may be similar — rejection of the alcoholic as a person.

A similar interpretation could be made of the results of a study reported by Reinehr (1969) who asked 50 male 'alcoholics' to choose from a checklist the adjectives they felt described themselves. Sixteen agents who had therapeutic responsibility for these clients were also asked to check which of the same list of adjectives they thought described 'the alcoholic client'. Over 70 per cent of the patients felt they could describe themselves by the adjectives 'civilized', 'clear thinking', 'considerate', 'fair-minded', 'healthy', 'honest' and 'reasonable'. None of their therapists believed that these adjectives applied to the typical 'alcoholic client'.

It was not that the agents were in disagreement amongst themselves. On the contrary, all 16 therapists checked 'self-centred' as a characteristic of the 'alcoholic client' compared to only 16 per cent of the clients describing themselves as such. 75 per cent of the therapists thought the 'alcoholic client' could be described as 'evasive' and 'hostile' compared to 6 per cent of the clients. 70 per cent of the therapists described the 'alcoholic client' as 'bitter' and 'complaining' compared to 10 per cent and 12 per cent respectively of the clients. Naturally, one would not expect clients to describe themselves in such uncomplimentary terms, but neither would one expect to find such complete agreement amongst a group of agents about the undesirable personality characteristics of a group of clients.

Such consistency in the agents' attitudes suggested that their perception of clients with drinking problems might be telling us more about agents and their working situation than about the clients. The consistency in agents' emotional reaction to clients with drinking problems could not be explained in terms of the personal prejudices of individual agents. Of course there were variations of degree according to the different personalities of agents, but so far studies have been limited to examining only one personality dimension, namely authoritarianism. The authoritarian personality has been characterized as rigid, aggressive, anti-intellectual, lacking self-confidence and feeling victimized. Mendelson *et al.* (1964) found that authoritarian personalities were more likely to believe 'alcoholics' had a 'character defect' and Chodorkoff (1967, 1969) indicated that the authoritarian personality was more likely to hold negative views of the 'alcoholic client'. It is perhaps predictable that such a personality type should be particularly low on therapeutic commitment. The authoritarian personality is likely to reject any deviant. The client with drinking problems is more threatening than other clients to the authoritarian agent, whose personal self-esteem is in any case somewhat tenuous and maintained by negativism towards out-groups. Poley described how this manifested itself in low therapeutic commitment to clients with drinking problems, manifested by failure to recognize and respond to them:

> It is suggested that armed service personnel who score high on authoritarianism tend to perceive a drinking problem in the armed services. However, they tend to see their own work in this field as not very important. They do not see the importance of educating others in the field; they tend to feel that the workshop will not be helpful in their own work and they are not confident of approaching and referring individuals with problems for treatment. (Poley 1975).

These findings confirmed our view that threats to self-esteem were probably the major determinants of the perspectives which agents adopted towards clients with drinking problems. The authoritarian personality was particularly sensitive to such threats and thus more likely to regard drinkers negatively and be unwilling to respond to them. But low therapeutic commitment could not be explained just in terms of personality types amongst agents. This could not explain why non-authoritarian agents also consistently perceived the alcoholic client in the same way as did authoritarian personalities. Taking all our agency studies into account, it was perfectly clear that low therapeutic commitment to clients with drinking problems was very much the rule, not the exception. Many agents who were quite comfortable in dealing with, and therapeutically committed to other types of client, felt insecure and uncommitted to helping clients with drinking problems. We argue that agents who in other situations were non-authoritarian adopted authoritarian perspectives when working with clients with drinking problems, because their situation when responding to drinkers led them to experience the same feelings as the authoritarian personality experiences with most people — a feeling of threat to self-esteem. When faced with a client with drinking problems, the threat to the agents' self-esteem was created by role insecurity — a composite of anxieties about role adequacy, role legitimacy and role support. They were unsure how to respond to drinkers, unsure whether to respond to drinkers and unsupported in this uncomfortable situation. They had little self-confidence and wished to avoid or withdraw from the situation.

Negative characteristics were attributed to the client. Just as the agents in Reinehr's study selected adjectives which described the 'alcoholic client' as a socially-undesirable person, so agents in our studies reported feeling that clients with drinking problems were 'distasteful', 'embarrassing' and 'threatening'. Some believed they were 'compulsive liars'. Such beliefs were easily aroused in agents who lacked information about alcohol and alcohol-related problems and had received no training in the skills required to work with clients with drinking problems. Such agents were at the mercy of their own fantasies about people with drinking problems, which as Kilty (1975) has shown, will be largely based upon the layman's concept of the 'alcoholic'; a concept which can easily provide a rationalization for believing that it is futile to respond to drinking problems, thus excusing the failure of the agent to respond.

The low therapeutic commitment of agents thus consisted of a series of safeguards against the threat experienced in responding to drinking problems. The threat emanated from having to respond under conditions where agents felt they did not have the ability or the right to respond. Not all agents would openly admit their sense of failure and inadequacy. They rationalized away their inability to respond and their lack of motivation to respond by believing that the clients themselves lack motivation and will power, that drinking problems were incurable and drinkers were degenerate, and therefore neither amenable nor indeed worthy of the 'skill' and time of the agent. The castigation of the client as unmotivated and worthless was a further rationalization for avoiding him, confirming the drinker as an undeserving client rated very low on the agent's scale of priorities.

PART FOUR   THEORIES ABOUT IMPROVING
THE RESPONSE

8 PREVIOUS THEORIES ABOUT IMPROVING THE RESPONSE

For some time, researchers, administrators and agents themselves have been aware of the inadequacy of the response to drinking problems. However, there has been no previous systematic examination of why agents felt negatively about drinkers and disinclined to respond to them. Accordingly, ideas about improving the response have not been based on an analysis of the reasons why the response was inadequate and what steps should therefore be taken to remedy the situation. Instead, previous theories about improving the response have been essentially opinionated and speculative, and as we shall see, they cannot really stand up to examination. In particular, these theories have not appreciated the range of factors which contribute to low therapeutic commitment and hence have only concentrated on isolated aspects of the inadequacy. Three theories of this sort have been put forward recurrently. The first was based on the assumption that agents did not fully recognize or respond to drinking problems because they were unaware of the facts about alcohol and alcohol abuse. It was presumed that if only they realized the extent of the prevalence of drinking problems then they would be more committed to respond. A second view believed the fault lay rather in the moralistic attitudes which agents adopted towards drinkers, considering them to be weak-willed, degenerate and undeserving. It was felt that agents would only become sympathetic towards drinkers and therapeutically committed to respond if they accepted that drinkers were ill and needed help. A third line of thought concluded that the response would best be improved by finding out which treatment was most effective. If we could determine which treatment system produced the best outcome and encouraged agents to follow this proven course, then the response would naturally improve.

How valid have been these previous theories about improving the response?

1. Can the Response be improved just by providing Agents with Information about Drinking Problems?

It has often been presumed that if only agents knew the signs and symptoms of drinking problems and the means of treating them, then they would obviously be better able to recognize and to respond to them. It has been implicitly assumed that education must be of benefit and that disseminating information and organizing courses must help to transform agent attitudes and therapeutic practices. This assumption was undermined by Kilty's (1975) finding that agents' attitudes to drinkers and drinking problems correlated more strongly with the attitudes of the communities of which they were a part than with the amount of information they possessed about alcohol and alcohol abuse.

Studies of training courses have confirmed that agents' attitudes are unlikely to be strongly influenced by objective information. Chodorkoff (1969) studied the effects of basic psychiatric training upon groups of nursing and medical students (Chodorkoff 1967). They spent between two and four weeks full-time training at a psychiatric institute, including special lectures about 'alcoholism'. Chodorkoff measured their knowledge on an Alcoholism Information Scale comprising 53 test items. He measured their attitudes on the Alabama Attitudes to Alcoholism Scale. By the end of the course both groups had increased their knowledge by approximately 50 per cent, but both groups recorded very small and insignificant changes in their attitudes to 'alcoholism'.

Cooke *et al.* (1975) reported on the effects of education upon the information and attitudes of 47 para-professionals undergoing training as alcohol counsellors. Training took place on three consecutive days a month over a ten month period: a total of 240 hours. Students completed scales of information and attitude prior to starting the programme, after the initial part of the course in which theoretical issues were discussed and again after completion of the programme. Their levels of information had increased quite dramatically after the early part of the course and were maintained after completion. Changes in attitude were more complex. After the initial part of the course in which theoretical issues were considered, the students adopted a significantly more rejecting attitude towards alcohol and 'alcoholics'. However, after the later part of the course covering more practical areas, their attitudes reverted back to those they had held prior to their training. So, like Chodorkoff's results, education increased their level of information but made no significant difference to their attitudes to 'alcoholics'. At the end of the course trainees were asked their subjective assessment of its impact upon them. Generally speaking, they agreed that the information they had gained had been useful and had influenced their approach to therapy. Yet they did not feel that the training programme had made them any more effective in responding to drinkers.

Our 1976 detoxification staff study measured the knowledge and therapeutic commitment of social workers, nurses and care assistants before and after a four week preparatory training course and then again three months after the unit opened. Over this four-month period, their knowledge of alcohol and alcohol problems rose by a statistically significant amount, but in common with the other studies their therapeutic commitment showed no change. In fact their scores of therapeutic commitment dropped.

The conclusion from these studies is clear: by itself, education about alcohol and alcohol problems is not sufficient to change agents' attitudes to drinkers and drinking problems or to make them more therapeutically committed to respond.

2. Can the Response be improved by promoting the Disease Concept of Alcoholism?

The reluctance of general community agents to respond to clients with drinking problems has sometimes been interpreted as a manifestation of over-moralistic attitudes. Agents did not want to help drinkers, it was argued, because they felt drinkers were weak-willed and unmotivated, that 'they had only themselves to blame' and were therefore not worthy of being helped. It has often been assumed that the disease concept of alcoholism was promoted directly to counter-balance such attitudes. For the disease concept argued that the drinker was powerless to control alcohol, that it was a force greater than himself and that he should not be blamed for succumbing.

The advocates of the pragmatic value of the disease concept have claimed that if agents believed that people with drinking problems were ill, they would be more sympathetic toward them and respond accordingly. It has been assumed that it would be incompatible for a person to believe 'alcoholism' was a 'disease' whilst simultaneously believing 'alcoholics' had a character weakness. However, Robinson (1972) has pointed out it is possible to hold both views. For the disease concept still implies 'alcoholics' have a defect, and defects tend to be stigmatized. Furthermore, if agents were to believe that this defect was incurable, they may be sympathetic but equally see no point in trying to treat it. The studies by Fisher *et al.* (1975) and Mackey (1969) confirm this interpretation. Fisher's respondents saw 'alcoholics' as 'sicker' and 'feebler' than the 'average person' but also as more 'foolish', 'hopeless' and 'dangerous' than the 'average person'. Mackey found that respondents who accepted the idea that 'alcoholism' was a disease still rejected the 'alcoholic' as a person. In our 1974 agency study, over half agreed with the statement 'alcoholism is a disease'. But of these agents 40 per cent did not disagree with the statement 'alcoholics are degenerate' and 49 per cent agreed that 'alcoholics are weak-willed'. A third of agents in our study thought 'alcoholism' was a mental illness, but of these 61 per cent did not disagree that 'alcoholics' were 'degenerate' and 74 per cent agreed that 'alcoholics' were 'weak-willed'. So it was actually fairly common for agents to agree both with statements suggesting 'alcoholism' was a disease and statements which suggested that 'alcoholics' had undesirable or defective characteristics. Acceptance of the disease concept did not guarantee positive attitudes towards drinkers or therapeutic commitment to responding to drinking problems. Agreeing with statements like 'alcoholism is a disease' seemed largely a matter of compliance, endorsed by agents because such statements have been recited continually in the media and in policy documents. The currency of phrases suggesting 'alcoholics' are 'sick' have made little impression on the set of generally unfavourable attitudes toward individual people with drinking problems. This conclusion was supported by the study of Cooke *et al.* (1975) which showed that agents' agreement with statements indicating they believed that 'alcoholism was an illness' had no correlation with statements indicating they believed in the 'worth of an alcoholic'. Bailey (1970) showed that when social workers were influenced by a training course towards accepting the disease concept of alcoholism, they did not necessarily change their negative feelings about clients with drinking problems or their unwillingness to work with such clients. At the outset of the course, 85 per cent believed 'alcoholism' was a 'disease'. During the course the few dissidents changed their beliefs, so that upon conclusion 97 per cent believed 'alcoholism' to be a 'disease'. However, this greater acceptance of the disease concept was not associated with any fundamental changes in their attitudes to 'alcoholics' or the ways in which the social workers intended to respond to such clients. In fact, Bailey noted that 'the more closely the attitude statements related to actual casework practice, the less responsive the change. Sometimes they moved slightly away from the desired direction'. In other words, an increasing belief that 'alcoholism' was a 'disease' did not fundamentally change the ways the social workers intended to act towards 'alcoholics' in their actual work.

Our 1973 Summer School study investigated this phenomenon from the other direction: what happened to therapeutic commitment when agents were influenced to question the disease concept? For the school aimed to provide not only factual information, but also to highlight ongoing debates in the field, including of course, the controversy over the disease concept of alcoholism. Initially, the majority of attenders believed that 'alcoholism' was a 'disease', but at the end of the school there were less respondents agreeing with each single statement implying that 'alcoholism'was a 'disease'. If it were necessary for agents to accept the disease concept to become therapeutically committed to respond, then it would be expected that the agents attending this school would have become more rejecting in their attitudes towards 'alcoholics'. But on the contrary, their therapeutic commitment did not change.

The evidence suggested that attitudes to clients with drinking problems – as people with whom agents dealt in their actual work – developed completely independently of whether agents believed these clients were suffering from a disease. Thus the fundamental assumption of many informational pamphlets and training courses must unfortunately be regarded as irrelevant in changing attitudes and behaviour applying in actual therapeutic practice. Therapeutic commitment to helping clients with drinking problems is unlikely to be improved by promoting the disease concept of alcoholism.

This tied in with our analysis of the anxieties of general community agents in the preceeding chapters, which indicated that negative and rejecting attitudes to drinkers were not in themselves the 'causes' of an inadequate response; rather they were manifestations of the threat to professional self-esteem created by difficulties in the agents' working situation. Believing drinkers to be weak-willed and undeserving was a safeguard against the threat to agents' self-esteem. Agents could excuse their own lack of motivation to respond by claiming that drinkers were unmotivated to accept treatment. If there were no fundamental improvement in an agent's working situation to help reduce the sense of threat experienced when dealing with drinking problems, then one set of safeguarding attitudes would merely be replaced by another set. If agents came to believe that 'alcoholics' were 'ill', they might still rationalize not responding on the grounds that it was futile to treat an incurable disease.

3. Can the Response be improved by discovering which is the Most Effective Treatment?

The third theory about improving the response has been, in a sense, a less rigid version of the second theory described above. It has been assumed that there must be some particular approach to drinking problems which can be proven more effective than others, and that if agents adopted this particular approach, then their response would naturally be improved. But just as we have seen that basing responses on the disease concept of alcoholism does not necessarily guarantee greater therapeutic commitment or a more effective response, so other studies have shown that no one approach or treatment philosophy can definitely be shown to be more effective than any other. Evaluative comparisons of different types of treatment services for clients with drinking problems have shown only minor differences in outcome. As Emrick (1975) suggested in his mammoth review of treatment evaluation studies, any treatment seemed likely to result in some improvement, but there was no evidence to suggest that any one programme was more likely to be effective than any other:

> A review of 384 studies of psychologically orientated alcoholism treatments showed that differences in treatment methods did not significantly affect long term outcome. Mean abstinence rates did not differ between treated and untreated alcoholics, but more treated than untreated alcoholics improved, suggesting that formal treatment at least increases an alcoholic's chance of reducing his drinking problem. (Emrick 1975).

Not only have Emrick's conclusions been supported by another comprehensive review of treatment effectiveness by Armor *et al.* (1976) but they have also been replicated by research findings from other areas of psychotherapy. For evaluations of treatment for other kinds of psychosocial problems have concluded that the theoretical perspective and the treatment programme adopted by agents do not predict whether or not a client is likely to improve. In reviewing the research literature on the effectiveness of different approaches to counselling and psychotherapy, Meltzoff and Kornreich (1970) concluded that:

> . . . while some differences in attitude may be found between therapists of different schools, these are perhaps differences which do not have a significant long term effect on the outcome of therapy. Each school of therapy probably provides patients with a specific line or philosophy and a different means of solving problems, and perhaps each solution is as valid as another.

This stagnant conclusion rules out the possibility of improving the response simply by finding the 'correct' treatment philosophy. Yet it leads us to a perhaps more incisive enquiry.

The Effect of Therapeutic Commitment

If differences in outcome are not related to different types of treatment programme, what are they related to? Why, for example, do some clients benefit less than others from the same treatment programmes?

In effect, this is a question we have already asked of clients being treated by general community agents. We concluded that the response they received was ineffective because of the low therapeutic commitment of general community agents to work with drinkers. Consequently, we may suppose that a similar factor could explain why the response of some specialist agents is equally ineffective. After all, other studies have shown that some psychologists and psychiatrists would rather give up their posts than deal with drinkers (Knox 1971) and that amongst psychiatrists treating drinkers is the least favoured activity (Macdonald and Patel 1975). If differences between treatment philosophies and programmes do not explain why some clients do not benefit from treatment, perhaps this can be explained in terms of the low therapeutic commitment of the agents who are dealing with them. The corollary of this argument would of course be that clients of agents with high therapeutic commitment would exhibit a consistently higher level of improvement.

This would concur with the conclusions of much research in the fields of psychiatry and psychotherapy. While research into the effectiveness of the responses to drinking problems has been almost entirely fixated with comparing techniques, a copious literature has developed elsewhere on the effectiveness of counselling and therapy which consistently demonstrates that the best predictor of treatment outcome is the inter-personal approach which an agent adopts towards a client. This dimension has been conceptualized in various constructs, such as 'warmth', 'empathy', and now 'therapeutic commitment'. Whatever the actual terminology used, there has emerged a distinct pattern of results which suggest that a certain type of inter-personal style on the therapist's part predicts a better outcome for the client – whatever the theoretical position and treatment goals adopted by the therapist.

It is beyond the scope of this chapter to review this considerable literature in detail and the interested reader is referred to those authors who have undertaken such reviews. These include Keisler *et al.* (1967), Swenson (1971), Meltzoff and Kornreich (1970), Luborsky *et dl.* (1971, 1975), and Cartwright (1977). They generally conclude that the effective counsellor is the one who feels optimistic about his work, likes his clients and feels positively about his contribution to helping them. In the terms used in this book, he is role secure and therapeutically committed. Clients of such therapists tend to feel that the therapist is able to relate to them as people of value and worth and that he considers them and their problems to merit his time and attention. The effective therapist understands how clients themselves feel about their problems, and he allows them their own perspective — even if he does not necessarily agree with them. From their interviews with a large number of patients about their experiences in psychotherapy and counselling, Strupp *et al.* (1969) concluded: 'The composite image of the good therapist drawn by our respondents is that of a keenly attentive, interested, benign and concerned listener. A friend who is warm and natural, is not averse to giving direct advice who speaks one's own language and rarely arouses intense anger'.

There has been considerable debate whether such attributes of effective therapists represent a single dimension or a number of different factors. Following Keisler *et al.* (1967) and Swenson (1971) we would suggest they probably represent a single, albeit composite, dimension. This composite dimension, whose characteristic components are described in Strupp's image of the good therapist, we conceptualize as high therapeutic commitment. Unfortunately, the previous preoccupation with comparing different types of treatment programme has precluded confirmation of the effect of this more sophisticated variable upon treatment outcome. However, a unique study by Chafetz *et al.* (1962) can be cited in this context.

Chafetz and his colleagues were particularly concerned that a large number of patients with drinking problems who attended an emergency clinic and were then offered appointments at an out-patient clinic never kept their appointments. Moreover, very few who did attend were ever successfully brought into treatment. Having examined the dynamics of this process, Chafetz *et al.* described the interaction between clients and agents thus: '. . . methods of initial approach to the alcoholic are as varied as the individual propensities of the personnel he sees . . . protractive evaluation involving delay and contacts with a number of different caretakers are usual . . . all of these contacts both in the emergency ward and the clinic involved considerable delay and some involved open hostility and rejection'. In other words, responses which we have seen are typical of agents with low therapeutic commitment. Whilst a control group of clients continued to be dealt with in this fashion, a 'Treatment Response Model' was designed to guide interaction between agents on an experimental group of clients. The experimental approach was somewhat different:

In handling the intial contact, consistent respect of the alcoholic's tenuous feelings of self-esteem and constructive utilization of his dependency needs are essential. This means treating the alcoholic with respect and consideration, reducing the frequency of frustrating situations and gratifying his requests . . . more specifically the psychiatrist and the social worker show the alcoholic that he is always welcome and demonstrate that he will be met with interest and respect whatever his problem.

These latter conditions seem almost a deliberate attempt to demonstrate to the client that the agents were therapeutically committed. By the end of the study period, approximately one year after patients' initial contact, 65 per cent of experimental group patients had made an initial visit to the out-patient clinic compared with 5 per cent of the control group. Furthermore, 42 per cent of the experimental group had made five or more visits to the clinic and were defined as having established a therapeutic relationship, compared with only 1 per cent of the control group. This study thus conclusively demonstrated that the motivation of the therapeutically committed agent could elicit increased motivation from the client. Yet it must sadly be concluded that few agents' responses to clients with drinking problems ever fit the description by Chafetz *et al.* or Strupp *et al.* of the committed therapist. In fact, therapeutic commitment is generally so low that many agents would prefer not to work with any drinkers at all. It is this dimension which, above all, accounts for the prevailing inadequacy in the response to drinking problems. Hence, we should reconceptualize the question of how to improve the response to drinking problems into the question of how we can raise the therapeutic commitment of agents to work with drinkers. As we have seen, this cannot be produced by education alone, or by promoting the disease concept of alcoholism.

In Part Three we concluded that the factors which created low therapeutic commitment involved anxieties about role adequacy, role legitimacy and role support. Having rejected other theories about improving the response, can we now go on to show that helping agents overcome these anxieties could increase their therapeutic commitment and hence make them respond more effectively to clients with drinking problems?

9 DEVELOPING ROLE SECURITY AND THERAPEUTIC COMMITMENT

To find out how the training and working situation of general community agents could be improved so as to remove their anxieties, we compared the characteristics of various agents from different backgrounds to discover which factors were associated with role insecurity and low therapeutic commitment, and which factors were associated with the development instead of role security and high therapeutic commitment.

The Alcohol and Alcohol Problems Perception Questionnaire was administered to 175 agents attending Summer Schools on Alcoholism in 1976. These agents indicated on seven point scales how far they agreed or disagreed with a series of statements measuring their

Therapeutic Commitment. E.g. 'I want to work with people who have alcohol-related problems.'

Role Adequacy. E.g. 'I feel I know enough about the causes of drinking problems to carry out my role when working with drinkers.'

Role Legitimacy. E.g. 'I feel that my clients believe I have the right to ask questions about drinking when necessary.'

Role Support. E.g. 'If I felt the need when working with drinkers, I could easily find a member of another profession who would be able to give me expert advice about any problem relevant to their area.'

High scores on these latter three scales were taken to indicate role security. Low scores were taken to indicate role insecurity, and this interpretation was validated by subsequent questionnaires used at the 1977 Summer Schools which correlated low scores on scales of role adequacy, legitimacy and support not only with scale items indicating low professional self-esteem when working with drinkers — e.g. 'All in all, I am inclined to feel I am a failure with drinkers,' but also with items indicating less sense of role adequacy, legitimacy and support when working with drinkers than with other clients — e.g. 'In general, I feel I have less skill in working with drinkers than with other types of client.'

164

Other data taken by the questionnaires included the agent's sex, age, profession, working situation, years of experience in their profession, experience in working specifically with drinkers, previous training in responding to drinking problems, and knowledge about alcohol and alcohol-related problems.

As predicted by our hypothesis, agents who expressed most anxieties about their role adequacy, role legitimacy and role support also felt least therapeutically committed to work with drinkers. We have already described this attitudinal syndrome as typical of most general community agents. However, other agents who completed the questionnaire recorded contrastingly high scores of therapeutic commitment and felt little anxiety about their adequacy, legitimacy and support. What factors distinguished these agents from the role insecure general community agents described in Chapter 6?

The agents who felt a high degree of therapeutic commitment were distinguished by four major characteristics:

1. They were *experienced* in working with drinkers. They had worked personally with a considerable number of people with drinking problems.
2. They were working, or had worked in the past, in a situation in which *role support* was available. Agents who reported feeling supported in their work with drinkers tended to come from two particular types of working situation — a specialist environment or one which provided ongoing supervision. Of the agents from specialist environments, agents from local councils of alcoholism and from psychiatric alcoholism treatment units tended to feel most supported, but with some degree of support being felt by agents working in other voluntary organizations. Of the agents working in non-specialist environments, those who received ongoing supervision when working with drinkers felt most role support, and this applied particularly to agents working within the armed forces.
3. They had received a *training in counselling,* usually of a formal nature, such as on courses and training programmes. The more hours of counselling training agents had received, the less anxious they felt about their role adequacy and role legitimacy.
4. They had *clinical knowledge* about alcohol and alcohol related problems. The areas of information which most helped to dispel anxieties about role adequacy were those covering the effects of alcohol on the individual drinker, such as described in Chapter 1. Agents with few or no anxieties about their role adequacy knew, for

instance, how to recognize acute withdrawal symptoms, to describe patterns of behaviour typical of the highly tolerant drinker, and the likely physical, social and psychological consequences of excessive drinking.

Each factor — experience, role support, counselling training and clinical information — contributed to reducing particular aspects of role insecurity. Agents experienced in working with drinkers had least anxieties about their role legitimacy. Agents who came from supportive working environments had least anxieties about the availability of role support. Agents who had counselling training and high clinical knowledge had least anxieties about their role adequacy.

However, these factors interacted. Clinical information, for example, was only found to significantly reduce anxieties about adequacy if agents were also experienced in working with drinkers and had received a training in counselling. Amongst agents who had little experience in working with drinkers, the possession of even quite substantial knowledge did not seem to reduce their anxieties about their role adequacy. Clearly then, the four factors distinguishing agents with high therapeutic commitment were of different relative strengths in helping them achieve this level.

Analysis of the questionnaire scores suggested that developing high therapeutic commitment to drinkers was a two-stage process, in which agents firstly developed a sense of role security and then a sense of therapeutic commitment.

Experience acquired under support and supervision appeared to be the key to the first stage. Inexperienced and unsupported agents always recorded scores indicating role insecurity, whatever their training or clinical knowledge. But inexperienced agents who felt supported seemed to feel role secure even when they were not too certain of their role legitimacy or confident about their role adequacy. Thus of the four factors distinguishing agents of high therapeutic commitment, role support was the only one which could be provided for inexperienced agents and be expected to make some improvement in their response. Without role support agents would safeguard themselves against responding, and would not gain the necessary experience. Knowledge and training could not be effectively applied until agents had worked with a considerable number of drinkers, and this experience, in turn, could only be gained if role support were available.

It was role support, then, which started agents off on the road towards therapeutic commitment. However, in practice, the other factors were often provided simultaneously. The highest level of therapeutic commitment of any of the groups of agents we studied was found amongst the experienced counsellors who worked with the United States Air Force in Europe. They had received not only a minimum of ten weeks' counselling training but had also received ongoing supervision from a more experienced agent while they themselves had gained experience in working with drinkers. Thus their higher therapeutic commitment was created by considerable support and supervision in conjunction with comprehensive training.

Other agents achieved slightly lower, but still quite high levels of therapeutic commitment within supportive working environments. These environments allowed agents to gain experience and become role secure, whilst also directly or indirectly providing training and clinical information as well. A social worker or a nurse, for instance, operating within a psychiatric alcoholism treatment unit could gain experience in dealing with drinkers without carrying too great a burden of responsibility, and whilst picking up clinical information and counselling skills.

The supportive working situation, whether a specialist environment or one providing ongoing supervision, allowed agents the time and security to develop knowledge, counselling techniques and a realistic appraisal of their role and abilities, under the umbrella of supervision. Agents newly recruited into such an environment did not feel isolated, so many of the safeguards were precluded. Most of the other staff were experienced and suffered few unrealistic feelings of threat from working with drinkers. Agents were drawn into a milieu of support, experience, low threat and high therapeutic commitment. Their gradual improvement in effectiveness and in therapeutic commitment produced more motivation from their clients, which in turn endorsed their optimism and reinforced their therapeutic commitment still further. Each element in the supportive working situation thus fed back positively upon the others; therapeutic commitment and effectiveness built up together.

General community agents on the other hand, were usually caught up in completely the opposite situation. They had no role support available and they became enmeshed in a negative spiral leading in the other direction. When faced with drinkers they felt anxious about their adequacy, legitimacy and lack of support: they felt isolated and unable to respond effectively. They avoided recognizing and responding to drinking problems for as long as possible; only recognizing cases when they were forced by circumstances to respond, or when clients were obviously highly damaged. Usually this 'recognition' was swiftly followed by referral to get rid of the drinker. Therefore, general community agents gained virtually no experience in dealing with drinkers, developed no therapeutic skills and derived no realistic sense of how to handle drinkers or what goals to set. Because of the agents' low therapeutic commitment, clients did not co-operate. This increased the threat to agents' self-esteem, but simultaneously reinforced their safeguarding attitudes. Agents became more antagonistic and moralistic towards drinkers, and more pessimistic about the possibilities of helping them.

The contrasting spiral between agents in supported working situations and agents in non-supported situations are conceptualized below. The recruit moving into a supported environment gradually improved until he reached a position of role security; the unsupported agent gradually declined towards a nadir of ineffectiveness and low therapeutic commitment. The motive force of each cycle was the presence or absence of role support.

The addition of clinical information and counselling training could make no impression on the role insecurity cycle, if support was still unforthcoming. However, if training in skills and clinical knowledge were added to the role security cycle, the cycle accelerated still further and agents began to develop from a position of role security to one of therapeutic commitment.

The fully fledged expert had travelled this cycle on numerous occasions. Once high therapeutic commitment had been reached, the cycle became self-perpetuating; and the original motive force of role support could be taken away without disturbing the cycle.

If the major responsibility for responding to drinking problems was to be transferred to community agents, then these agents would have to be helped to break out of their negative cycle of role insecurity and to develop instead within the positive cycle. Unfortunately, the development of role security and therapeutic commitment only seemed possible for agents working in supportive situations such as specialist environments. Obviously, general community agents could not all be temporarily transported into such environments. The answer therefore would have to be to transplant the crucial elements of such environments into the working situation of general community agents. One factor was of the utmost importance — role support. Without role support, there would be little possibility of general community agents learning how to help people with drinking problems. Our analysis had shown that information and training were necessary but not sufficient; the advantages of knowledge and counselling techniques only accrued

Figure 9.1 Role Security and Insecurity Cycles

ROLE SECURITY CYCLE

Positive Development of Agents in a
Supportive Working Situation

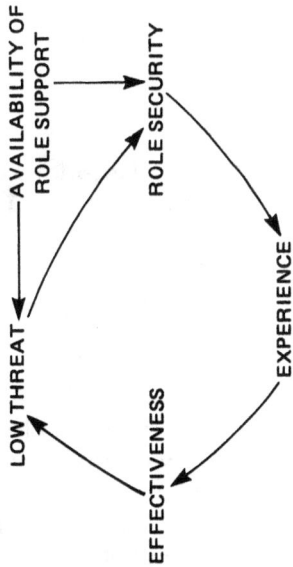

ROLE INSECURITY CYCLE

Negative Development of Agents in a
Non-Supportive Working Situation

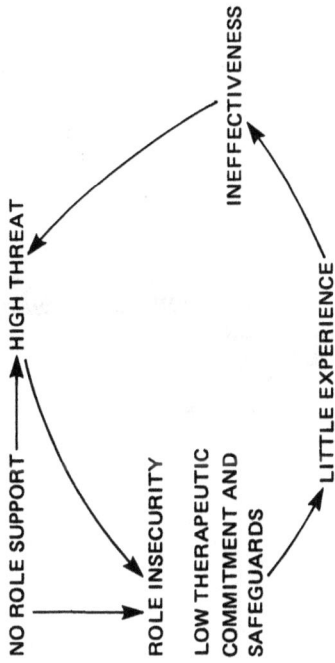

Figure 9.2 The Therapeutic Commitment Cycle

The continuation of Positive Development of Agents in a Supportive
Working Situation

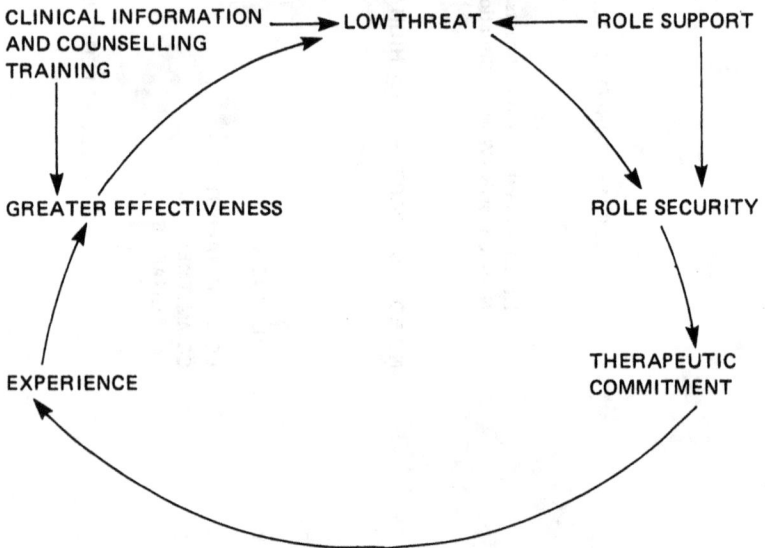

CLINICAL INFORMATION ⟶ LOW THREAT ⟵ ROLE SUPPORT
AND COUNSELLING
TRAINING

GREATER EFFECTIVENESS   ROLE SECURITY

EXPERIENCE   THERAPEUTIC
                                              COMMITMENT

to agents who had gained experience in responding to drinking
problems. General community agents were precluded from gaining
this experience because of their anxieties and sense of threat which
arose when they were faced with drinkers. The analysis indicated
that only role support could help agents break out of this negative
cycle.

This involved considerable implications at a time when general
community agents had been exhorted to respond more actively to
drinking problems. At the end of Chapter 4, for example, we raised
the question as to why the Department of Health and Social Security
had been led to rebuke social workers for 'shrinking away' from the
attempt to help people with drinking problems (Department of
Health and Social Security 1975). In answer now we can see that the

social workers' lack of role support when dealing with drinkers created anxieties about their role adequacy and role legitimacy which threatened their self-esteem. In turn, they safeguarded themselves by avoiding drinking problems. Unsupported inexperienced agents were unlikely to do anything else but 'shrink away'. This was not primarily a reflection of their education or their personalities and whether or not they believed in the disease theory of alcoholism seemed to be of no particular relevance one way or the other. The inadequacy of the community response was not primarily due to educational deficiencies or personality deficiencies, but rather to organizational deficiencies. The whole question of how the response of general community agents could be improved hinged on how these agents could be provided with support and supervision while they gained experience in working with drinkers.

PART FIVE   EXPERIMENTS IN IMPROVING
            THE RESPONSE

Based on our analysis of the inadequacies of the existing response, reported in Part Three, and our analysis of strategies for improving this response, reported in Part Four, we decided to test the hypothesis that providing role support for general community agents would help them become more effective in responding to drinking problems. Two of the research team took on full-time responsibility for providing this support, and they adopted the name 'Community Alcohol Team' (CAT).

The CAT was referred to as a *community* team because its focus of operation was in the community, not in hospitals.

The CAT was called an *alcohol* team rather than an alcoholism team, because it was attempting to help agents respond to a variety of problems associated with alcohol as described in Parts One and Two.

The CAT was called a *team* because it involved agents from different professions. The two full-time members were a consultant psychiatrist and a senior social worker who both had a special interest in problems of alcohol abuse. When the team worked with agents other than social workers, respective members of the profession or group involved who also had a special interest in drinking problems were drafted into the team to help provide support for their colleagues.

The purpose of the CAT was to improve the response of general community agents to drinking problems in the manner suggested by our research analysis. It attempted experimentally to provide role support for groups of general community agents, whilst simultaneously providing information, training in skills, and helping them gain some experience in responding to drinking problems. The CAT also attempted to deal with the attitudinal manifestations of community agents' role insecurity, namely their low therapeutic commitment, safeguarding attitudes and sense of threat when working with drinkers. This was attempted in two ways: by training courses and by a consultation service. Both differed from the usual sort of activities implied by these terms, because both were designed in terms of our theoretical analysis of the inadequacy of the response.

175

The training courses were not aimed just to provide a factual background, but rather to deal with the practical difficulties agents experienced in dealing with their actual cases. The courses were aimed more at counteracting the agents' lack of therapeutic commitment than providing facts and figures about alcohol abuse. The consultation service was not piloted to help clients directly, but rather to help agents to help clients. Agents were to be helped not only by advice, but also by ongoing support, training in counselling skills and clarification of rights and responsibilities.

There was clearly a major difference then between the CAT approach to encouraging agents to respond to drinking problems and the previous attempts via official circulars or formally structured academic courses. For our research indicated that merely giving agents a rational account of the size of the problem and their responsibility to respond was not sufficient to encourage them to respond. The CAT experiments were based on our research conclusions that agents must be actively helped in their work, that their rights and responsibilities must be clarified, that they must be given information about the specific problems involved in actual cases, that they must be given concrete proposals as to how to translate this information into therapeutic responses and most important of all, they must be supported and supervised when carrying out their response.

Thus three clusters of questions were to be asked of the CAT experiments:

1. Were they practical methods? Was there any demand or need amongst agents for training courses and a consultation service? Were there any agents prepared to accept what the CAT had to offer? Could CAT attempts to encourage therapeutic commitment in this way be practically established and administered in a workable form?
2. Would both types of experiment fulfil our hypotheses? Could the CAT reduce the sense of threat which agents felt in dealing with drinkers? Would this make them more therapeutically committed to work with clients with drinking problems?
3. How far did each service go towards achieving this aim and what were the particular strengths and weaknesses of each approach?

10 THE CAT TRAINING COURSES: IMPROVING THE RECOGNITION OF DRINKING PROBLEMS

The research analysis had shown that role insecurity affected different groups of agents in slightly different ways. Social workers and probation officers, for example, scored higher than GPs on our measures of skill in handling the personal crises of clients with drinking problems, while doctors were the least anxious about their clinical knowledge of drinking problems. This suggested that it would be more effective for our purposes to run separate courses for different professional groups rather than to organize the sort of multi-disciplinary course which tends to be popular in alcohol education. We decided to provide separate training courses for social workers, probation officers, GPs and nurses, and we felt that the optimum number on each course would be about ten agents. This number would allow a range of backgrounds and experience without being so large as to hinder discussion and proper participation. Each course was divided into a series of two-hour sessions. The major part of each session dealt with ongoing cases of the agents attending the courses. Each agent was asked to present to the group one such case in which they felt drinking problems were playing a part, or in which they suspected drinking might be involved but were not sure. These latter cases proved the more fruitful in dealing with the major issues of their inadequate response, since uncertainty over recognition usually highlighted all the agents' anxieties.

The CAT asked each agent not simply to present a case history of the client's problems, but also to present a history of their own personal and professional difficulties in responding to that particular client. The agent was asked what goals and approaches they had tried and what further methods they had in mind. The rest of the group were then asked in turn how each of them would handle the case. The CAT channelled this discussion to bring the agent's anxieties into the open, and to challenge each agent's safeguards within a group context, which made it difficult for them to hang on to any irrational positions. The rest of the group could contribute to this clarification process because they were not as emotionally involved in that particular case. Nevertheless they could generalize from this particular agent's experience to help overcome some of their own difficulties in handling clients with drinking problems. The CAT then provided relevant clinical information and tried to elicit a group view of the approach the agent should take to make a proper assessment of the role of drinking. Sometimes the CAT suggested which questions the agent should ask and in what way. The agent was then asked to try to carry out these suggestions and report back to the group in the next session. This simultaneously exerted a form of group pressure on the agents to try out the recommendations whilst supporting, encouraging and advising them. Some agents were clearly reluctant to make the attempt at recognition and assessment but the CAT had created a group structure which obliged them to report back on this. The courses also provided a role model for trainees because on each course the CAT training staff included a member of the professional group being trained; a colleague who could be seen to be role secure in working with drinkers. This precluded the safeguard that alcohol abuse was a special problem which could only be dealt with properly by psychiatrists. Since the group ethos was also turned against unnecessary referrals, this put the agents in a position where they began to appreciate their potential roles in responding to the particular case being discussed. So agents were not being constrained to operate against their will. The group and the CAT discussed the case and worked out goals and would thus have shared any of the responsibility for the failure of the suggested strategy. Yet interestingly, when agents did go back into the field and tried the recommendations, they discovered that the experience was not as difficult or traumatic as they had feared it might be. Clearly their previously held safeguards had exaggerated the difficulties to justify to themselves why they should neither recognize nor respond to drinking problems. Support and supervision removed the anxieties which created such safeguards.

An Example of a Case Discussion

The type of discussion described above is best illustrated by a specific case. One of the social workers presented to her group the case of a 50 year-old client with three children aged seven, eight and eleven. His wife had left him two years previously and had herself become a vagrant drinker. The social worker selected this case because she 'was not sure' if the man was drinking excessively or not. She reported that the client's previous social worker had decided that the client was 'not an alcoholic' because he had a good relationship with the social worker and would have admitted any such problem to her. Other agents had wanted the children to be taken into care, but the previous social worker had opposed this. When the social worker attending the CAT course had taken over the case, drinking did not seem to be playing

much of a part. However, she had noticed bottles of cider lying around
the house and on some recent visits, the client had seemed 'the worse
for drink'. His children had also appeared to be embarrassed by this,
but yet felt protective towards their father. On one visit the client's
speech had been very slurred and the social worker had tried to find
out how much he was drinking. The client rebuffed the social worker's
questions and claimed that 'cider was not alcohol and that anyway he
did not drink much'. This exposed the social worker's anxieties about
her role adequacy, since she was uncertain whether it was true or not
that cider contained alcohol. Like many agents working with drinkers,
she felt that the client probably knew more about drinking and its
effects than she did herself. She suspected that drinking was causing
problems but she could not justify this nor deal with the client's
manoeuvres. For the client also played upon her anxieties about her
role legitimacy, by teasing the social worker, (a Welsh Methodist) that
she was prejudiced against drinking. 'I'd actually talked to him about
drinking and he denies he does it, whenever it comes up in conversation
now he just adopts this teasing approach that I am after him for his
drinking . . .' The social worker had nowhere to turn for information
about alcohol or advice as to how to deal with the client's 'teasing'.
She was unsure how to utilize the clues to recognition, she had
become highly uncomfortable in bringing up the subject with him, and
yet felt a need to establish some kind of diagnosis regarding drink
because of her concern for the children.

The CAT firstly used the group discussion to go over the clues
already presented and to draw out any further ones. This demonstrated
the recognition process and helped the social worker feel more role
adequate. The social worker was informed of the precise alcoholic
content of cider and this was linked with the client's drunken
demeanour. The group themselves interpreted the children's embarrassment and protective behaviour as possible clues that their father was
often the worse for drink. They felt that the client's need to create a
false relationship with the social worker whenever she enquired about
his drinking was also a possible sign of guilt about his drinking, since
he avoided any straightforward discussion about it. The CAT then
asked the social worker to examine the case history and current situation for any other major problems. It transpired that a number of these
could also have been alcohol-related. In particular, the client was
reported to often feel depressed and to suffer continual bruises from
falls. There was evidence of liver damage in the past. Their likely
relationship to excessive drinking was explained by CAT to the group.

Moreover the social worker realized during the discussion that she had never seen him doing any housework; it was all being done by the children.

Various suggestions for her management of the case were then discussed within the group. The points of issue were how the social worker should utilize clues when bringing up the subject, how she should use the children to help the assessment, and what approaches should be made to his drinking. The group made various suggestions:

1. She should not deal with the case until he was prepared to acknowledge his drinking problem. If he would not acknowledge it, then she should consider what should be done about the children.

2. She should find a way to say as a statement of fact, 'I know you are drinking excessively'.

3. She should confront him with the fact that he was drinking and state that 'If you go on drinking you are going to lose your children . . .' thus compelling him to accept the social worker's professional authority via the threat of taking the children away. Some of the group felt this dramatic approach was necessary because the subject had been avoided for so long.

4. She should attempt to see the children by themselves and ask them to help her in establishing a diagnosis. However, the social worker reported that she had attempted this before and failed because the children were too loyal to their father and pretended that all was fine.

Having discussed these possible approaches, the CAT then attempted to help the group to establish an approach for the social worker which was investigative, but not critical. First, she was advised to seek the co-operation of the client's GP. (Although she had been unsure whether his physical and psychological problems had been caused by drinking, she had not contacted the GP to ask for a diagnosis or informed him of the client's other problems.) Second, the question of role legitimacy was discussed in terms of her general feeling of threat in bringing up the subject. Following our theoretical analysis, the CAT knew that the core of her anxiety was the threat to her professional self-esteem. In this particular case, discussing her feeling of threat with her elicited its two major manifestations. First, the social worker felt a sense of hopelessness and pessimism about bringing up the subject and approaching it. This was an expression of her need to safeguard her self-esteem by rationalizing that diagnosis was pointless. This was 'justified' by her further feeling that there was no therapeutic response which could follow a firm diagnosis anyway: 'Even if you can get him to admit that drinking is a problem, is there really a lot that can be done to help him?' Second, the CAT interpreted her feeling of being unable to discuss drinking with him as much in terms of her own reluctance as the client's. Her reluctance emanated from her sense of 'looming as a figure of authority' whenever she tried to discuss drinking, whereas her idealized image of the social worker was as warm and accepting. This only involved her in further difficulties because she was reluctant to pursue the subject. His constant denials made her doubt that he was drinking excessively and he further confused her by joking and teasing her — playing a game. The group felt she should analyse the game to see why he felt compelled to behave this way. Was he trying to cover up his problems? Was he testing whether she could handle the situation? The social worker admitted, 'I have become more and more incompetent about tackling the problem and I have found it more and more difficult to go and visit'.

The CAT attempted to resolve this lack of therapeutic commitment created by her role insecurity. The CAT tried to impart the feeling that diagnosis was a worthwhile procedure because there were therapeutic responses which could follow recognition. But she had to be helped to bring up the subject in such a way as not to appear to herself or to the client as a figure of authority, since this obviously made them both unable to discuss drinking rationally. It was therefore suggested that she should begin by discussing with him the good effects of his drinking and try and link up the reasons why he drank with the other problems in his life, so that the client felt that he was being understood and not lectured. If the social worker moralized, this would only worsen the client's fears of revealing any drink problems there may be. Any injunctions like 'you ought not to drink' should be avoided. However, it was important to assess with some accuracy the level of his drinking and its relationship to his problems. The social worker was given the opportunity to role-play her next contact with the client.

The social worker then broached the subject of drinking with the client in the suggested manner. She reported back to the group two sessions later that she had felt disappointed with the client's reaction, but her self-mocking tone revealed her realization that her expectations had been unrealistic, 'I think partly my expectations were of going in there and saying something which would make him go down on his bended knees, confess everything and say, "I've been lying all along" . . . and it didn't happen like that'.

The group then discussed these feelings and concluded that she had been expecting to act out a 'rescue' fantasy, which made discussing drinking seem more important to her than to the client. By now the group was coming to realize that her avoidance of the subject had been as much a reflection of the social worker's reluctance as the client's. The client had not perceived discussing drinking as such a dramatic breakthrough; the social worker had expected it to be more difficult and more effective than it turned out to be. Bringing these feelings out into the open again clarified her expectations and imparted a more realistic sense of success or failure. The support and supervision of the course prevented her feeling further disappointment and helped her to maintain a sense of adequacy and commitment even though she had not achieved the results which her rescue fantasy demanded. She began to adopt a more realistic attitude to the case — 'One can't expect anything to happen terribly rapidly' — and became resolved to continue visiting the client and to discuss drinking in the hope that at some point in the future she might be able to help him to deal with his alcohol abuse.

The major part of the CAT training courses revolved round cases like this: using the agents' experiences to draw out their safeguards, using the problems in the case to practically demonstrate clues to recognition and assessment and encouraging and training them to pursue the process of recognition, assessment and treatment.

The Effect of the CAT Training Courses

A research evaluation of the CAT training courses, based on agents' responses to the AAPPQ questionnaire before and after each course, showed that attenders reported significantly increased scores on scales measuring their role security. As would be expected from our hypothesis, this was accompanied by substantial increases on the scale measuring therapeutic commitment. When the agents felt less anxious about their role adequacy, role legitimacy and role support, clients with drinking problems became less of a threat to professional self-esteem.

These results were compared with responses of students to the AAPPQ before and after a more formal educational course — the 1976 Basic Summer School on Alcoholism organized by the Alcohol Education Centre. Summer School students were selected to match the CAT students in terms of personal characteristics, professional experience and experience with drinkers. Before their respective courses, there were no fundamental differences between the students' scores on the scale of therapeutic commitment or on scales measuring anxieties about role adequacy, role legitimacy and role support. After the courses, the

questionnaire showed that the Summer School had been more successful in increasing agents' information about alcohol and alcohol-related
problems, especially clinical information about the effects of alcohol.
The CAT courses, on the other hand, had been more successful in
increasing agents' knowledge of therapeutic skills in handling clients
with drinking problems (the type of information best covered within a
casework approach) and had also been more successful in reducing
anxieties about role legitimacy. More importantly, the agents who had
undergone CAT courses felt considerably more supported in their work
and consequently much more therapeutically committed to responding
to drinking problems. This comparison was not intended to show
whether one course was better or more effective than another, but
rather to reflect the extent to which these different courses achieved
their different aims. The Basic Summer School on Alcoholism intended
to increase agents' information about alcohol-related problems. In this
respect it was more successful than the CAT courses. On the other hand,
the CAT courses set out to reduce agents' anxieties about role adequacy,
role legitimacy and role support. Consequently these courses were more
successful than the Summer School in improving agents' therapeutic
commitment to work with drinkers.

The questionnaire measured the success of the CAT courses in terms
of changes in attitudes and subjective feelings. To discover the effect
of increased role security and therapeutic commitment upon behaviour,
an interview schedule was designed to elicit agents' responses to ongoing
cases before and after their training course. In particular, the interviews
were designed to measure any increase in agents' rates of recognition of
clients with drinking problems, since this was likely to be the best
numerical indicator of a practical improvement in the agents' therapeutic commitment. The group we chose to interview were the social
workers since our 1974 survey had shown they were less willing than
GPs or probation officers to label their clients as having drinking problems. For example, when the social workers in the 1974 survey were
asked to talk about one client with drinking problems whom they had
seen in the three months prior to interview, only eight out of 28 social
workers felt that they could name such a client. Yet the alcohol-
related problems of the eight clients who were discussed were measured
to be as severe as those of clients in our 1975 study who were attending
an alcoholism clinic. The social workers as a group were also less likely
than GPs or probation officers to feel they had got the right to raise and
discuss the subject of drinking. They were reluctant to discuss drinking
unless either the client brought it up or the relationship 'felt right'.

Social workers were also particularly prone to avoid attaching importance to the recognition of drinking problems by pessimistically dis-
missing them as inevitable or unalterable.

These manifestations of low therapeutic commitment hindered both
stages of the recognition process — not only the cognitive realization
that certain problems could be related to drinking, but also then
obtaining information from the client to discover if or to what extent
drinking was involved. Clearly, any increase in the social worker's
ability to recognize drinking problems amongst their clients could be
taken as a most forcible demonstration of the effect of increased therapeutic commitment upon their actual work.

The Interview Schedule

Each of the 12 social workers trained by the CAT was interviewed
before and after the course. Each interview lasted at least an hour and
was based around an investigation into the last eight cases with which
the social workers had been dealing prior to interview. Social workers
were asked only to select cases which they considered to be upon their
active caseload. For each case, they were asked to describe in detail the
major and subsidiary problems, the responses which they had made to
them, their goals in dealing with the case and their expectations about
being able to achieve these goals. This interview material thus painted a
spectrum of how the social workers were responding to 96 ongoing
cases. It elicited drinking problems from the social worker's overall
perspective and it supplied a background pattern of their overall work
within which their response to drinking problems could be compared to
their response to other sorts of case.

For each of the eight cases, the social worker was asked whether they
saw drinking as playing any part in the total set of problems, whether
drinking had ever been discussed and what information they had about
their client's drinking. If a social worker perceived any drinking problems were involved in a particular case, then a further series of questions were asked about the social worker's recognition and responses to
these problems, and their goals for dealing with the drinking involved.
To trace any changes which occurred, each of the social workers completed a follow-up interview about the same eight cases approximately
one month after completing the CAT course.

Changes in Recognition Rates

In strict numerical terms, the CAT social worker course had a very
marked impact upon the rate of recognition of drinking problems.

(Since there were nearly 100 cases discussed altogether, each of the numbers cited hereafter can be taken as virtually a percentage score.)

Increased Recognition of Cases definitely involving a Serious Drink Problem

Before the course, only two cases were recognized by the social workers as definitely involving a serious drink problem. After the course the number of such cases had risen to 13.

Increased Assessment of Cases in which Drinking possibly played a Part

Before the course, a further 29 cases had been seen by the social workers as possibly involving drinking problems. However, the social workers had neither acquired enough information nor discussed the subject enough with the clients to make a definite decision one way or the other. After the course, the social workers had been able to decide about 19 of these cases. In 12 cases, the previous suspicion of a drinking problem had been discounted, but in 7 cases drinking problems were confirmed.

Increased Recognition of Cases in which Drinking possibly played a Part

After the course, the social workers had begun to suspect that drink might be playing a part in a further 8 cases not suspected before the course began, although at the time of the follow-up interview the social workers had not made firm assessments.

A General Shift towards Increased Recognition

In itself, this numerical increase in recognized cases demonstrated a great improvement in the social workers' recognition and assessment of drinking problems. Recognition of serious drinking problems had substantially increased whilst a number of clients with possible problems had begun to be assessed and the role of drinking either confirmed or discounted. Improvements of course, were not absolute; there were still cases where the social worker was unable to come to a decision. However, the improved recognition rate represented a general shift. It was not due to particularly dramatic improvements in the performances of just two or three social workers. Before the course began, ten of the social workers said that none of their eight cases involved a definite drinking problem, but after the course only three social workers remained who did not feel that at least one of their eight cases involved a serious drinking problem. Moreover, there were eight cases considered to involve no drinking problem before the course, but suspected after the course as possibly involving drink: each of them belonged to a different social worker, again demonstrating a general shift in increased awareness across the group. Although recognition rates might increase over time irrespective of the agents' improved ability to recognize, the increase was so marked that the improvement must have been attributable to the effect of the CAT course. Moreover, the recognition rate had increased despite the fact that some formerly suspected cases had been assessed and agents had definitely discounted the possibility of drinking problems. Improved recognition was therefore not just indicated by more cases recognized as definitely involving drinking problems, but also by more cases recognized as definitely not involving a problem, i.e. the recognition rate had become more accurate.

The improvement is perhaps best demonstrated in the light of particular examples:

1. Cases recognized as definitely involving a Serious Drinking Problem

The only two cases recognized before the course as involving definite drinking problems were both cases who had been labelled as 'alcoholics' by other agents. This accorded with our previous data on social workers, who had been shown to be unwilling to label clients as 'alcoholics' or as 'problem drinkers' and were also uncertain about the criteria which other agents used to justify applying these labels. Consequently, social workers would only consider drinking to be causing problems when it was highly obvious, and often only when clients had been labelled as 'alcoholics' by some other agency.

The two cases recognized as having drinking problems before the course had both been diagnosed as 'alcoholics' by psychiatrists, and had histories of continually being in and out of mental hospitals.

Of the 11 cases recognized in the period between the interviews, seven had been suspected before the course, but four had been completely unsuspected. Amongst the 7 previously suspected cases, the recognition process had generally been triggered when the social worker acquired some new information about a problem which could have been caused by drinking. This clue was then linked up with other bits of information the social worker had previously acquired so that a pattern of harm related to alcohol emerged, rather than just a disparate collection of problems. Many of the clues to aid recognition had been there all along. But only when provided with clinical information and advice on how to raise problems with the client had the social workers become able to tie up the clues and realize there were a range of problems in the client's life which were probably being caused or aggravated by drink.

For example, between the interviews one social worker had two clients diagnosed as having liver damage. Before the course the social worker had known that both clients drank most nights, but she had not known anything more than that and the subject had only been discussed superficially. By the follow-up interview the social worker had realized the liver damage might be connected to the clients' regular drinking and had discussed this with them. One of the clients had turned out to be frightened about her drinking. The social worker had assessed the case more fully and had related the client's drinking to physical, mental, family and sexual problems. She concluded that 'I know just what I'm doing with it now, whereas I didn't three months or so ago.' She had become therapeutically committed to the case and said, 'I put as much into that case as any other case I've got . . . I'm surprised how much is being done.' The social worker had also gained much more information about the other client's drinking and in the follow-up interview presented a knowledgeable list of problems which she believed drinking to be causing, including loss of weight, listlessness, neglect of children and marital problems, wrapped up with sexual problems and jealousy precipitated and intensified by drinking. The social worker was dubious about the client's claim that he was not in financial difficulties and she was surprised that it did not seem to cause work problems. She expected the situation might deteriorate when the two children went away from home, since she felt that their presence might be restraining the client's drinking somewhat at the moment. Since the subject had never been discussed before the course began, this highly raised level of information represented a major improvement in the social worker's assessment of the case. Her therapeutic commitment imparted optimism that something could be done about the drinking: 'It has opened out some sort of relationship but I think there is quite a lot that can be done'.

In other cases, the social workers had changed their assessment because of gaining further information about the client's drinking itself, which they had then linked up with problems in the client's life. One discovered that her client, a divorced man with two children, often indulged in drinking sessions until 4 o'clock in the morning. She then linked this up with a report that one of his children had gone to school in his pyjamas and further investigation revealed that because the father was often incapable in the mornings the children had often gone to school in a neglected condition or had not gone at all. Another social worker who also discovered that one of her clients was drinking till 3 or 4 o'clock most mornings linked this with him developing a stomach complaint. Further investigation revealed a whole series of alcohol-related problems about which the social worker had been previously ignorant. It transpired that in the past the client had been arrested while drunk and disorderly. When questioned by the social worker, the client's son revealed that his father had been violent after drinking and this was also confirmed when the social worker questioned a local policeman. The social worker had begun to attribute loss of sleep, lack of concentration and chronic depression to drinking and she had changed her interpretation of how the drinker himself perceived the drink: 'He is quite defensive about it because I tried to visit him one evening, fairly early on, about half past six and he wasn't there. He came in and saw my senior the next day and said, I hardly ever go out for a drink . . . you don't make excuses like that unless you feel a bit guilty about it.'

Probably the widest range of problems emerging when a social worker followed up clues to drinking problems was a case in which only one problem related to drink had been mentioned in the first interview. The son, 14, had attempted to take and drive away a car when drunk. By the follow-up interview the social worker had found out that this boy's drinking was much more serious than he thought and that his twin brother had also been charged for being drunk. Meanwhile, both the social worker and a probation officer had visited the mother and found her too, 'the worst for liquor'.

In all fairness the probation officer involved in the case discovered her before I did, but she [the probation officer] seriously never told me. I never realized that drinking played such a part in the family. It plays a much bigger part than I thought, and obviously they are getting high on drink. It also says why they have to steal, you know, the reasons behind this. I think perhaps the lads are not stealing so much for themselves but when the mum is laid up sick they tried stealing for mum for drink. You know this is a possibility, and more than a possibility, it is a serious possibility and it puts a different complexion on the case and it means I've got to work at it in a different way. Also dad died of kidney trouble, so this drink problem I'm sure has been there for a long time, but it has just not been picked up by anybody.

The social worker perceived he was 'just beginning to get into the drink' but was using information he had previously not connected with drinking. He felt guilty about not having realized it before and embarrassed when it came out in court that the boy had attempted to take and drive away after drinking a whole bottle of gin. 'My feelings about that court case, when I thought about my report when he said he drank a bottle of gin, I wanted to creep under the desk in front of me, because I was trying to make myself look smaller and get away from the magistrate because my report was immediately devalued.' After the court case the social worker asked the boy how much he drank and found that it was common for him to drink a bottle of gin in the morning and that he was served in numerous local pubs: 'It really did shock me.' He drank 'quite regular and it's getting to be a serious drinking problem'. As for the mother, the social worker had now begun to discuss it with her as well and concluded that 'she is an alcoholic, my feelings at the moment are that she is definitely an alcoholic. She denies drinking, and I've seen her drunk, it's just not on.' The social worker felt that the mother's drinking was straining the family finances, which would not be alleviated by the boys going out to work. 'I think in fact it is going to escalate instead of decreasing. As soon as they get more money in their hand, they are going to do more drinking.' In total, the social worker felt he had to 'admit at the moment, the family fills me with foreboding and horror and I really haven't sat down to think about the future, or any future plans for them.' However, he was still committed to respond. 'I think that I will approach them, yes.'

As if such revelations were not startling enough, there were four cases in which social workers had not perceived any drinking problems whatsoever before the course, but by the follow-up interview they had come to recognize serious drinking problems. In two of these cases the social worker was informed directly about the drinking problem by someone else, in one case by the client's spouse and in another case by the former probation officer. In this latter case the social worker had said before the course that drinking definitely played no part in the case because the father never went out at night. He had no information about the client's drinking, had never discussed drinking and thought it was irrelevant to the case. By the time of the interview after the course he had been alerted by the former probation officer that 'in fact, the father has quite a severe drinking problem' and two years previously the client had been drinking half a bottle of spirits a day. Again the social worker had then realized that other problems in the client's history must have been caused by alcohol abuse. He had recently collapsed in the street and been taken to hospital from where he had been referred for psychiatric treatment. The social worker also now believed that drink caused financial, legal and work problems. Yet, the drinking had not been discussed with the client, and the social worker was unsure what to do next. Another social worker who had just become aware that a case involved a serious drinking problem was still establishing the extent of the drink-related damage before discussing it with the client. Again, the social worker had previously dismissed drinking as irrelevant but reported in the later interview, 'That's the one thing that's altered. She's been arrested for being drunk and disorderly just recently and her drinking has increased rapidly over the last three months.' The social worker had not assessed the client's drinking behaviour, but she felt that this should be done. The social worker's recognition and assessment of the extent of the problem had probably not been fully conceptualized. For example, just before the interview, the client had been admitted to hospital with a drugs over-dose, but the social worker did not seem aware that this could possibly be associated with drinking as well.

However, in the final case in which there had been no problem what-soever seen before the course but severe problems recognized after, the recognition had been a combination both of the client bringing up the problem and then the social worker actively pursuing it. The client was an unmarried mother with a son who had told the social worker at one point that she was drinking very heavily and was worried about it and then two weeks later she said she was not drinking at all. Whereas the usual tendency of a social worker working without advice and support would have been to let the matter drop there, the social worker with the CAT's assistance had gone on to discuss the drinking in depth with the client and had acquired much information. The client was drinking every day both at the pub and at home, and the social worker felt the client's inability to cope with her child, her depression and her financial problems were all probably caused by drinking, and she had suggested to the client that her loss of appetite and severe headaches were prob-ably due to her drinking. She had discussed it at length 'to get it accep-ted as a topic' and to discuss its ramifications.

2. Cases which might involve a Drink Problem

There were eight cases where the social workers had originally said that the drinking was not playing any part, but after the course they had recognized the possibility of a drink problem. The pattern was similar in each case; the social worker had noticed that consumption was increasing, that there were episodes of drunkenness or that the consump-tion had been more than they previously realized. They had therefore become suspicious about the possibility of drink causing problems and were 'keeping an eye on it'. This reflected their adoption of the CAT perspective that heavy drinking was itself a strong clue of the possibility of drink problems. For example, one social worker who thought drinking was irrelevant in a case before the course said afterwards that she had 'become suspicious' of the client because he went out drinking every night. She felt she had picked up 'little allusions' to his drinking from the rest of the family and although the drinking may have been worse in the past, she was still watching in case it was currently affecting the client or the family. Another social worker had become suspicious because a client's wife had brought up the subject of her husband's excessive drinking and because the husband was an Italian waiter.

The increased alertness to the possibility of a drink problem on the part of these 8 different social workers reflected quite strongly the way the CAT course had increased their tendency towards greater recognition. They had become aware of the possibility of drink being involved in cases where there were relatively minor clues or no clues at all except for drinking itself. This had become sufficient to make these social workers 'keep an eye on the drinking' in case it should be causing other problems or get worse in the future. It also reflected an increased ability of the social workers to discuss drinking with the client when it first arose and to extract information from the clients to help them assess whether the drinking was excessive and whether it was causing problems. This is well illustrated by the case of a divorced man living with his two boys whose problems had previously been assessed as basically financial. The social worker thought that he did drink a bit but it was not in any way contributing to his problems. However, after the course, the social worker reported being alerted when 'He mentioned getting half drunk on his own and rolling into bed, which having been to this course, I pricked up my ears and said something about drink.' The social worker was quite surprised that it had been relevantly easy to talk to the client about it. 'I wasn't sure whether he saw it as a problem or not, except that he said about sitting there and getting drunk, he brought it up, and when I asked him in fact he did tell me an awful lot about it, with really no prompting on my part.' She was sceptical when he said, 'I don't worry about that', because she felt 'you don't say you don't worry about something unless you do really'. She then asked how much he was drinking and concluded the expense was possibly making him unable to meet his electricity bills. Since her major goal with this man had been to help him budget, she realized why much of her previous efforts, which had not allowed for the financial effect of his drinking, had been unproductive. Since she felt his drinking was connected with losing his wife, the social worker considered it might continue to get worse: 'I feel it is something to be watched, keep an eye on it and find out as much as possible and watch.'

3. Cases in which Recognition was Not Pursued

The improvement in the social worker's recognition practices was not all-inclusive. There were 10 cases in which there had been some mention of the possibility of a drinking problem before the course but the recognition process had proceeded little further by the time of the second interview. No proper assessment of the client's drinking behaviour had been made. These cases probably represent the inability of the course by itself to fully reorientate the social worker's attitudinal 'set' towards recognizing drinking problems. The role insecurity and lack of therapeutic commitment usually typical of social workers had been retained in these particular cases. Some still felt anxieties about their role legitimacy: 'I would like to discuss it with them, but they don't see me as the person to do this for them.' In some cases the social worker expressed a general disinclination to pursue the issue, 'I would only respond if it got a lot worse', accepting the client's face view that drink was no problem, and further investigation was pointless. Some felt that unfortunately the time when they would have been most able to discuss drinking had passed, and one particularly rued that she had not known 'a little bit more about the clues earlier on'.

4. Cases where Drinking Problems were No Longer Recognized

In 12 cases, the course had the effect, not of helping the social workers to discover drinking problems, but conversely to decide that drinking was not playing a part. In 10 cases, suspicions had been followed by investigation and a firm assessment had allowed the possibility of drinking problems to be discounted: 'I did wonder but I don't now. Definitely not, I still have the fear that she could become a sneak drinker at home on her own. There must be a question mark because of her in that situation, but I felt reassured about it after I did the interview.'

Two cases where the social worker had said that there was some form of drink problem before the course, but not after, went against the grain of the general shift. For in neither case did there seem good reason to be certain that drinking was no longer playing a part – quite the opposite. Both social workers had been told by other agents that the client had a drinking problem but they seemed loathe to explore or to recognize this. One reported that, 'they said there were drinking problems, but there does not seem to be now from what I know of'. However, when questioned she did not actually know anything about the client's drinking behaviour. The other social worker reported that the wife had threatened to leave the client if he kept on drinking and the social worker believed that he had then cut down on his consumption. However, he had no information about it. Neither had he enquired into the possibility that drinking might be related to the psycho-sexual difficulties which which were the client's major presenting problems. The reasons why such anomalies still persisted within the general shift towards increased recognition will be examined in the following section.

The Relationships Between Recognition, Role security and Therapeutic Commitment

Reductions in the social workers' anxieties about role adequacy, role legitimacy and role support each contributed to different aspects of improved recognition.

(a) *Role Adequacy, Recognition and Therapeutic Commitment*

As explained in Chapter 9, agents' anxieties about their role adequacy were reduced when supplied with clinical information and training in counselling skills. The questionnaire results also showed that some of the general counselling skills which social workers developed in their casework were applicable in working with drinkers. Therefore providing clinical information was the more important aspect of reducing social workers' anxieties about role adequacy. Social workers expressed particular discomfort about recognizing and dealing with physical and psychological problems related to drinking, and were also anxious to find out about the medical aspects of treatment, particularly about any drugs used. These areas had not been covered in their training.

After the CAT course the social workers' increased clinical knowledge helped them to make not just a more knowledgeable and active response to their clients' social problems, but to their physiological and psychological problems as well — 'At the moment, I must get Mr. T round to his GP to get some vitamins inside him.' The clinically informed social worker was able to interpret to the client what was happening to him and knew about possible medical help: 'He's frightened of the withdrawal period. I have told him he can get Valium for that, and if it got really bad we could perhaps fit him up in hospital.'

Increased role adequacy also enabled the social workers to make a more thorough and knowledgeable assessment of the client's drinking history. For example, one social worker discovered that a client had been diagnosed in the 1950s as 'possibly an epileptic'. Following a further interview with the client, the social worker concluded that her fits had probably been related to alcohol consumption and that the woman's drinking problems had developed a lot earlier than anyone had previously supposed. The social worker realized that drinking had probably been involved in the breakup of the client's marriage over 20 years previously which gave the social worker a completely different perspective on the client's drinking. She felt this would help her to plan the case more effectively and to set more appropriate goals.

(b) *Role Legitimacy, Recognition and Therapeutic Commitment*

Unless agents felt they had the right to raise, discuss and ask questions about the subject of drinking, and also felt that clients accepted these rights, agents were unable to elicit the necessary clinical information, no matter how knowledgeable they were.

The reduction in these anxieties about role legitimacy amongst the social workers by the end of the course was indicated by the fact that ten out of the 12 social workers had discussed drinking with at least one more client with whom they had never discussed the subject prior to the course. In all there were 18 more cases in which drinking was being discussed after the course. The social workers admitted their previous reluctance to investigate thoroughly: 'I have started talking to a lot more people about their drinking in a way that I would have avoided before.'

Some attributed their widened view of the legitimate sphere of a social worker's rights and responsibilities to the realization that drinking problems involved social causes and effects – 'I would have thought before, that a drinking problem was someone else's job to do something about more than mine. As I wouldn't pry into a physical thing, so I think I would have felt a bit interfering to have asked about the drinking, whereas now I think it's maybe necessary that I'm interfering, so that I included it more in the social problems than I did.' While this quote demonstrated reduced anxieties about role legitimacy, it also indicated that the social worker's anxieties had not been completely eradicated. The notion that enquiry might be construed by the client as 'interfering' still lingered. There were other such instances in which, after the CAT course, the social workers felt they should investigate drinking problems more thoroughly but still worried whether clients would accept this. So although drinking had been discussed with more clients than previously, some of the social workers still believed that drinking should not be discussed until the client brought it up or until the relationship felt right. Fortunately, these remaining doubts about role legitimacy were offset by feelings of increased role adequacy which at least allowed the social workers to decide whether the client was telling them the truth or not. 'There is this case which I'm awfully worried about because he said that he didn't drink and I always thought he did, he was such a con man and tried to persuade me that I was making a mistake, that I wasn't sure if I was coming or going and as a result of the course, at least I feel definitely sure in my own mind that he is a heavy drinker, which helps.' Other social workers reported that their clients had previously been able to negate their role legitimacy by becoming 'flippant', 'teasing' and 'condescending' whenever they tried to investigate drinking. After the course, the social workers were no longer being put off by these ploys. For instance, one client had always tried to ward off investigation by dominating the therapeutic relationship and thus denying the social worker's authority. The social worker discussed this difficulty with the CAT group, and in the follow-up interview she believed that she had overcome it. 'I think we've got over very much this nice little girl coming to see me bit which was getting away from the question of drinking.'

All the social workers commented that when they had brought up the subject of drinking with clients for the first time, they had found the situation to be more comfortable and the discussion more open and straightforward than they had imagined possible. They had been anxious that clients would not accept the intrusion into their privacy, that they would be angered by it or even that the therapeutic relationship might be destroyed altogether. Without exception these fears proved unfounded. All the clients with whom the subject of drinking was raised seemed quite accepting of the social worker's more active response. This confirmed our view that fears of disturbing the therapeutic relationship were more of a rationalization for avoiding and not recognizing drinking problems than an accurate perception of the relationship between agent and client. The exaggerated fears of client hostility to being asked questions about drinking was a safeguarding strategy, an excuse for not bringing up the subject — even at times to the client's obvious detriment. The same point was made in a letter written to the CAT by a GP who had attended the GP course:

I am amazed how forthcoming patients are about how much they drink now that I have the courage to ask them. I am also very surprised to discover how much young males drink these days. The other thing I've discovered since the course is how many of my depressed middle-aged women have alcoholic husbands who they haven't been able to talk about until directly questioned. Thank you very much for opening my eyes, or should I say, my mouth.

Some of the social workers had so dispelled their anxieties about role legitimacy that they had come to perceive themselves as the drinker's lifeline, their one outlet for discussing their drinking – even if at times the client behaved as though he was rejecting this idea: 'I think he's riddled with guilt and he won't do anything about it, except talk to me. He obviously feels that I don't preach to him. When he packs up talking to me about it, that's when I'm really going to get worried.'

(c) *Role Support, Recognition and Therapeutic Commitment*

In the case quoted above, the social worker felt unworried about his role adequacy and role legitimacy because he also felt an increased sense of the crucial requirement which promotes role security – the feeling of having role support. This case had been discussed upon the CAT course and the social worker's role and potential range of responses had been considered. His increased role adequacy allowed him to recognize and assess the drinking problems, his role legitimacy allowed him to discuss it with the client, and his role support allowed him to continue responding to the drinking even when his efforts seemed very unlikely to produce any dramatic improvement. Another social worker remarked how support would allow social workers to carry on when all seemed lost: 'I think it's a very specific problem which on courses for social work training you hardly cover at all, but really it's a problem which comes up time and time again, and I think most people do feel pretty helpless and unable to help, I think it gives you reassurance there isn't much more you can do, in a way you feel better than dealing helplessly with the case.' This quote highlighted one of the most important aspects of role support. When given encouragement, advice and supervision, the agent developed a more realistic sense of what could and could not be achieved. Failure to produce immediate changes became less of a threat to professional self-esteem and did not result in the social worker giving up. Without role support agents were easily dissuaded from responding to drinking problems, and again this was most noticeable in their ability to pursue recognition. For the absence or presence of role support was the key in determining whether or not the social workers could recognize drinking problems amongst their cases.

When the CAT supported an agent's handling of a case, the agent felt role secure enough to recognize and to pursue drinking problems. If an agent's response to a case was not supported and supervised, then the agent felt role insecure and this sometimes precluded the agent using his generally increased ability to recognize drinking problems. This produced the anomalies which, as we have reported, punctured the general shift towards improved recognition.

The point is best illustrated by comparing two clients of the same social worker. These two clients were very alike; both unmarried mothers whose drinking had begun to escalate, causing them physical and psychological problems and interfering with the care of their children. Before the course the social worker felt both cases possibly involved drinking probelms. After the course the social worker had decided that in both cases drinking was definitely a serious problem. Her response to one of these cases had been supported by the CAT; the other had not. The case which had been discussed, planned and supported by the CAT group was marked by a highly raised level of information about the client's drinking and all the problems related to it. The subject had been discussed between the social worker and the client herself. The social worker felt it had been an achievement, 'to make it a subject that was possible to talk about . . . that took some doing actually. But I thought that was pretty successful.' 'She's responded very well to my talking about it.' The social worker felt 'really good' about the progress made in this case. In the other case where her response had been unsupported, the social worker admitted that she had not done much to respond to the drinking and she had never discussed it with the client. She had not even raised the subject during an interview to compile a social report on the client when she had suspected the client to be either drunk or hungover at the time. She felt her response to this case had been 'futile and not very effective really'.

Quite clearly, the support and supervisory function of the CAT group was crucial to the responses to individual cases made by this social worker. When supported, she pursued recognition and assessment, felt role secure and derived rewards from working with the client. When unsupported in dealing with a virtually identical case, she could not pursue recognition and assessment, felt insecure and derived only a sense of failure from working with the client. The process of recognition then did not merely depend on how much agents knew or what they believed were their rights. The agent who felt no sense of role support avoided recognizing and responding to blatant drinking problems. Obviously the social worker was unable to generalize her sense of support and success in one case to another similar case. This emphasized still further the importance of role support in helping an agent become an effective worker. It bore out the analysis that agents were unlikely to become generally more effective until they had been supported in handling a considerable number of cases of drinking problems, thus acquiring the experience which consolidated role security. With clinical information and counselling training this could then lead to higher therapeutic commitment.

(d) *Recognition, Therapeutic Commitment and Attitudes to Alcohol Abuse*

Nevertheless, there were some indications of more general shifts, in attitude at least, in a direction more akin to therapeutic commitment.

Some social workers said they realized they had changed their prejudices and stereotypes of drinkers:

> I suppose I thought before that if you met someone to whom drinking was a real problem so it was affecting their lives it would be obvious on meeting them . . . I suppose I thought someone with a drink problem was going to look like a drinker or something like that. I was inclined to ignore it unless someone was falling off the edge of the pavement and rolling about.

This was accompanied by a change in their attitudes to drinking problems and their views as to how widespread and severe these were likely to be, especially within their own casework. Indeed, most of the social workers remarked that during and immediately after the course they had perhaps temporarily held a somewhat exaggerated view of the importance and prevalence of drinking problems:

> I think for the first couple of days you were looking for alcoholics underneath beds and things but slowly that calmed down and now it's a more constant looking for them . . . I think at one point it might have made me too suspicious, the mere mention of the word drinking but at least it altered my attitude that way.

As they stated, their increased awareness tended to level off to a realistic consciousness of the potential importance of drinking in causing or aggravating problems.

I think I've realized that it plays more of a part in their problems
than I had before. For example, in this area a lot of people drink
culturally because there are a lot of Irish and Scottish and I think I
tended to dismiss a lot of the drinking as a cultural thing rather than
accepting it as a drinking problem which is probably one of the most
important revisions for me.

This revised perception of the scope and importance of alcohol abuse
was a prerequisite attitude for producing a general shift towards increasing recognition, and reducing anxieties about role legitimacy:

I'm certainly looking out for it much more, whereas before I wasn't
unless it was so obvious that you couldn't avoid it. I wasn't actually
looking for it or even noticing it. In a sense, as a result of making a
conscious effort to see alcohol as a possible element in the situation,
I'm definitely more confident of actually raising it, because I've been
willing to actually look for it in the first place.

Moreover after the CAT course, there was a clear sense of confidence,
realistic optimism, and a concern for clients with drinking problems
which was quite different from the general picture drawn from our
1974 study of social workers who had not been trained in responding
to drinking problems. The social workers who had attended the CAT
course had increased their therapeutic commitment, and lost some of
the sense of despairing hopelessness. They were feeling optimistic about
responding to their clients with drinking problems – 'I think there is
quite a lot that can be done.' Instead of tending to push drinkers low
down on the list of priorities, they had begun to see them as equally
deserving of the social worker's time and energy as any other case: 'I
put as much into that case as any other case I've got.' Instead of
tending to blame drinkers for their condition and to disapprove of them
as people, there was more concern for the drinking client and a sense of
a need to encourage an adequate response from others too, 'it is other
people's problem not her problem.' Even a client whom the social
worker believed was lying to him about his drinking, who was thought
unlikely to improve in either his drinking or his problems and who
battered his son when drunk, was still considered by the social worker
to merit a response. In the place of nihilism was a slight glimmer of
hope, with a realistic expectation that in cases of drinking problems,
improvements often took a long while to engender:

I cannot see Mr C giving up drinking. There is a very, very, I'm being very optimistic, well, there is a very, very small hope of a chance, there is one thing that gives me hope is him keeping on talking to me about it. I'm pleased though it may sound nothing, I know a lot more, nothing was done beforehand, at least we've made a start and it's better late than never.

11 THE CAT CONSULTATION SERVICE: IMPROVING THE RESPONSE TO INDIVIDUAL CLIENTS WITH DRINKING PROBLEMS

The previous chapter described how the CAT attempted to overcome agents' role insecurity on the training courses by asking them to discuss cases of drinking problems from their current caseload. The consultation service, on the other hand, allowed agents to bring up cases whenever they wanted. The courses attempted to deliberately challenge agents' safeguards to increase their recognition rates and actively encourage them to respond; the consultation service waited for them to bring their cases to the CAT. It was expected that agents would tend to consult the CAT when their professional self-esteem was threatened so much that their usual safeguards such as avoiding or blaming the client were no longer working or were no longer possible in the situation. We expected then that agents might approach the CAT, in a sense, for the wrong reasons; perhaps hoping to relieve themselves of responsibility.

However, the goal of the CAT consultation service was not to take cases away from general community agents, but to help these agents to carry on dealing with cases by themselves at a primary care level. The CAT would refuse to take on the client unless there were special circumstances. They would try instead to clarify the situation for the agents, give them information about their client's problems, advise them what clues to look for and what questions to ask, talk the agents through their own problems in responding, and suggest alternative responses which they could try out with CAT support and supervision. This would enable them to acquire experience under supported conditions, and thus help them, in the terms of our analysis, to move towards a position of greater role security.

There were other possible benefits besides the training function. We were interested to see if such a service might prove a suitable alternative for clients reluctant to attend psychiatric out-patient clinics, Alcoholics Anonymous or any service with potentially stigmatizing and offputting labels of 'alcoholism' and 'problem drinkers'. Of course the experiment could only indicate if a supportive system could reduce the number of unnecessary referrals to specialist services. The service described was embryonic and the following chapter is intended to provide ideas about how such a service might get off the ground and how it would be likely to operate. It is not a formal research evaluation of a full scale consultation service. Perhaps the most interesting questions of all were simply – would anybody use it, and if so, who and why, and with what sort of client with what sort of problems did which agents need what sort of support?

1. Administrative Arrangements

The period for which the experimental service operated varied with each professional group, since it had been decided only to offer the service to each group of agents when some of their members had completed their training course. There were two reasons for this. First, we wished to assess the training courses' effect upon recognition and therapeutic commitment, without the added variable of consultation.

Second, we felt the consultation service would develop more fruitfully and realistically through personal contact, rather than through formal letters publicizing its existence. We had expected that the consultation service would be used primarily by agents who had got to know the CAT members personally on the training courses. As it turned out, such agents were not in the majority of agents requesting help, although some did use the service and others recommended it to their colleagues.

It had been planned to offer the consultation service to each group of agents for a twelve-week period. If necessary, any cases presented in that time which required consultation beyond the 12 weeks were to be dealt with until the CAT members left their posts. Although the nurses and GPs were offered consultation services, their training courses only finished when the social worker member of the CAT had already left the project and the psychiatrist was about to take up his new post, so the service for GPs and nurses only effectively ran for 4 weeks. But because of the personalized nature of the service, other agents such as clergyman and hostel wardens, who had not been involved in the training courses, also contacted the consultation service.

2. Requests for Help from the Consultation Service

There were requests for help from the CAT consultation service from 34 different agents concerning 42 different cases. As can be seen from the table below, the requests came predominantly from social workers and probation officers, which reflected the longer period of time for which the service was available to them. There were two types of request. There were 32 requests for support: asking for advice about goals, help over assessment and so forth, and 10 requests purely for information.

The following figures refer to the initial request for help with a particular case. Some agents requested help over some of these cases on more than one occasion.

Table 11.1 Requests for Help from CAT

Agents Requesting Help	No. of cases for which support was requested	No. of cases over which information was requested	Total
Probation officers	11 11	3	14
Social workers	13 11	4	15
General practitioners	4 4	1	5
Hostel warden	1 2	–	2
Health visitor	1 1	–	1
Clergyman	1 1	1	2
Marriage guidance counsellor	1 1	–	1
Social science student	1 –	1	1
Wife of a drinker	1 1	–	1
	34 32	10	42

1 probation officer requested support with 2 cases; 1 probation officer requested information about 3 cases; 2 social workers each requested support with 1 case and information about another case; 1 general practitioner requested support with 1 case and information about another.

Table 11.2 How Agents knew of CAT

Been on CAT training course	6
Recommended by someone who had been on a CAT course*	3
Recommended by another agent in the field	9
Agent had previous or current personal or professional contact	7
Client had previous or current contact with hospital in which CAT based	9
	34

* Not necessarily a colleague of the same profession. 1 probation officer consulted CAT on the recommendation of a GP who had attended the CAT course.

Since only a small proportion of requests for help came from agents who had attended courses, it would seem that social workers and probation officers were more likely than other general community agents to use the consultation service, irrespective of the fact that they had the consultation service on offer for longer.

3. Requests for Help over Information

In 10 cases the agent required straightforward advice rather than consultation over ongoing difficulties in case-handling. For example, there were requests for information about AA and Al-Anon, hostel places and criteria for hospital admissions.

4. Requests for Support

There were requests for support over 32 cases. The reasons for contact were so varied that no overall classification could be made, but certain traits clustered in different professions.

(a) *The Probation Officers*

Ten probation officers requested support:

Table 11.3 Use of CAT Consultation Service by Probation Officers

Why initial request for help	Main problem(s) related to drink	Joint Interviews conducted	Other action
Court report required	Legal (fighting after drinking)	JI	Court report made
Court report required	Legal (property damage after drinking)	JI	Court report made
Court report required	Legal (taking and driving away after drinking)	JI	Ongoing advice and court report made
Had the client got a drink problem?	Legal (theft after drinking)	—	CAT suggested court report and probation order
Client requested help	Legal (theft after drinking)	—	Advice
Client needed detox*	—	—	Detox arranged — ongoing advice
Client drunk in probation office	Financial	JI	Advice on how to get him sober
Client being evicted	Accommodation	JI	Help with accom. and advice
Hostel place required*	Accommodation	—	Hostel place arranged
Hospital referral required	—	—	Referral arranged
Marital crisis	Marital, violence, care of children, legal (drunk and disorderly)	—	Advice

* Requests made by the same probation officer.

Half the requests concerned legal problems concerned with drinking. In three cases the agent had to respond because the magistrates had requested psychiatric and medical opinions in conjunction with social enquiry reports. All three clients were teenage males. The court wished to know if two of them had a drinking problem which required specialist help. The other client had a record of committing crimes while drunk and since he had not completed his community service, the court wished to know if this was because of a drink problem. In another case, the court only requested a report on the client's social circumstances, but the probation officer himself wanted to assess the client's drinking. He did not want to submit a court report on the relationship between the client's drinking and the offence, but the CAT themselves recommended this because each time the client had been arrested he had been drunk.

These probation officers required help in answering four major questions:

1. What was the relationship of alcohol to crime?
2. Did the client recurrently drink to excess?
3. What kind of help would be appropriate?
4. What would be the effect of a custodial sentence upon the client and upon his drinking?

The fifth and sixth cases in Table 11.3 also involved probation orders. One probation officer contacted the CAT because the client had admitted to drinking problems just as the probation order was due to expire. The agent wanted advice as to whether he should review the ending of the order. Another officer felt he would have to ask the court to revoke an order unless the CAT were prepared to provide ongoing support. The probation officer said he had only accepted the client — a 37 year-old female ex-nurse, 'in blissful ignorance' at the recommendation of a psychiatrist. The client had continued to drink and to get into trouble with the law so the psychiatrist now thought that a custodial sentence would be more appropriate. The probation officer acknowledged feeling utterly confused and overwhelmed by the number of crises which had arisen. He was floundering because he lacked the necessary knowledge to plan realistically. On the day he rang the CAT, the client had been drinking heavily and was due to attend court the following day. The probation officer wanted the CAT to find somewhere to detoxicate her overnight as an emergency. He did not realize that because the client had resumed drinking within a week of discharge from hospital, it was very unlikely that any other hospital would readmit her immediately. By planning inappropriately he was getting no help from any agency and becoming increasingly desperate. This case illustrated that requests for help from the CAT were made not just when the client was experiencing a crisis, but also when the agent was experiencing a crisis — a crisis of threat to professional self-esteem. This was equally true of the seventh case in Table 11.3. The probation officer was thrown into confusion when the client arrived drunk in the probation office, and the officer had no idea how to deal with him.

Three further requests were for practical assistance over arranging accommodation and hospital referrals. The remaining request for help came when a hospital refused to admit a client's wife who had drinking problems and the situation became intolerable for both client and probation officer. Clearly then, the majority of requests from probation officers were made when they were being forced to respond to drinking problems, but felt inadequate to do so. Anxiety about role adequacy was suddenly intensified when the probation officer had to assess a client's drinking problems, handle drunken clients or deal with clients who asked for help about their drinking problems.

These situations seemed particularly threatening to probation officers' self-esteem and their role insecurity drove them to seek role support.

(b) *Social Workers*

Eleven social workers made requests for support from the CAT service.

The first six cases in Table 11.4 involved social workers requesting help when their client had in turn sought help from their social workers over their drinking. The first three clients were all female and all worried about their growing excessive consumption. One admitted drinking over half a bottle of whisky a day which she believed caused her chest pains and other physical problems. The other two clients were both worried about the effect of their drinking on their care of their children. Both asked the social worker for help over their drinking when the social worker had first brought up the possibility of taking the children into care. The social worker had been aware for some time that one of these clients might have serious drinking problems, but all previous attempts to discuss the subject had failed. When the client eventually admitted drinking excessively, the social worker felt unsure how to proceed; it was important not to break the trust she had slowly built up, yet she felt obliged to respond to the drinking because of the

Table 11.4 Use of CAT Consultation Service by Social Workers

Why initial request for help	Main problem(s) related to drink	Joint Interview JI or without agent WA	Other action
Client requested help	Child neglect	JI	
Client worried about drinking	Child neglect	JI	
Client worried about drinking	Physical (duodenal ulcer & cardiac risk)	—	Referral to hospital
Client requested support after hospital discharge	—	WA	
Client's husband admitted drink problem	Marital	JI	
Possible violence from client's husband	Marital & violence	JI	
Assessment required	Marital & violence	JI	
Assessment required	Legal		Involved PO
Child battering	Child battering	JI	
Client drinking in dry house	—	WA	Replaced with day care. CAT eventually took over case
Client requested money	—	WA	Advice on how to prevent his spending on drink

children. When the other client requested help, the social worker had wanted to refer her to the psychiatric services, but the client had previously seen a psychiatrist whom she felt had not understood her fears of becoming aggressive towards her son when drunk. These fears had been noted in the psychiatrist's letter to the client's GP, but no enquiry into the woman's drinking had been recorded. The client refused to accept any further referral to a psychiatric hospital; she was asking for help specifically from the social worker. However, the social worker felt unable to respond without advice and support. The CAT consultation service thus provided a way out of this impasse.

The fourth client above asked for continued help with her drinking after discharge from an out-patient alcoholism service, whilst the next two cases involved the client's husband. One had been causing chronic marital disharmony and the client felt she could no longer cope with her husband's constant drunkenness, but she did not wish to leave or divorce him. The social worker also felt unable to handle the husband when drunk and disinclined to discuss drinking with him when he was sober and denying that he drank excessively. Her goals were just to support the wife, even though she felt this was really doing little to help preserve the marriage. Only when the husband eventually admitted that drink was a problem did the social worker feel forced to respond, but was still uncertain how to respond. Another client was worried about possible violence following her husband's imminent release from prison and had asked the social worker how she could protect herself and her children. The social worker felt anxious in case any poor advice from her resulted in violence, and she therefore turned to the CAT for advice and support. There were three requests from social workers for help with assessments. Two wanted to know if their clients were 'alcoholic or not'. The other was unsure how much of the marital disharmony and also the family's financial difficulties were due to drink. The two remaining requests for support both occurred when social workers were faced with a dilemma in their handling of a drinker. One client had started drinking in a dry house and the social worker was unsure of the likely repercussions or how to deal with the client. The other social worker asked for advice over a client who had asked the social worker to claim more money for him. She suspected that this money was wanted for drink or drugs.

As with probation officers, the requests for help from social workers were largely triggered when responding to the drinking became unavoidable, especially when the clients themselves forced the issue. The social workers' anxieties about their role adequacy and role legitimacy made obtaining role support imperative in these situations. Like probation officers, social workers also used the CAT for help with assessment, but without as much concentration on formal reports. Most of the social workers felt inadequate in assessing drinking problems and were anxious lest any inappropriate enquiries or responses might disrupt the relationship with their client.

(c) *General Practitioners*

Although consultation was offered to GPs for only one month, four GPs still availed themselves of this service.

Table 11.5 Use of CAT Consultation Service by GPs

Why initial request for help	Main problem(s) caused by drink	Joint Interview conducted	Other Action
Client needed detoxication	—	—	Advice over detoxication then long term advice
Client's daughter asked for advice	Accidents when drunk	JI	——
Client asked for help	Psychological and marital	JI	——
Client's wife asked for help	Depression in spouse	——	CAT took over case

The first GP requested help when a patient required detoxication. He particularly wanted to know whether it was possible for the patient to be detoxicated in her home. After this crisis had passed, he then asked how to plan a long-term response. The other three cases were all cases in which the doctor had been asked to respond but felt unable to do so without CAT support. One patient's daughter asked the doctor to 'do something' about her father's drinking because he kept having accidents when he was drunk. The second patient asked for help over her own drinking. Three months before asking for help she had had a baby and following the birth she had suffered depression interspersed with bouts of panic. Her sleep had been continually disturbed. At first she had found that alcohol helped her relax, but her consumption had begun to increase markedly and she had begun to worry that she was becoming addicted to alcohol. In the final case, a wife had asked the GP to respond to her husband's drinking.

From these few examples then, it would seem that the GPs were requesting help from the CAT consultation service in similar situations to the social workers. They were obliged to respond to clients' direct pleas for help but felt a need for role support in order to make such a response.

(d) *Other Agents*

Six other requests were made for help from the CAT.

Table 11.6 Use of CAT Consultation Service by Other Agents

Agents requesting help	Why initial request for help	Main problem(s) related to drink	Joint Interview	Other action
Hostel warden	Client worried by mood swings	Psychological and occupational	JI	GP informed drugs prescribed
Hostel warden	Client irritable and Vit. B deficient	Physical	JI	GP informed drugs prescribed
Health visitor	Wife suddenly drinking excessively when client abstained	Marital	—	CAT took over case
Clergyman	Client being evicted — violence	Accommodation and violence	—	Help obtaining hostel place and letter to client
Marriage guidance counsellor	Spouse threatened to leave alcoholic husband	Marital	JI	—
Wife of client	Wanted advice about handling drunken husband	Marital and violence	—	Advice given

The warden was concerned on both occasions about clients within his hostel. One had asked the warden for help because he was frightened by his constant mood changes and his psychological problems which he felt precluded him going out to find work. The other client had become exceedingly irritable and had been diagnosed by his GP to be suffering from vitamin B deficiency. In both these cases the hostel warden wished for a psychiatric opinion and chose the CAT because he knew the CAT psychiatrist would be willing to visit the hostel. The clergyman asked for help over a man who was being removed from one hostel because of his continual drunken violence and no other hostel would accept him. The remining three cases involved married couples. The health visitor requested help with a case in which the husband, who had a long history of excessive drinking had recently become abstinent, upon which his wife had begun to drink excessively. This had thrown the health visitor into complete confusion, and she was also very anxious lest the husband might return to drink. The marriage guidance counsellor was faced with an ultimatum from a wife who had threatened to leave home if her husband did not seek treatment for his drinking. A wife of a client also rang up the CAT to ask how she might handle her husband, who was drunk at the time, and how best she might protect herself and her child.

5. Method of Operation

When agents first contacted the CAT, details about the client were noted down and hospital records were checked to see if the client involved had any previous contact with the psychiatric services. After the agent had outlined the problem, the CAT member would usually offer one of two courses of action. If the request was primarily for support over investigation, management and treatment, then the CAT would firstly propose to discuss the history and current difficulties of the case with the agent. If the request was primarily for help over assessment and review, the CAT member straight away made an offer of a joint interview involving the CAT, the agent, the client and any significant others involved, such as the client's spouse. As shown on the previous tables, a similar joint interview was sometimes conducted for cases involving consultation over management. The CAT recommended that either the joint interview or the initial assessment with the agent be conducted at the agent's place or work, although when necessary the consultations took place in the CAT offices or in the client's home. The CAT explained that although they were willing to interview the client this must be in the presence of the agent if at all possible. Certain principles were always spelled out to the agent requesting help. The CAT emphasized that it was not a referral service on to which clients could be off loaded, but that the agent was expected to retain the main therapeutic responsibility for the case unless there were exceptional circumstances.

Some crises, of course, such as threats of violence from a drunken husband required advice straight away, but the CAT also attempted to make some initial response to any problem within a week of the initial contact.

There were four basic assessments to be made by the CAT in the first consultation. These were to assess:

1. The client, either from the agent's account of him or from the joint interview.

2. The relationship between the client and the agent.
3. The agent's needs as regards information, skills, legitimacy and support.
4. The relationship between the CAT and the agent, and the ways in which the CAT could best support the agent.

(a) *The Joint Interview*

Sixteen joint interviews were conducted. Most followed a set pattern. The CAT told the agent concerned that they would like to discuss the situation with him first, without the client being present. This provided the CAT with the history of the case and some idea of the agent's therapeutic commitment to the client. The agent was then asked to bring in the client. The CAT explained to the agent that they would prefer the agent himself to conduct the interview and this was usually, but not invariably, accepted by the agent concerned. The CAT felt it would be more relaxing for the client if the agent conducted the interview. It also provided an opportunity for the CAT to observe the agent's therapeutic style and his working relationship with the client. For from the CAT point of view, the interview was as much an assessment of the agent as it was of the client. The CAT members would gradually participate more in the interview, directing questions at the client not just to gather information necessary for the assessment of the case, but also to educate the agent into the skills of questioning drinkers, by demonstrating which clues to look for, what questions to ask and how to interpret the answers. When the CAT felt they had gathered enough information to make basic decisions they asked the client if he would mind leaving the room while they talked over the situation with the agent. The CAT discussed the case with the agent with two major goals in mind — to help the client, and to help the agent to help the client. The CAT would then suggest various possible approaches to improve the situation and assure the agent of continuing support and advice while he tried out these approaches. Wherever possible, the CAT attempted to spend not more than an hour upon the whole session and it was usually possible to make a thorough assessment within this time. Usually a specialist has to spend a considerable time over routine questions about the client's history, but the agent had usually passed on the most relevant information to the CAT already. It was thus possible to get to the key aspects of the case fairly quickly, leaving time for the equally important task of assessing the agent's needs and using the situation as a practical educational and training exercise for the agent.

Following either the joint interview or the consultation with the agent alone, the CAT sent back to the agent a summary and their main conclusions. Again, this served both practical and educational purposes. The clarification letter usually began by setting out the major problems involved in the case and the CAT assessment of their relationship to drinking. This was generally followed by a CAT prognosis of the drinking and possible goals which the agent could pursue. If the agent was not a GP the CAT would ask permission to inform the GP of the discussion, the conclusions and the possible treatment methods to be followed. An explanation of CAT involvement and a copy of the clarification letter were sent to the client's GP. To give a sense of the consultation interviews, the types of cases dealt with and the types of approaches suggested by CAT we have reproduced two of these clarification letters.

The first letter concerned a social worker's client whose husband was about to leave prison. While he had been away both the social worker and the wife felt that the family situation had much improved. Both were equally anxious that the return of the husband, who was often violent when drunk, would return the family to its former circumstances. Both social worker and wife were particularly worried about the possibility of him physically assaulting the family but neither knew what to do.

Dear Miss E,

Re: Mrs A

This is a report on the meeting we had together with her in your office last week.

It was quite clear from Mrs A's description of her husband's drinking that, indeed, he has a serious drinking problem. His consumption is extremely heavy, there is much harm from his drinking and he shows early morning withdrawal symptoms such as shakiness and nausea, which indicate a moderate degree of physical addiction to alcohol.

The severity of his drinking problem, together with the history of repeated failed attempts to reduce his drinking indicates to me that this man is extremely unlikely to return to normal drinking. I think that he is faced with the alternative of total abstinence or continual trouble.

Mrs A is quite clearly very frightened about when her husband comes home. She feels that almost certainly the situation which held before will repeat itself. I felt very strongly that she does not want her husband back home for this reason but that she is basically frightened of rejecting him. She said that she would not dare to turn him out of the house and continue to live there because she knew that he would come back and cause trouble. Although he has not been violent to her so far, I feel sure that she is right to be afraid of his violence if she stands up to him. I think she has only escaped his violence so far by continually giving way to him. She seemed to feel that the best thing was for her to see how his drinking went when he came home and then leave him if it got too bad. I think, however, this is unrealistic. I think she will find herself trapped in the old pattern if she does this. I explained to her that he was extremely unlikely to return to normal social drinking and that she should only be prepared to have him back if he becomes totally abstinent. I explained to her that it was only fair to put this to him while he is in prison so that he has time to think it over rather than wait until he arrived home. By the time he arrives home from prison he might well already be drunk, in which case to confront him with the situation then would be very dangerous. She said that she had tried to discuss the matter with her husband in prison but he had just laughed the matter off. I agree with your suggestion that she should put down the terms of her conditions on paper and write to him in prison about it. She is clearly very frightened of doing this and I think she will need your constant support in order to prepare herself and the family to take this very tough line.

It is sad that such a tough line has to be taken, but I feel that Mrs A and the children will suffer greatly if he carries on drinking as he has done in the past. Furthermore, the taking of such a firm line with him can in fact be very helpful to him. Sadly, many men have to really be turned out by their wives (or by their employers) before they really believe that they have got to do something about their problem. If she does this I would not be at all surprised if he stops drinking and picks himself up. In this connection it was very interesting that when Mrs A had walked out on him and the children some time ago he had remained completely sober and looked after the children well during her absence.

I feel that you should also talk with Mrs A about discussing the future with her children. It is important that the children should be aware of the forthcoming crisis and that they should if possible support their mother in her actions.

Please keep me informed as to what happens. If Mr A wishes to see

me then if Dr H (his GP) agrees then I would be very happy to see
him.

Yours sincerely,

CAT

The second letter was a report on a joint interview between the CAT,
a probation officer and a client about whom the probation officer had
to make a court report. It particularly illustrated how the consultation
service was sometimes consulted about clients whose drinking problems
were at a relatively early stage but at some risk of becoming worse. The
CAT attempted to increase the probation officer's sense of role legitimacy in pursuing the question of drinking by recommending he discuss
with the client the good as well as bad effects of alcohol and to avoid
any moralistic approaches, whilst reducing the officer's anxieties about
his adequacy by providing clinical information together with the offer
of future support.

Dear ——,

Re: Mr F

Here is a report of the joint interview we had with Mr F last week.
The court had asked for a social enquiry report and a medical report
on Mr F following his appearance in court charged with assault.

Mr F came across to me as a fairly sensible 18 year-old who,
having done reasonably well at school, has now settled well into a
job as a computer programmer. From his own account he appears to
enjoy the job and to have the respect of his bosses. He clearly has
ambitions in this direction and intends to take evening classes two
nights a week to advance himself. He seems able to make friends of
both sexes.

He appears to me to have two related problems. First, he has an
obvious tendency to get into fights and on two occasions these fights
have brought him into contact with the law. He has clearly been
involved in many fights, particularly in pubs and in association with
his fellow Millwall Football Club supporters. The second problem in
his life relates to his family. He seems worried about his father who
has a long standing tendency to drink excessively. Last year the
father had a heart attack and was strongly advised to either cut
down or stop his drinking. However, the father has been unable to

do this and still comes home drunk. Mr F's main anxiety about this appears to be the effect it has upon his mother and the rest of the family. When his father comes home he is verbally aggressive and the rest of the family look to Mr F for protection, even though Mr F Sr does not appear to be physically violent to any of them. Mrs F seems very anxious lest her husband has a further heart attack. Mr F finds this situation very frustrating since he is unable to talk to his father about it or to change the situation in any way.

I would next like to consider Mr F's own drinking. The question I feel needs to be answered is this. Is his drinking causing harm or likely to do so in the future? The first point to note is that on both occasions when he has been caught by the police he has been drinking beforehand. Furthermore, he said during the interview that he has been charged for being drunk and disorderly once before which did not appear on the court record we received. People do not recurrently get into trouble after drinking unless they are drinking fairly heavily and regularly and in my judgement Mr F's drinking is excessive. He admits to drinking about five pints on most nights and on some nights he drinks as many as nine or ten pints plus about three glasses of spirits. This level of consumption is only reached by less than one in fifty of the adult population. He already shows a degree of tolerance to drink, since most 18 year-olds would not be able to drink as much as the amounts he is capable of drinking without becoming completely insensible. The danger of such heavy consumption is of course that he will gradually become more tolerant, his consumption will further increase and eventually he might start getting noticeable withdrawal symptoms which may further increase his consumption. We do not know what proportion of 18 year-olds who drink as heavily as this progress in this manner and what proportion will settle down, get married and cut down their consumption markedly. I would think that in Mr F's case the risks of progression are very real. He could easily get into a circle of fights, drinking, legal trouble, loss of job, further trouble in the home and further drinking.

The fact that his father also has a very serious drinking problem makes me feel even more concerned about him because we know that the sons of alcoholic fathers have a high chance of developing severe drinking problems themselves later on. I think therefore that it would be well worth spending some time trying to help Mr F at this stage, particularly in view of the fact that he has quite a lot of things going for him, such as his job and his ability to relate to people.

I would advise that you concentrate on three areas — his drinking, his tendency to violence and the problems within the family. I cannot advise you particularly about the violence as I am sure you have much more experience than me. On the other questions, I would approach the matter as follows. In addition to your usual casework skills, I would encourage him to talk about the good things he gets from his drinking. Unless you understand what he is getting from his drinking you will not be able to understand him or to handle the situation with him, and also he will be unlikely to accept your advice when you recommend that he cut down his drinking. Unless he really feels you understand what his drinking is about and can sympathize with his need to drink, he will not take seriously any attempt you make to show him the harmful effects of his drinking. He will just see you as a person representing authority who says 'thou shalt not' and the relationship will be characterized by denial on his part which would totally disrupt any therapeutic relationship. When he is able to talk very freely with you about his drinking then I think you can gradually begin to share with him your anxieties about the effect it is having on him now and in the future.

As for the parental situation, I feel that in some way his tendency to aggression might be linked up with his frustrations with his father, though in what way I cannot say exactly. I think that talking to you about his father's drinking may be very beneficial to him and if you are able to give him practical guidelines as to how he might approach his father on the matter then I think that this may be of great value to him. He will almost certainly learn to talk to his father about his father's drinking in the same way as you talk to him about his drinking. He will learn how to approach his father without making his father feel guilty or humiliated about his drinking and may find himself positively able to help his father. I may be a little over optimistic here but I certainly think it is worth trying.

I will be happy to discuss his progress at any time you wish and I hope that this letter is of some value to you. In reading it you must remember that my experience of handling people at such an early stage in their drinking problem is limited and therefore I may get things out of perspective.

I would be most grateful if you could ring me following your interview with his mother and your contact with his firm in case something turns up which would seriously modify my present opinions.

Yours sincerely,

CAT

Following the initial consultations and the assessment of the problems and goals by letter, follow-up consultations were available at the
request of the agent, and when appropriate other agents would also be
introduced into the case. In some cases, a considerable number of consultations took place and the case was dealt with under the support of
the CAT for a period of some months. Such a case is fully described in
the following chapter.

(b) *Other Methods of Operation*

If no joint interview were possible, the CAT attempted to make the
assessment by interviewing the agent alone. This applied to 13 cases and
the goals and procedures followed were roughly similar to those employed in joint interviews.

There were only three cases in which the CAT interviewed the client
without an agent being present. All three clients were the subject of
requests for help from social workers. Two clients from other health
districts requested support after their imminent discharge from hospital
and it proved more convenient for the CAT to see them in hospital and
send advice and plans for rehabilitation to their social workers by letter.
In the third case the social worker could not attend the interview with
the client in a hostel and so the CAT carried out the interview without
her.

The only other anomaly to the general method of operation was that
the CAT took over the main therapeutic responsibility for three clients.
One was the hostel resident just mentioned. He later became psychotic
and was admitted to the hospital where the CAT was based, so the CAT
took over the main responsibility for him. The second case, from the
health visitor, was one where the wife had suddenly started drinking
very heavily when her husband had become abstinent.

The health visitor was due to leave the area and did not know of
any other colleague who would be able to adequately take on this
difficult case. The GP felt unable to take on the main responsibility
because he was an old friend of the husband. The CAT therefore
decided to accept the case, and made arrangements for the husband
and wife to be visited by a nurse in charge of an alcoholism in-patient
unit.

In the final case taken over by the CAT, a GP was called by a
colleague to see his wife who had become depressed. The wife then
explained that her husband had a serious drinking problem and asked
for help. The GP who requested help from the CAT felt that he could
not easily treat his colleague and that a specialist consultation might be

more appropriate. The CAT felt this was not an unreasonable request and took over the main therapeutic responsibility for the case.

(c) *Disadvantages and Advantages of the Different Places of Consultation*

The CAT consultations took place in three settings — the client's home, the CAT offices and the agent's work place. Each had advantages and disadvantages; the suitability of each setting depending on the individual case.

(i) *The Client's Home.* Conducting interviews in the client's home can be particularly useful in helping agents to understand the client's social setting. This might be particularly valuable for a hospital trained psychiatrist to whom the importance of the client's environment might not be immediately obvious. In at least one case dealt with by the CAT the client's drinking was related to her refusal to have her child home from care on the grounds that her housing was unsuitable. The client claimed her drinking was caused by her poor housing since she was totally unable to stay in the house by herself at night because she was frightened, and that the only other place that she could go to locally was to a pub. When the CAT and the agent visited her home it became quite clear that her housing was indeed quite appalling and very likely the cause of many of the problems in the case. There was every reason to believe that she was frightened of remaining in that place at night. The CAT then supported the agent's attempt to get the client rehoused, and this enabled the agent to help with her drinking. Without seeing her in her home, the CAT's assessment could have been quite inappropriate. Sometimes visits to the client's home entailed certain disadvantages. They were usually more time consuming for both the CAT and the agents involved than meeting at either of their offices. It was occasionally awkward to organize a meeting between agent and CAT beforehand to have a discussion before entering the client's home.

(ii) *The Hospital Setting.* Some agents and clients preferred having the consultation at the hospital. This was naturally time saving for the CAT and made it easier for them to control the situation. For example, they were able to ensure on every occasion that they were able to speak to the agent before bringing the client into the room. The hospital setting was conversely less time saving for agents and clients and sometimes seemed to confuse both of them about the nature and approach of the CAT. Some clients refused point blank to come to the hospital and two clients did not attend a joint interview arranged for the CAT offices.

(iii) *The Agent's Place of Work.* Most consultations were conducted in the agent's work place. Agents and clients generally preferred this, feeling more comfortable within an office they knew and in which they did not perceive the CAT as a threat. Apart from the practical convenience, agent and client seemed complimented that a specialist team came out to meet them, taking it as a mark of respect and commitment. Very often it increased the general community agent's esteem in the eyes of their client. Notes were within easy access and could be consulted quickly. The total consultation including travelling times took the CAT little longer than a standard psychiatric interview where it is usual to spend about one hour in assessing a new case.

One possible disadvantage of this setting was that the CAT could not always control the structure of the joint interview. Sometimes the agent invited the client in at the same time as the CAT, which did not allow the CAT to glean basic background material first or to agree with the agent on a procedure for the meeting. Probably the most important advantage of going out to the agent's work place had nothing to do with the interview *per se*. It was that invariably the CAT met the agent's colleagues. This seemed to be the best way of getting to know other members of the agency and spreading information about the presence and uses of the consultation service. A general community agent was much more likely to consult a specialist whom he had met and seen helping his colleague in his office than he was to contact someone who was just a name associated with a hospital.

6. The CAT Consultation Service and Psychiatric Hospital Services

Some speculation can be made about the potential role and clientele of a service like the CAT consultation service in relation to psychiatric hospital services.

(a) *CAT Clients' Contact with Psychiatric Hospital Services*

The table below demonstrates that help was requested from the CAT for consultation over 4 cases which at the time were in contact with psychiatric services — in all 4 cases a hospital counselling service for people with drinking problems (which was itself being largely directed by CAT members). Apart from these 4 cases, the CAT consultations were divided equally between cases in which clients had contacted psychiatric services in the past and others in which the clients had never had any such contact.

Table 11.7 CAT Clients' Contact with Psychiatric Services

Past contact with psychiatric services	12
Past contact with Emergency Clinic alone	2
Current contact with counselling service	4
No previous contact with psychiatric services	14
	32

(i) *Clients with Past Contact with Psychiatric Services.* Of the 12 clients who had past contact with psychiatric services, three had never actually been diagnosed as having drinking problems although the role of alcohol had been noted. The other nine had all been labelled at some point as having drinking problems, although the diagnosis had usually been shared with other psychiatric conditions. Only two had ever been admitted to an alcoholism in-patient unit. Contact with psychiatric services had ended in various ways.

Table 11.8 Ending of Client Contact with Psychiatric Services

Lapsed	3
Own discharge	2
Referred back to GP or Social Services	3
Referred to hostel	1
Discharged for drinking in alcoholism unit	1
Unknown	2
	12

The consultation service thus seemed to function to an extent as an alternative response to clients whose previous contact with psychiatric services had been rather unsuccessful and for whom further contact seemed likely to be equally unproductive. Some had refused offers of new referrals to the hospital services. It was also striking to note that 9 of the 12 cases had been clients of social workers and probation officers when they had been initially referred for a specialist assessment. Not only had these referrals sometimes failed to improve the client's drinking, but they had tended to increase the community agent's role insecurity, since the referral appeared inappropriate, and the specialists did not support the agent's actions, as implied in a letter from a hospital registrar to a probation officer:

> Dear Probation Officer,
>
> Thank you for referring this patient whom I saw in the emergency clinic on the 2nd June. I understand from the patient that his GP did not know that he had been referred here. However, I have sent a full report to him and suggested a course of treatment.
>
> I think in future it might be better if you get a patient's GP to refer him/her to the hospital who can then give us any medical history that we require when seeing a patient.

(ii) *Clients with No Previous Contact with Psychiatric Services.* There were requests for help from the CAT consultation service over 14 clients who had no previous contact with psychiatric services. This demonstrated the potential of a support system to encourage recognition in both greater numbers and at an earlier stage. For there was good reason to suggest that these clients would never have been definitely recognized nor received any help with their drinking problems if it had not been for the consultation service. In most of these 14 cases, the agent contacted the CAT when they were uncertain as to whether or not the client was drinking excessively or how far drinking was contributing to the client's problems. Without the aid of the CAT it was quite possible that these clients would never have been recognized, assessed or helped with their drinking.

(b) *Some Advantages of the CAT Consultation Service Relative to Hospital Services*

The figures suggested that in its embryonic stages, the CAT consultation service functioned equally as a first point of contact for newly recognized clients at an earlier stage, and as an alternative means of responding to clients whom hospital services had failed to help. The number of clients of both types for whom help was requested in such a relatively brief period compared very favourably with the numbers of new attenders at the out-patient alcoholism clinic in the hospital in which the CAT was based. A consultation service might deal with greater numbers after its embryonic stage when its existence was known to all general community agents most of whom had some contact with the CAT. It is feasible that in such a situation, cases with no previous history of treatment would come to form a greater proportion of the total number of cases for which help was requested. It would be virtually certain that a CAT consultation service would then be dealing with considerably more clients with drinking problems than psychiatric hospital services.

There proved to be various ways in which the consultation service was more efficient than corresponding hospital treatment. In the CAT consultation system, clients could receive some psychiatric care and advice without ever attending a hospital or ever seeing a psychiatrist. (This is important in responding to drinkers who frequently refuse both of these alternatives.)

It is worth noting that of all the CAT consultations involving joint interviews with both agents and clients together, there were only two occasions on which the client did not turn up. Both these were for appointments at the CAT offices in the hospital grounds. This was a highly creditable record compared with attendance records of clients of alcoholism out-patient clinics. The CAT consultations avoided the breakup of the client/primary agent relationship which often occurs when the client is referred to a hospital. The CAT system allowed a maximization of any relationship that had been built up between the drinker and primary agent over a long period of time. It might take a specialist taking over the case a great deal of time to create as productive a relationship. Equally, the system avoided unnecessary doubling of therapeutic endeavour which sometimes occurs when the client is treated by both his primary agent and by a hospital in a more or less independent but concurrent fashion. When specialist and general community agents worked together, especially in joint interviews, the specialist could understand the reality situation of the agent and the agent could gain a proper understanding of what the specialist could and could not offer. Communication between referral agent and specialist via a third party, namely the client, tends to become very disjointed. When agent and specialist met face to face to discuss a case, a large number of possible misunderstandings were removed.

12 A CASE ILLUSTRATION OF THE CAT CONSULTATION SERVICE

To illustrate the CAT consultation service in practice, there follows a description of the first case for which an agent requested help from the CAT. The account is based partly upon case notes from the Social Services Department and the local psychiatric hospital, and partly upon a series of tape recordings of interviews between the CAT and the social worker, Miss B. The client was never seen by a CAT member.

The case contrasts the ineffective response of hospital services and of an unsupported community agent in comparison to the more effective response of a community agent where supported and supervised. It illustrates how role support can overcome the agent's sense of threat to professional self-esteem created by a client with drinking problems and can allow the agent to continue responding to the client in trying circumstances, thus gaining both experience and the opportunity to put newly acquired knowledge and skills into practice.

Client problems at time of initial contact with CAT.	The social worker, Miss B first made contact with the CAT for advice over the ongoing management of Mrs Y a 26 year-old widow, living with a cohabitee and her two children aged three and six. Both children were on the At Risk Register because of a previous history of neglect by the mother. Mrs Y was drinking heavily, generally run down and on sleeping pills from her GP. The domestic situation was deteriorating rapidly. No cooking was done, the flat was filthy, the children were left unwashed.
Client used a crisis to try and make drinking a legitimate focus of discussion.	To try and lessen the strain, the social worker had offered to take the two children into care until Mrs Y felt more able to cope. When the social worker mentioned taking the children into care, Mrs Y began to talk of her fears that

drinking was harming her own life and her ability to cope with the children. To the consternation of the social worker, she finished by asking Miss B to help her over her drinking. It was at this point that Miss B telephoned the CAT saying she felt unable to give Mrs Y the help she needed.

The CAT first of all clarified that Miss B would be prepared to retain the overall responsibility for the case and then offered to meet her.

In the first interview the CAT asked Miss B to recount the case to discover the type of difficulties involved and the way the situation had been handled so far. It appeared that Mrs Y and her late husband had been known to a number of helping agencies for several years. Her husband had a long history of offences for which he had been on probation and then eventually imprisoned. Mrs Y had first become known to the Social Services Dept. when the caretaker of her estate reported that the children had been left alone in the flat. Miss B visited the home and stayed with the two very dirty children until their mother returned home drunk. Miss B discovered that the family was heavily in debt, with arrears of rent, electricity and gas. She arranged to help sort out the financial difficulties, and to provide some general practical help. A similar incident occurred two months later when Mr Y was found drunk and brought home by a neighbour. The police were called in and took out a Place of Safety order on the two children who were then taken into care by the Local Authority. A distraught Mrs Y pleaded to

Initial contact provoked by social worker's anxieties about her role adequacy.

Drink had been a theme from the start but never selected as a legitimate focus of enquiry.

Phase I: Palliative help provided. A second incident involving drink and neglect of the children. Action taken on the issue of neglect but not on the drink.

Client again asked for help over drinking.

have her children brought home and at the same time asked for help with her drinking. As a result she was given an out-patient appointment at the local psychiatric hospital and the children were returned home.

The psychiatrist only saw Mrs Y on two occasions before discharging her back to the Social Services Department. In his discharge letter he commented that Mrs Y still had a number of serious problems, but that they 'seemed to fall more within the province of the Social Services rather than formal psychiatry.'

Agents adopted perspective that client was drinking because of difficult life situation. Drink problems seen as effect not cause, therefore no response made to the drinking.

His conclusion about Mrs Y's problem with alcohol was equivocal: 'The extent to which she has a real problem with alcohol is unclear to me and can only be elucidated by independent informants'. As no such informants were available, once again Miss B took charge of the case and a child abuse case conference designated her the key worker. Miss B said she tried to help Mrs Y by providing extensive social and emotional support. As well as

Social worker tried to help improve client's life situation.

visiting regularly to discuss Mrs Y's difficulties, a number of practical measures were taken to improve Mrs Y's social situation and reduce the strain of coping with two young children single-handed. (This was before the cohabitee moved in.) A home help visited regularly to do the family's shopping and to keep the home in order. The children started at the local day nursery to ensure they had regular meals and proper care, and to give Mrs Y some time to herself. Miss B helped budget for the household and some financial assistance was also made available. Yet despite this extensive support, little changed in the Y home. Only five months later the day nursery staff reported that the children frequently did not attend, and looked unkempt and neglected when they did appear. They complained that Mrs Y

Practical material help did not improve the situation.

sometimes appeared drunk, was argumentative and aggressive with the staff, and criticized their standards of care. Mrs Y complained to the social worker that she preferred to look after her children by

Pattern repeated. Possibility of taking children into care triggered client to request help over her drinking.

herself and would no longer send them to the nursery. Because it was clear to Miss B this would not work, she offered voluntary reception of the children into care to which the client responded by asking for help with her drinking.

Like the psychiatrist, the social worker conceptualized case in terms of client's deprived circumstances and vulnerable personality. No mention of drinking in this formulation.

When asked by the CAT to summarize the causes of the problems in the case, Miss B said that she felt the fundamental problem lay in Mrs Y's complete lack of self-esteem coupled with her genuinely deprived and difficult life circumstances. By relieving some of the stresses Miss B had hoped her client would start solving some of her other problems which would in turn modify her low self-esteem.

Phase II. Role insecurity when agent realized palliative help has failed. Forced by her failure, and by client's requests, to respond to alcohol abuse. Sought help from CAT. Social worker in crisis of threat to professional self-esteem because unable by herself to meet client's needs, but could not avoid the issue because request came from client, and because of statutory obligations over the care of the children.

The CAT then asked Miss B where she felt her client's drinking might fit into the picture. She answered that she had always felt, much as the psychiatrist had done, that Mrs Y was drinking 'because of her situation, because she was immature and not very good at managing her money. If I could take away the practical side of things she would stop drinking. And I struggled along trying to do that and it just wasn't working out at all'. The failure of this strategy had left Miss B completely stuck, but since Mrs Y had isolated the drink problem, Miss B felt obliged to respond, but equally felt unable to do this.

CAT assessed agent's anxieties and how they could be reduced. Anxiety about role adequacy: social worker lacked information.

Anxiety about role legitimacy: social worker lacked counselling skills.

Dishonesty in the relationship. Agent unable to get through the defence. Sense of role insecurity — "unnerves me completely".

Agent's feeling of failure over drink generalized to a pessimism about her general efficacy.

Phase III. Responding under CAT support and supervision. CAT tried to boost agent's role security by providing reasons why CAT believed her to be the best person to help the client.

CAT tried to clarify with Miss B why exactly she felt unable to respond. She said she felt she had no idea what kind of information she needed as she had never worked with drinkers and their families, nor had she ever received any kind of education on the subject. Furthermore when she had tried to broach the question of drink with Mrs Y before, the client had always changed the subject. Yet Miss B reported feeling sometimes that Mrs Y had almost been wanting to raise the subject because 'there have been times when I've been to see her and she's been drinking in front of me and saying at the same time she doesn't drink. It just unnerves me completely because I don't know how to get through that; saying "I don't drink" and at the same time tippling it back.' Miss B had so far presented an extremely negative picture of her own role in this case and had repeatedly stressed that she felt a failure. Yet as she had outlined the case the CAT had gradually been impressed by the strength of the relationship between agent and client. CAT felt Mrs Y must trust Miss B to expressly ask her for help for her drinking and to give Miss B permission to talk with CAT about her. Miss B had been closely involved in the case for well over a year and had more understanding of the total situation than any other agent.

CAT pointed out to Miss B that she started off with many advantages. While this seemed to encourage her she still felt her lack of knowledge was an immense handicap.

At this stage CAT tried to provide the necessary clinical information and

Support of assessment procedure began by partializing the difficulties and suggesting the areas of exploration. Provided clinical information.

CAT attempted to further reduce anxieties about role legitimacy by suggesting approaches to reduce agent's sense of discrepancy between ideal social worker role and having to assess a client's drinking. CAT had to work through social worker's safeguards against responding.

CAT provided clinical information and practical advice about how to assess.

Agent had valuable information but unable to use it till CAT helped systematize knowledge.

CAT stressed importance of sharing response when necessary.

Reporting back an integral part of supervision system. Agent and client began to discuss drinking.

suggested to Miss B the areas that she would have to explore with her client. CAT explained that she needed to understand (1) how and why the client was drinking (2) how much she was drinking and (3) how the drinking related to other difficulties in Mrs Y's life.

The agent felt she could not really begin to explore consumption levels with her client until she herself felt more certain of her own mastery of the facts. She preferred to explore with the client why she was drinking and in particular welcomed the CAT suggestion that drinking might have good effects for the client. She admitted that in her previous approaches she had felt moralistic saying implicitly to the client 'If you drank less there'd be more money, and if you drank less you wouldn't leave the children alone'.

To guide Miss B she was given an assessment schedule to follow together with facts about the good and bad effects of alcohol as set out in Chapter 1.

Miss B was then able to piece together the information and saw that she already had answers to certain important questions. CAT suggested that Miss B contact the GP to discover any further relevant information and to attempt a co-ordinated strategy. The first interview ended here with the agent agreeing to try and broach the subject of drinking with Mrs Y. No goals had been set and it was agreed that these would be left until Miss B had collected the necessary information. Two weeks later the social worker contacted the CAT again following a further two interviews with the client. Miss B described how she had tried to feel her way into discussion about alcohol by asking what sort of drink Mrs Y preferred. Although forthcoming on this, Miss B's direct questions about the client's consumption had been evaded. Mrs Y admitted feeling ashamed about her drinking.

With support from CAT, social worker took lead and used cues in situations where she had previously hesitated.

When Miss B arrived for the second interview, a glass of alcohol had been left conspicuously on the mantelpiece. Miss B used this as a lead into discussing drinking. Whereas on earlier occasions Miss B's attempt to discuss drinking had been rebuffed by the client, Mrs Y now began to talk more freely about drinking and gave examples of situations in which

Client became defensive and showed her ambivalence in discussing drinking.

she drank to gain confidence, although she immediately asserted that she had recently managed to cut down her drinking. The CAT discussed with Miss B her reactions to these interviews. Miss B felt she had made a real breakthrough, 'We've got over a hurdle now that the topic has been broached.' She was sur-

Agent felt much more confident. Client had frequently been on her guard and evasive but agent now beginning to understand why and to emphathize with client. Developing sense of role adequacy and role legitimacy together.

prised the client had volunteered the information so easily and felt that for the first time in this area the relationship had been set on to a more honest footing. 'Before we both knew it was a problem and she knew I thought it was a problem but I don't think she wanted me to come out and say "you've got a problem" because I suppose she couldn't cope with it herself.'

Began to feel her role was legitimized by being able to use cues appropriately.

Miss B felt she had begun to understand her client's behaviour and that conspicuous signs of drink around the flat had meant, 'She's been quite anxious to talk about it.'
CAT asked for a very detailed reporting back, sometimes even asking for a verbatim account, to gain as accurate a des-

cription of the agent/client interaction as possible, to establish whether the agent was fully understanding information. For example, in this consultation session Miss B remarked *en passant* that Mrs Y 'was being quite silly about it . . . saying she needed a bottle now before it had any effects'.

Lack of clinical knowledge about drug effects of alcohol led social worker to misinterpret information given by client.

The CAT spent more time explaining to Miss B that this indicated Mrs Y had a high tolerance level and discussed other possible implications of this.

Enough information had now been gathered to begin to formulate some new goals for Miss B and Mrs Y. Miss B felt she had a far clearer understanding of why her client was drinking and that together they had been able to establish the various problems which seemed to link up with Mrs Y's use of alcohol. She hoped that by discussing together in further detail the reasons for client's drinking this would be sufficient to bring it under control. 'What I was envisaging was that she wouldn't abstain from alcohol completely, but that she would feel more in control and better when she did drink'.

Social worker's safeguards and lack of clinical information prevented her from setting realistic goals.

The CAT explained that setting goals around drinking needed to take account of the client's consumption levels and linked this with the information on Mrs Y's high tolerance. Drawing together all the information, the CAT suggested that a goal of temporary abstinence might be more appropriate to allow Mrs Y to sort herself out a little better. Miss B was very doubtful that she could persuade Mrs Y to give up drink altogether and brought up a

Agent anxious about pursuing a goal which she saw as too authoritarian and moralistic for a social worker. CAT explored with agent her own subjective reactions which prevented her from making an objective assessment of client's needs.

Reaction formation safeguard: intellectually able to accept client's drinking was harmful but emotionally unable to accept this. Slipped into typical lay underestimation of possible bad effects of alcohol, since 'criticizing' client's behaviour discrepant with her view of social work role.

Phase IV: Supporting the agent through a period of rejection by the client. Further crisis of threat to professional self-esteem when client rejected agent's response to her drinking. Agent shrank away completely and support system had to re-approach agent to get the response resumed.

CAT assesses agent's difficulties in counselling.

number of reasons why it would not work. When the CAT asked Miss B about her own attitude to abstinence she summed up the situation, 'I feel it's a bit mean. I can go out drinking in the evening.' The CAT and Miss B examined this reaction together and linked it up with the kind of relationship Miss B had established with her client, whereby the emphasis was entirely on giving – whether it was practical help or emotional support. It was agreed that Miss B would try to discuss this area with Mrs Y and report back.

Six weeks elapsed. The CAT decided to ring Miss B. She was very disappointed to report that she had only managed to see her client three times and that Mrs Y had stopped keeping her appointments. Miss B said she felt very confused and 'a bit of a failure' and therefore had not got in touch with the CAT. Discussing the case over the phone, Miss B felt that her earlier fears that Mrs Y would reject her if she discussed drinking had materialized. In the last contacts between Miss B and Mrs Y the client had grown increasingly hostile about discussing drinking and in a final outburst had declared 'Your visits made me drink.' Subsequently she had never been at home for appointments with Miss B. The CAT explored with Miss B factors which could have accounted for the client's rejection of her. It emerged that similar crises had too much space. characterized earlier stages of Miss B's handling of the case and that Mrs Y experienced some difficulty in discussing other sensitive areas of her life, besides drinking. Miss B felt that Mrs Y had a history of unhappy deprived relationships with her parents and late husband and found it difficult to trust people easily. CAT reaffirmed to the agent that she was in a better position than anyone else to gain Mrs Y's trust and to respond to her drinking.

Miss B became confident that her client would re-contact and that moreover 'If she returns in a crisis state, it is likely to be to do with drink.' Miss B realized that upon re-contact she would have to focus on drink because avoiding the subject would undermine the honesty of the relationship and would not be in the client's best interests.

Agent no longer avoided the subject of drink despite the difficulties in the present situation. Formulated her goals in terms of needs of client not in terms of safeguards to protect her own professional self-esteem.

CAT protected agent from 'rescue fantasy' which could easily lead to apparent failure and result in avoidance of drinking in the future.

However, the CAT felt it was important to set a time limit on the attempts to renew contact and suggested ways of keeping observation on the children in the interim. Liaison with the school and the GP were encouraged and Miss B tried to think up ways of keeping in contact with the children. After six weeks Miss B re-contacted CAT to say that she had now re-established contact with the client, who had improved dramatically. During the period in which the client had not been in contact, her relationship with her cohabitee had deepened and the couple were discussing marriage. She had reduced her alcohol intake and was not drinking at home. As a result Mrs Y had put on weight, had become more even tempered and was caring better for the children. Miss B felt quite confident about the progress of the case and arranged to ring the CAT within a month. Successive reports from Miss B indicated that the family as a whole continued to maintain their improvements and

Phase V: Conclusion of drinking problems.

as a result Miss B had begun to think of removing the children from the At Risk Register. She invited the CAT to attend the Social Services Child Abuse Review Conference to advise on drink related criteria which would be used to assess the present and likely future stability of the family.

The quite startling improvement in this client is not presented as an endorsement of the CAT consultation service, although it does show that improvements can occur in apparently intractable cases. The resolution of this client's difficulties was in a sense unimportant for the purpose of this chapter, which was to demonstrate how role support could help an agent to continue responding to drinking problems despite considerable anxieties about role adequacy and role legitimacy. The CAT could claim no responsibility for the changes in the client's circumstances, but the CAT could congratulate itself on significantly affecting the response to this case before the dramatic improvements. The CAT moved the response out of the futile cycle of palliative help interspersed with crises involving the police and emergency hospital treatment; help which had had no effect on the client's drinking. As a result of blocking this ineffective help and supporting the agent instead to make a more direct response to the client's drinking, the CAT probably helped to prevent the children being taken into care.

This case has also served to illustrate some of the most important points made in this book. The CAT experiments indicated that, in its infancy, a role support system would be largely preoccupied with helping agents overcome their safeguards against raising and discussing drinking problems with their clients, and seeing alcohol as a possible cause of their client's problems. Drinking featured in each of the crises which arose in the year preceeding Miss B's request for support from the CAT, but drinking had been conceptualized as an effect of Mrs Y's social and personality problems, not a potential cause of them. Social worker, general practitioner and psychiatrist had all tried to alleviate the social difficulties which were seen as a cause of the client's drinking but had made no effective response to the drinking itself. The CAT had to help the agent reconceptualize the role of alcohol in the case. This reconceptualization was instigated in the first place by a demand from the client, although the initial request for help from the social worker had been sidetracked by the safeguard of referring the client to a psychiatrist.

As the social worker said, 'I don't think it ever occurred to me that I could do anything about it'. However, when referral failed and a second crisis occurred, the responsibility for responding was forced onto the social worker who felt she 'ought to do something about it'. The availability of the CAT consultation service made this a possibility.

Nevertheless, various other safeguards remained in play. Miss B, claimed, for example, that discussing the client's reasons for drinking with her would be sufficient to help the client bring her drinking under control – a belief which safeguarded Miss B from having to suggest a goal of abstinence, which she perceived as punitive and moralistic. Safeguards like this arose even when the agent was obviously very concerned to help the client over her drinking. Whenever the CAT challenged or blocked such safeguards, the agent's sense of threat was increased, and throughout the CAT experiments, this stage in the process of support and supervision seemed to require particularly careful negotiation. Although agents' anxieties about role adequacy and role legitimacy could be assuaged to an extent by providing information and advice about techniques, the CAT experience backed up research findings described in Chapter 9 that such resources only helped to reduce role insecurity when agents gained experience. With inexperienced agents, the dynamics of dealing with the sense of threat operated more at the level of emotional factors. Four interconnected strategies developed to overcome the agent's sense of threat.

Firstly, the CAT 'permitted' the agents to feel threatened by suggesting that their feelings were not a reflection of personal failure – which was the way Miss B saw it – but rather an understandable response to a situation requiring resources which agents had never had the opportunity to acquire. Secondly, the CAT tried to demystify the nature of drinking problems and the resources required to respond to them. When supporting general community agents, a supervisor should not adopt the image of a charismatic expert. The CAT personnel pointed out instead that their expertise was not some purely intuitive ability but a product of their greater knowledge, training and experience in working with drinkers, thus hoping to encourage agents to acquire these advantages themselves. Thirdly, the CAT offset threats to self-esteem by helping agents develop realistic expectations. Miss B, for example, and another social worker described in Chapter 10 both held fantasies of 'rescuing' their client. Such agents had to be helped to distinguish between what they would ideally like to achieve and what they were likely to achieve in practice. In this respect, the CAT assessments, described in Chapter 11, of agents, clients, and the relationships between them were of considerable importance.

The final strategy used in breaking agents out of the role insecurity cycle was encouraging them to act as if they were therapeutically committed before they had actually embraced this perspective. The CAT suggested to Miss B and other agents if they approached drinkers hesitantly or with overt anxiety, then the clients were unlikely to have much confidence in their agent and might reinforce the agent's anxieties about role adequacy and role legitimacy by not co-operating. If however, agents approached clients with an air of confidence and concern, then clients would be less likely to reject the agent's intervention. Sure enough, when Miss B became able to discuss drinking with a degree of confidence and therapeutic commitment, the client became less evasive. Yet Miss B was still not able to cope with the client's sudden rejections of her approaches. Almost certainly, the client's increasing hostility was an indication that the social worker was making inroads into an area about which the client felt highly sensitive. Although the inexperienced social worker interpreted the client's reaction as a personal rejection, the subsequent improvement in the client's condition and the rapid re-establishment of a relationship where drink could be more easily discussed, suggested rather that the rejection had been part of the therapeutic process. Without role support, the inexperienced agent would have been unlikely to ride these sudden shifts in the therapeutic relationship when the client attempted to deny the agent's role adequacy and role legitimacy. The intensity of the threat to professional self-esteem was perhaps best demonstrated in that when the social worker felt a failure, she avoided not only the client, but the CAT as well.

However, continuing role support managed to again overcome these acute phases of role insecurity and gradually reduced the agent's role insecurity and her need for safeguarding strategies, although some uncertainty still remained.

> I don't know whether I've actually more awareness of what the danger signals are but I'll let myself see them . . . maybe before I would have turned a blind eye.
>
> I might not feel comfortable but I would feel more comfortable that I was doing the right thing and I would certainly feel I had more ways of getting at it.

The encouragement of the CAT to plug away at the case when all seemed hopeless was dramatically justified in the end. How far this reduced the agent's sense of threat when working with other drinkers would be a matter of conjecture, but the data from Chapters 8 and 10 would suggest that the experience of working with this one case under support and supervision would have gone some way towards changing the agent's general perspective about responding to drinking problems, but by itself the experience would not have been sufficient to make a major impression on the agent's effectiveness. Chapter 8 showed that an agent could not feel role secure until he or she had gained much more experience in dealing with other drinkers, and would not become a fully effective, therapeutically committed agent unless this experience was further supplemented by clinical information and a training in counselling. However, the consultation service was vindicated as a viable and practical way of providing agents with support and supervision while they acquired information and skills and gained experience. These experiments in providing role support also had a beneficial effect on the clients involved, and in the final analysis, this was the most important vindication of our theoretical analysis. The provision of support and supervision encouraged Miss B to maintain the main therapeutic responsibility and respond at a primary care level to a client whose drinking had not been helped by a psychiatrist. Role support allowed the agent to respond to drinking problems which otherwise would have been dealt with inadequately or ignored altogether.

Part Five has described the dynamics of providing support and supervision as they came to light during the CAT's brief period of operation. Because the CAT's aim was primarily to test the feasibility of initiating systems of role support, the lessons learned were largely in how to actually begin the process; how to help agents break out of the negative cycle of role insecurity and instead begin to make their first faltering steps in responding to drinking problems. Our other research described in Part Four showed that if a CAT aimed to make more permanent improvements in the effectiveness of general community agents, then they would have to supervise individual agents in dealing with a considerable number of clients with drinking problems, and would have to provide a thorough training in clinical information and counselling drinkers. Whether these recommendations become enacted or not, the evidence of this research in combination with the account of the CAT's experience has considerable implications for any attempt to improve the response to drinking problems. It is to these implications, and their relationship to the other arguments advanced in this book, to which we shall now turn.

PART SIX   CONCLUSION

13 TOWARDS A COMMUNITY RESPONSE

Chapter 1 described the wide range of severity and type of problems associated with alcohol consumption. Chapter 2 concluded that concepts of alcohol abuse, particularly the disease concept of 'alcoholism', had drawn attention away from the extensiveness and variety of drinking problems. Part Two then presented an alternative model for conceptualizing prevalence and etiology. Part Three reported that as ideas about the nature and extent of drinking problems had changed, so had ideas about the required response. Administrators and planners of services had concluded that the target population of people labelled as 'alcoholics' was a relatively small proportion of all the people experiencing various social, psychological or physical problems associated with their drinking. It was noted that the specialist psychiatric alcoholism services were inappropriate and in any case logistically incapable of dealing with this wider target population. Our 1975 report to the Department of Health and Social Security (Cartwright *et al.* 1975) recommended that the solution to the inadequacy of the response could not lie in pouring more resources into existing specialist services or in the widespread creation of new forms of specialist service. If a response was to be made to all those people harmed by their own drinking or the drinking of others and if help was to be forthcoming as quickly as possible in a person's drinking career, a way had to be found to make more effective use of a very broad range of existing resources especially community resources.

Up to the mid-1970s, the 'community response' had largely been centred around voluntary work. Voluntary community services included Alcoholics Anonymous, hostels and shelters, usually run by churches, counselling services, usually run by local councils on alcoholism and a variety of organizations which tended to concentrate their efforts on specific groups of drinkers, particularly drinkers of no fixed abode. All these services put together only helped a minority of people with drinking problems, whereas the call for a community response envisaged a much broader target population being helped by less specialist organizations. It was recognized, of course, that there was an important role for AA, local councils, and other such community-based organizations, but the term 'community response' implied much more than this. It implied that wherever possible clients with drinking problems should be

helped while they continued to live and function in their own homes;
if necessary, the response should involve a client's family, and ideally it
should be the responsibility of general community agents such as GPs,
social workers, community nurses and probation officers. The primary
health care team was seen as the fundamental element upon which a
community response could be based, since these agents would have the
best opportunity initially to recognize and assess the problems, to
understand drinkers and their behaviour within the context of family
and environment and to act as the main focus of support for both
drinkers and their families.

But as we have seen throughout this book, it was precisely these
general community agents who were most unlikely ever to become
effective in working with drinkers. As our analysis showed, agents
could only learn to respond effectively through being supported and
supervised while they gained experience. To develop further to a position
of high therapeutic commitment, they required clinical information
about alcohol and alcohol related problems, and a training in counselling. The majority of general community agents we studied had
received none of these requirements and were anxious about their role
adequacy in dealing with drinkers. They were also unsure about their
rights and responsibilities when working with drinkers and thus
experienced anxieties about role legitimacy. Most important of all, they
felt isolated when faced with drinkers who were frequently difficult
and demanding clients who played on agents' uncertainties. General
community agents had little access to other agents with more
experience who might have been able to advise them, clarify their
situation, and encourage them in their work. In short, general community agents were ill-equipped by their working situation to achieve any
of the basic goals of the helping professions when working with clients
with drinking problems. This constituted a major threat to their sense
of professional self-esteem. To assuage this sense of threat, agents
developed a series of safeguarding strategies. Some denied, for example,
that any of their clients had drinking problems; others argued that
responding to drinking problems was futile whilst others felt that
drinking problems were self-inflicted and therefore undeserving of time
and attention. If forced to recognize and respond to drinking problems,
general community agents still tried to safeguard themselves by getting
rid of drinkers as soon as possible. Sometimes this shrinking away from
responding was relatively inconspicuous, but sometimes it was quite
overt, although couched in cynicism and guilt. The only completely

'successful' safeguarding strategies were those which precluded recognition altogether or allowed an agent to pass on a drinker to a specialist who then responded successfully. Unfortunately, as we have seen, these latter safeguards, which were the most likely to offset agents' anxieties, were also simultaneously the factors which most prevented them ever becoming able to make an effective response themselves. For low recognition rates and hasty referrals precluded agents ever gaining vital experience in working with drinkers and this inclined them to recognize only the most damaged clients as having problems from drinking. These clients in turn, were the most difficult to treat and the most unlikely to improve, and therefore the most threatening to the agent's professional self-esteem. The more difficult and damaged the client, the more the agent felt inadequate in responding. An agent's interaction with such a client was marred by tentativeness, trepidation and hostility, conveying to the client his own low therapeutic commitment and low expectations of success. The client encountered an agent who adopted an essentially negative approach towards him, a person lacking in confidence and emanating a sense of hopelessness and futility about the client's prospects. Not surprisingly, the client was reluctant to accept the agent questioning or advising him. The client might then ward off the agent by evasive answers, by colluding with him, by lying to him, or by bluntly refusing to accept the agent 'interfering'. This unrewarding experience for both client and agent confirmed to the agent that he did not have the ability or the right to help people with drinking problems. Drinkers came to represent an ever-growing threat to the agent's professional self-esteem and the agent became enmeshed in a spiral leading him to low levels of therapeutic commitment and effectiveness. The agent was caught in the negative cycle of role insecurity.

So many agents travelled down this negative spiral on so many occasions that the safeguarding attitudes of pessimism and hostility towards clients with drinking problems became part of the mythology conveyed by members of each profession to new recruits. A stance of low therapeutic commitment was considered acceptable and indeed the 'realistic' perspective to adopt towards drinking problems.

Yet agents developed in a completely different manner if they were recruited into a working situation where their colleagues had high therapeutic commitment to working with drinkers. Recruits into such an environment were encouraged to develop a high sense of therapeutic commitment themselves, and were usually provided, directly or indirectly, with clinical information, training in skills and the opportunity to put these into practice under support and supervision. In these conditions an agent experienced little threat in working with drinkers, even with chronic and crisis-ridden cases. The agent's role security encouraged the client to trust, respect and co-operate with him. The agent's sense of security was thus reinforced, and he was encouraged to acquire further experience, becoming more effective as he progressed. It should be re-emphasized here that this experience in working with drinkers was quite independent of general professional experience, and the sense of professional self-esteem engendered by role security was only slightly related to general personal self-esteem.

The conclusion then was obvious: if we are to develop a community response to drinking problems and if we expect general community agents to respond effectively to clients with drinking problems, we must create for them working situations in which they can gain experience whilst working under support and supervision. How could this be achieved? From whom could they receive the support and supervision necessary to get through the period when they were acquiring experience?

As our analysis has pointed out, this was a question of organization and training. Agents who had become effective in working with drinkers had achieved their expertise through being supported and supervised themselves while they were acquiring their experience. The same solution should therefore apply to agents working in the community. They too should have access to support, advice and encouragement from known experts. They must have somewhere to turn for clarification of their obligations, for clinical information, for specialist advice, help and support during crises and for advice over referral. At present, they have few or none of these things.

The CAT experiments described in Part Five were an attempt to provide these resources for general community agents and to test out the hypothesis that this could begin to improve their response. The results of those experiments showed that when a team of agents experienced in working with drinkers provided the necessary role support, general community agents could be encouraged to make a more effective response to their clients with drinking problems. For the agents on the training courses not only increased their sense of adequacy and of therapeutic commitment as measured by questionnaire scores, but also increased their recognition rates of drinking problems amongst clients on their caseloads. Agents who approached the CAT consultation service when they had reached crises in their ability to handle clients with drinking problems became able to retain the main therapeutic responsibility for these clients whilst being supported by the CAT.

How Much Support?

Whilst the research analysis of agents supported and supervised by the
CAT showed that they came to feel more role secure, the analysis also
revealed that this had not been a wholesale shift.

The social work case illustrated in Chapter 12 demonstrated that even
an agent provided with considerable ongoing support and supervision
could still get into profound difficulties in handling a client with drinking
problems. The studies described in Chapter 10 agreed that after attending CAT training courses, agents still exhibited discrepancies in their
ability to recognize and assess cases. This was only to be expected in
terms of our theoretical analysis. A brief period of information and
training provided with role support could not be expected to rapidly
change general community agents from ineffective to effective workers.
The questionnaire analysis showed that agents did not become role
secure enough to operate effectively without support and supervision
until they had acquired considerable experience. The experiments did
demonstrate that role support could break general community agents
out of the negative cycle of role insecurity and initiate them instead into
the positive cycle, but because the experiments were short-lived, it was
not possible to say whether these agents would have continued to progress after the CAT experiments finished. The other data compiled in
this book suggest that their response would not have continued to
improve without role support. For the CAT only supported and supervised each individual agent's response to one or two clients with
drinking problems, and so each agent only had the opportunity to
circulate the positive cycle once or twice. The evidence from the other
studies reported in Part Four strongly suggested that agents needed to
travel the positive cycle of rewarding experiences many times – perhaps
with as many as 40 or 50 clients – before they came to feel completely
role secure. So within the existing pattern of training and organization,
the only agents who had been able to go around this self reinforcing
cycle on sufficient occasions to become role secure and effective in
working with drinkers were agents who had been weaned in working
situations providing role support – usually within psychiatric alcoholism
services. This latter working situation had usually provided new recruits
with most of the resources necessary for an agent to develop effectiveness in working with drinkers. More experienced colleagues had supported and supervised them while they gained experience, and had encouraged the development of therapeutic commitment and skills. In
such a situation, there was little threat to agents' professional self-
esteem and so there was little need to develop safeguarding strategies.

Who Could Provide Role Support?

(i) *The CAT*

How would it be possible for agents working in the community to acquire the advantages which accrued to agents working in specialist environments? From whom could general community agents receive ongoing support and supervision whilst they acquired experience? One answer to these questions could be to create teams along the lines of the CAT teams operating in the community with the explicit aim of providing role support to general community agents. For although the CAT support system was short-lived and embryonic, it had clearly begun to move general community agents out of their role insecurity cycle, and to help them begin responding more actively and optimistically towards drinkers. In effect, the CAT was recreating for general community agents the conditions of specialist environments which promoted a sense of role security. The CAT took the advantages of the supportive working situation out into the community.

If we wished then to help general community agents become more effective in responding to drinkers, perhaps teams like the CAT should be generally applied on a more permanent basis. Naturally, the actual staffing and mode of operation of such teams would probably have to vary from place to place. Each area has its idiosyncracies in the prevalence and type of drinking problems, the quantity and quality of staff and the existing structure of services. Each area would have to judge the applicability of the CAT approach to their own particular problems and needs. However, it is not the purpose of this chapter to consider specific organizational issues such as who would pay for a CAT or to whom the team would be accountable; these are not the important points at issue. For the *raison d'être* of a role support system would be the same whatever the actual name of the organization, whatever its structure, or whatever its precise staffing. If we consider that it would be more appropriate and efficient for drinking problems to be dealt with at a primary care level then we must accept that this would not be possible unless agents providing primary care were helped to gain experience in dealing with their clients with drinking problems under conditions of support and supervision. To be able to attain high therapeutic commitment, they would also require clinical information and a training in counselling drinkers. If these requirements were not supplied, it would be unrealistic to continue to call upon general community agents to make a more active personal attempt to help people with drinking problems.

The aims of any role support system would therefore have to be similar to those of the CAT even if its organization differed from the model we have suggested in matters of detail. The personnel providing this role support would also have to be similar to the CAT membership in that they would have to be experienced and therapeutically committed to responding to drinking problems. Such agents would usually be found in psychiatric alcoholism services although scores of high therapeutic commitment were recorded on the questionnaire by other agents such as AA members, hostel staff, counsellors and other specialist agents. Which of these agents might be expected to act as supervisors for general community agents? It is unlikely that AA members would wish to fulfil this task and it would probably prove inappropriate for voluntary workers to supervise professionals. In any case, if we wish to improve the community response methodically, it would seem more logical to design role support systems in terms of the existing ranges of statutory services, rather than to rely on services which may or may not be present in particular areas. But neither could statutory community medical and social services be expected to reliably provide suitable supervisors. Although members of teams providing support and supervision could, in principle, include various community agents, such as nurses, GPs, probation officers, priests or voluntary counsellors, it is unlikely that there would be many agents of this type who had the requisite training, experience and therapeutic commitment. Therefore it would seem that the major onus for developing an on-going role support would have to lie with the statutory specialist services.

(ii) *Psychiatric Alcoholism Services*

Psychiatric alcoholism services were the most frequent source of agents with high therapeutic commitment and yet these agents only came into contact with a small proportion of people with drinking problems. Although this was partly because few drinkers were recognized, it was also partly because psychiatric resources have tended to be deployed in an inefficient and inappropriate manner. It would be beyond our research focus to make detailed comments on this, but it could be pointed out, for example, that costly psychiatric facilities and manpower have often been used to provide custodial and convalescent services in default of appropriate community services. Protection of clients' families or of clients themselves from environmental pressures could often have been adequately provided more cheaply by hostels or day-care services with psychiatric backing. Similarly, Chapter 4 discussed studies which showed that in-patient psychiatric treatments were no more effective than other forms of treatment. Whatever the advantages of in-patient facilities, it should be recognized that, in principle, most of the specialist treatments of drinking problems such as individual counselling, group and family therapy, behaviour therapy, medication and educational and social retraining programmes, do not necessarily require a hospital setting, and certainly not in-patient facilities. There would be a case then for a general redeployment of psychiatric manpower, and it would seem reasonable to argue that agents working in psychiatric services should spend less of their time in highly labour-intensive care of a minority of clients with drinking problems and instead direct more effort towards helping general community agents become able to respond themselves at a primary care level to a much larger pool of clients with drinking problems. For general community agents could only begin to respond more effectively under the support and supervision of experienced, trained and highly therapeutically committed agents and the most logical and appropriate source of such agents would be the psychiatric alcoholism services. The personnel of hospital services; psychiatrists, psychologists, social workers, nurses and others could deploy some of their expertise in the community by providing role support to general agents and, ideally, also by providing in-service training in clinical information and counselling skills. This is essentially what was attempted by the experimental CAT training courses and consultation service. A consultant psychiatrist and senior social worker, both from specialist hospital services, both therapeutically committed, trained and experienced in dealing with drinkers, went out into the community to support and train agents to deal more effectively with their own clients with drinking problems. As a result, more drinking problems were recognized and cases were more adequately assessed and handled, even though, as was reported, the two specialists themselves saw very few of the clients involved.

The proposed redeployment of psychiatric manpower then, as visualized in the CAT style of approach, would imply a departure from the traditional concept of a multi-disciplinary team. Although multi-disciplinary information and skills are required when dealing with drinking problems, drinkers and their families are sometimes treated by a confusing array of many different professionals. Multi-disciplinary responses have sometimes degenerated into undisciplined responses, resulting in confusion for clients and antagonism and professional jealousy between agents. The CAT style of approach aimed to prevent this by encouraging the general community agent, who had the most background knowledge and the strongest therapeutic relationship with a client, to maintain the prime therapeutic responsibility for responding to the client's drinking. Yet clients still benefited indirectly from the specialists' expertise and clinical knowledge. Of course the specialists' non-treatment functions should never come to completely dominate their treatment functions for, unless they regularly and actively treated drinkers, families and groups themselves, their ability to provide role support and advice to community agents in their own treatment would gradually atrophy. Nevertheless, if specialists were going to have time to perform their educational, organizational, supportive and advisory role, then they would have to restrict their participation in individual treatment. And after all, the CAT experience indicated that it would only be a small minority of clients who could not be treated at a primary care level given the provision of psychiatric back-up. When general community agents felt they were going to be adequately supported by readily available specialists, most of them were prepared to maintain responsibility for their own cases. In many such instances, it would be a far more valuable use of a specialist's time to spend an hour talking with a general community agent about the management of a case rather than just seeing the client for an hour in the psychiatric out-patient clinic. Clients would then also begin to receive more appropriate ongoing treatment from the agent most knowledgeable about their background and in the best position to help them on a long-term basis.

Although various types of agent working in psychiatric services could act as supervisors to general community agents, the CAT's structure of a psychiatrist and a senior social worker was probably the most suitable pairing to form the nucleus of a role support system. Certainly, any role support team should comprise at least one agent with a medical training and one agent with a social work training, since drinking problems are invariably a combination of medical and social problems.

(iii) *The Psychiatrist*

The ideal medically-qualified member of the team would probably be a psychiatrist who specialized in drinking problems. He would be likely to be effective, experienced and therapeutically committed to working with drinkers. In setting up and running the CAT experiment, the prestige of the psychiatrist also appeared advantageous when negotiating with administrators and training officers and in convincing general community agents of the usefulness of the CAT services.

Unfortunately, relatively few psychiatrists have specialized in drinking problems, and in some areas role support would have to be supplied by general psychiatrists who might perhaps be encouraged to develop part-time interest in supervisory work. Whilst a psychiatrist providing a full-time service would obviously be more accessible, it might be that a part-time psychiatrist in contact with local agencies for other problems besides alcohol abuse, could sometimes develop a more intimate contact and more rounded assessment of agents in the local community. Whatever the case, any psychiatrist hoping to provide role support would have to spend more of his time than usual in casualty departments, general medical wards, health centres, social work area team offices, probation departments, prisons, day hospitals, hostels, marriage guidance clinics and reception centres to appreciate the range and variety of drinking problems, to comprehend the responses made to them by different agencies and to learn how best to assist other agents.

In this respect the major difficulty in expecting psychiatrists to support general community agents would be that, traditionally, psychiatrists have been trained to understand behaviour within the context of a hospital setting and within the context of psychiatric language. This would often be more of a hindrance than a help in communicating with clients and agents in community settings. If psychiatrists specializing in drinking problems were to be expected to involve themselves more in the community, then they would be better prepared by a training which was more dynamically than phenomenologically orientated.

(iv) *The Social Worker*

If a psychiatrist was unable to provide a full-time CAT service, then this could perhaps be balanced out with the full-time services of a social worker. Like psychiatrists providing role support, social work CAT members would have to be not only experienced and therapeutically committed to working with drinkers, but also skilled in co-operating at a personal level with a variety of agents. There could be difficulties here for social workers just as there would be for psychiatrists. For example, our 1974 agency study noted that GPs tended to be critical of social workers and to be unwilling to accept them as colleagues.

However, there are other factors which suggest that a social worker would be the most suitable type of agent to form a role support team with a psychiatrist. In the first place, social workers tend to share certain psycho-social perspectives with psychiatrists, particularly social workers with some mental health training. However, in the field of responding to drinking problems social workers would hold certain advantages over psychiatrists, and other medically trained agents. Social workers are likely to be more sensitive to environmental pressures on a client, such as the unemployment situation or tensions in the neighbourhood where the client lives. The social worker might also be able to make a more thorough assessment of immediate causes and effects of a client's drinking problems, such as emotional disturbance and material deprivation amongst children, or depression in the spouse. The ability to appreciate the potential importance of such factors might be crucial in helping other agents set realistic goals. A social worker would also be likely to be better placed to assess practical problems caused by drinking, such as financial difficulties and to know how best to relieve these difficulties through social work skills (e.g. help over budgeting) and via access to material social security benefits. A social worker would probably be more conversant with obtaining access to community based resources such as day centres, nurseries, or rehabilitation programmes. If the client's material and emotional problems become so gross as to endanger children, then the social worker would be the most appropriate agent to arrange for them being taken into care. Above all, then, social workers are probably more orientated than any other agents to respond to whole families in their community setting; an orientation often facilitated by statutory responsibilities which allow social workers access to family settings over the long term.

The second major advantage which social workers would hold over other agents in the field of providing role support would be that social workers themselves tend to be trained under support and supervision, and would therefore be in a good position to appreciate the concepts and the dynamics of providing support and supervision.

(v) *Other Agents with a Special Interest*

In the CAT experiments, the nucleus of psychiatrist and social worker was occasionally augmented by other agents who could contribute to specific tasks. For example, teaching on the training courses for probation officers was supplemented by two senior probation officers, who worked locally and who happened to be particularly interested and experienced in working with probation clients with drinking problems. The GP training courses and consultations were run by the psychiatrist in conjunction with a local GP who conducted a weekly session in the hospital alcoholism out-patient clinic. In providing an information course for community nurses, and in answering the request for consultative help from the health visitor, the CAT was assisted by the sister in charge of the alcoholism in-patient unit. The availability of these agents reflected the tradition of interest in drinking problems amongst various agencies within the district in which the CAT operated, but there would doubtless be some experienced and therapeutically committed agents in various districts who could usefully assist the training and consultative functions of a role support system. Moreover, in the long term, it might be that an organization such as a CAT could develop such agents of a special interest for itself, by helping particularly interested general community agents to become as experienced in working with drinkers and as therapeutically committed as agents working in specialist environments. Together with practical experience acquired under support and supervision, some general community agents might develop their expertise to such a level that they could themselves provide a consultative service for their immediate colleagues, as was suggested by local authority social workers in our 1974 agency study:

> A case for further training, there are other fields which require specialization and this could be one. Specialization in the future would be an internal thing, good on this level . . . good to have someone support others with their clients with drinking problems.

It is probable that some of the inputs required to fully develop therapeutically committed agents with a special interest would be beyond the scope of role support teams. Clinical information and training in counselling might be more efficiently provided by national educational bodies, though it should be re-emphasized here that such training could only be effectively deployed by agents who had already achieved a sense of role security through experience gained under support and supervision. However, the task of encouraging general community agents to make a more worthwhile response to drinking problems would be assisted by a greater concern within professional training to cover basic aspects of responding to drinking problems. Although our research clearly indicated that in-service training was the more effective in increasing agents' role security, some of the more straightforward aspects of drinking problems, particularly clinical information, could be usefully expanded within the basic training of general community agents.

Towards a Community Response

These latter pages of the book may have seemed somewhat speculative, but this has been inevitable in considering the potential and the limitations of establishing teams such as the CAT on a more widespread and permanent basis. However, it should not be considered speculative to recommend that some form of role support for general community agents must be introduced if the response to drinking problems is to be improved. For the range of evidence provided in this book, culled from accounts of the effects of alcohol to general population surveys, from studies of general community agents to evaluations of the characteristics of specialists, from studies of labelled 'alcoholics' to reviews of the literature on the effectiveness of professional training, all point to the major conclusions that the most appropriate and effective way to deal with the majority of drinking problems is at a primary care level, but if the call for a comprehensive community response is to be answered, then general community agents must be helped and encouraged to respond by being given role support. Without role support inexperienced agents were trapped in the negative cycle of role insecurity. The only way they could be extracted from this cycle was through being supplied with support and supervision until they became role secure and experienced enough to respond actively by themselves. Since the CAT experiments proved to be a viable means of initiating this process, the CAT approach could therefore be used as a model for further trials with more ongoing systems of role support.

The choice then is clear – are we content to allow the majority of people with drinking problems to remain unrecognized and unhelped or do we wish to encourage more active and effective recognition and treatment? If we decide on the latter, then the development of role support systems like the CAT will be requisite. Without them, we cannot expect to achieve the goal of a comprehensive community response, for without systems of role support, the call for a more active response to drinking problems will continue to fall on the unreceptive ears of agents who see responding to drinking problems not as an interest, a duty or an obligation, but as an anxiety-provoking area which threatens their professional self-esteem. In the final analysis, improving the response to drinking problems will not be a matter of providing more specialist facilities or finding the most effective treatment programme; it will depend rather on improving the effectiveness of individual agents working in the community. This in turn will be made possible only by improving their working situation. Agents must be helped away from a position of unsupported insecurity fraught with anxieties about adequacy and legitimacy into a supportive situation in which they could gain experience, develop a sense of role security and eventually attain the prime characteristic of effective agents – high therapeutic commitment.

REFERENCES

Alcoholics Anonymous (1939). *The Story of How Many Thousands of Men and Women have Recovered from Alcoholism* Second Ed (1955), Alcoholics Anonymous World Services Inc., New York

Anmark, C. (1951). *Acta. Psychiat. Neurolog, Scand.* Supp, 70.

Anderson, D.J., (1967). 'A History of our Confused Attitudes to Beverage Alcohol,' *Mayo Clinic Proceedings*, 42, 705-23. Rochester, Minn.

Armor, D.J., Polich, J.M. and Stanbul, H.B. (1976). *Alcoholism and Treatment*, Prepared for the US National Institute on Alcohol Abuse and Alcoholism, Rand Corp, Santa Monica, CA.

Bailey, D. (1975). 'The Alcoholic Content of Some Commonly Prescribed Medicines', *J. Alcoholism*, 10, 2. London

Bailey, M.B. (1970). 'Attitudes Towards Alcoholism before and after a Training Programme for Social Workers', *Quart, J. Stud. Alc.*, 31, 669-83.

Bastide, M. (1954). 'Une enquête sur l'opinion publique à l'égard de l'Alcoolisme', *Population*, 9, 13

Blyth, W.G., and Marchant, L.J. (1972). 'A Self-weighting Random Sampling Technique', *J. Market Research Soc.,* 15, 157-62.

The Brewers Society (1976). Statistical Handbook, Brewing Publications Ltd, London

Bruun, K. *et al.* (1975). *Alcohol Control Policies in Public Health Perspective*, Finnish Foundation for Alcohol Studies, Publication No. 25, Helsinki

Cartwright, A.K.J. (1977a). Population Surveys and the Curve in *The Ledermann Curve, Report of a symposium held in London, January 1977*, Alcohol Education Centre Publications, London
The latter has been summarized in Cartwright, A.K.J. and Shaw, S.J., 'Editorial: Trends in the Epidemiology of Alcoholism', to be published in *Psychological Medicine*

Cartwright, A.K.J. (1977b). 'The Effect of Role Insecurity on the Therapeutic Commitment of Alcoholism Counsellors', MAPP Internal Paper

Cartwright, A.K.J. Harwin, J.E., Shaw, S.J., and Spratley, T.A. (1977).

Implementing a Community Based Reponse to Problems of Alcohol Abuse, Final Report to the Department of Health and Social Security by the Maudsley Alcohol Pilot Project. London

Cartwright, A.K.J., Shaw, S.J., and Spratley, T.A. (1975). 'Designing a Comprehensive Community Response to Problems of Alcohol Abuse', Report to the Department of Health and Social Security by the Maudsley Alcohol Pilot Project, London

Cartwright, A.K.J., Shaw, S.J., and Spratley, T.A. (1976). 'The Relationship between Illness and Moralistic Models of Alcoholism', MAPP Internal Paper

Cartwright, A.K.J., Shaw, S.J., and Spratley, T.A. (1976). 'Changing Patterns of Drinking in a London Suburb', in Royer, R.J. and Levi, J. (eds.), *Proceedings of the Anglo-French Symposium on Alcoholism*, Editions INSERM, Paris, 41-55

Cartwright, A.K.J., Shaw, S.J., and Spratley, T.A. (1977). 'The validity of per capita alcohol consumption as an indicator of the prevalence of alcohol related problems; an evaluation based on national statistics and survey data', in Madden, J.S., Walker, R. and Kenyon, W.H. (eds.), *Alcoholism and Drug Dependence*, Plenum, New York

Chafetz, M.E., Blane, H.T., Abram, H.S., Golner, J., Lacy, E., McCourt, W.F., Clarke, E. and Meyers, W. (1962). 'Establishing Treatment Relations with Alcoholics', *J. Nerv. Ment. Dis.*, 134, 395-409

Chapman, L.F. (1970). 'Experimental Induction of Hangover', *Quart. J. Stud. Alc.*, Supple., 5 67-86

Chodorkoff, B., (1967). 'Alcoholism Education in a Psychiatric Institute. I – Medical Students: Relationship of Personal Characteristics, Attitudes towards Alcoholism and Achievement', *Quart. J. Stud. Alc.*, 28, 723-30

Chodorkoff, B. (1969). 'Alcoholism Education in a Psychiatric Institute. II – Student Nurses: Relationship of Personal Characteristics, Attitudes towards Alcoholism and Achievement', *Quart. J. Stud. Alc.*, 30, 657-64

Clark, W. (1966). 'Operational Definition of Drinking Problems and Associated Prevalence Rates', *Quart. J. Stud. Alc.*, 27, 648-68

Cooke, G., Wehmer, G. and Gruber, J. (1975). 'Training Professionals in the Treatment of Alcoholism: Effects of Knowledge, Attitudes and Therapeutic Techniques', *J. Stud. Alc.*, 36, 938-48

Cumming, J., and Cumming, E. (1955). 'Mental Health Education in a Canadian Community' in Paul, B.D. (ed.), *Health, Culture and Community*, Russell Sage Foundation, New York

London Suburb I: Correlates of Normal Drinking'. *Quart. J. Stud.
Alc.*, 6, 69-93

Edwards, G. and Gross, M.M. (1976). 'Alcohol Dependence: Provisional
Description of a Clinical Syndrome', *Brit. Med. J.*, 1, 1058

Edwards, G., Gross, M.M., Keller, J., Moser, J. and Room, R. (1977).
Alcohol-Related Disabilities, WHO Offset Publication No. 32,
Geneva

Emrick, C.D. (1975). 'A Review of Psychologically Orientated Treatment of Alcoholism. 2. The Relative Effectiveness of Different
Treatment Approaches and the Effectiveness of Treatment Versus
no Treatment' (Abstract), *J. Stud. Alc.*, 36, 88-108

Engle, K.B. and Williams, T.K. (1972). 'Effect of an Ounce of Vodka
on Alcoholics' Desire for Alcohol'. *Quart. J. Stud. Alc.*, 33, 1099-5

Evans, M. (1977). 'Books and Publications Review', *Brit. J. Alc. Alcsm.*,
12, 2

Fisher, J.C., Mason, R.L., Keeley, K.A. and Fisher, J.V. (1975).
'Physicians and Alcoholics: Factors Affecting the Attitudes of
Family Practice Residents Towards Alcoholics', *J. Stud. Alc.*, 36,
626-33

Glatt, M.M. (1961). 'Drinking Habits of English (Middle Class) Alcoholics', *Acta. Psychiat. Scand.*, 37, 83-113

Glatt, M.M. (1973). 'The Hazy Borderline of the Loss of Control',
Paper presented at Thirtieth International Conference on Alcoholism
and Drug Dependence, Amsterdam

Gross, M.M. (1977). 'Psychobiological Contributions to the Alcohol
Dependence Syndrome: A Selective Review of Recent Research', in
Edwards, G. *et al.* (eds) (1977). *Alcohol-Related Disabilities*, WHO,
Offset Publication No. 32, Geneva

Hore, B.D. (1977). 'Aims of Treatment', in Madden, J.S., Walker, R.
and Kenyon, W.H. (eds) (1977). *Alcoholism and Drug Dependence*,
Plenum, New York

Huss, M. (1849). *Alcoholismus Chronicus eller chronisk alkoholssjukdom*
(Alcoholismus chronicus or the chronic alcohol disease), Stockholm

Jellinek, E.M. (1942). 'Seneca's Epistle LXXXIII: On Drunkenness',
(Classics of the Alcohol Literature), *Quart. J. Stud. Alc.*, 3, 302-7

Jellinek, E.M. (1945). 'The Problems of Alcohol' in Yale University
Centre of Alcohol Studies: *Alcohol, Science and Society*, rep. 1972,
Greenwood, Connecticut

Jellinek, E.M. (1952). 'Phases of Alcohol Addiction', *Quart. J. Stud. Alc.*, 13, 673-84

Jellinek, E.M. (1960). *The Disease Concept of Alcoholism*, Hillhouse, New Jersey

Keisler, D.J., Mathieu, P. and Klein, M. (1967). 'A Summary of the Issues and Conclusions in Rodgers C.R. *The Therapeutic Relationship and its Impact*, Univ. of Wisconsin Press, Madison

Keller, M. (1976). 'The Disease Concept of Alcoholism Revisited' *J. Stud. Alc.*, 37, 11

Kellermann, J. (1974). 'AA: A Family Affair', in Addictions, Vol. 21, No. 1, Addiction Research Foundation, Ontario

Kenyon, W.H. (1972). *About the Illness Alcoholism*, Merseyside Council on Alcoholism Booklet

Kessel, N. and Walton, H. (1965). *Alcoholism*, Penguin, Harmondsworth

Kilty, K.M. (1975). 'Attitudes towards Alcohol and Alcoholism Among Professionals and Non-Professionals', *J. Stud. Alc.*, 36, 327-47

Kissin, B., and Begleiter, H. (1974). *The Biology of Alcoholism*, Vol. 3, Clinical Pathology Plenum, New York

Knox, W.J. (1971). 'Attitudes of Psychiatrists and Psychologists Towards Alcoholism', *Amer. J. Psychiat.*, 127, 1675-79

Kreitman, N. and Chowdhury, N. (1973). 'Distress Behaviour: A Study of Selected Samaritan Clients and Parasuicides ('Attempted Suicide' Patients)., *Brit. J. Psychiat.*, 123, 1-21

Leake, C.D., and Silverman, M. (1974). 'The Chemistry of Alcoholic Beverages' in Kissin, B., and Begleiter, H., *The Biology of Alcoholism*, Vol. 1, Biochemistry, Plenum, New York

Ledermann, S. (1964). *Alcool, alcoolisme, alcoolisation mortalité. morbidité, accidents du travail*, Cahier No. 41, Institut National d'Etudes Demographiques, Travaux et Documents. Presses Universi-taires de France, Paris

Lester, D. (1966). 'Self-selection of Alcohol by Animals, Human Variations and the Etiology of Alcoholism. A Critical Review'. *Quart. J. Stud. Alc.*, 27, 395-438

Levinson, T. (1975). 'The Donwood Institute: A Five Year Follow-up Study', Paper presented at 31st International Congress on Alcoholism and Drug Dependence, Bangkok

Levinson, T. (1977). 'Controlled Drinking in the Alcoholic: A Search for Common Features', in Madden, J.S., Walker, R. and Kenyon, W.H. (eds) (1977). *Alcoholism and Drug Dependence*, Plenum,

New York

Litman, G. (1977). 'Once an Alcoholic Always an Alcoholic. A Review and Critique', Addiction Research Unit Manuscript, London

Logie, H.B. (ed.) (1933). National Conference on Nomenclature of Disease. 'A Standard classified nomenclature of disease'. Commonwealth Fund, New York

Luborsky, L., Chandler, M., Averbach, A.H., Cohen, J. and Bachrach, H.M. (1971). 'Factors influencing the Outcome of Psychotherapy: A Review of Quantitative Research', *Psychological Bulletin*, 75, 145-85

Luborsky, L., Singer, B. and Luborsky, L. (1975). 'Comparative Studies of Psychotherapies', *Arch. Gen. Psychiat.*, 32, 995-1008

Ludwig, A.M., and Wihler A. (1974). ' "Craving" and Relapse to Drink,' *Quart. J. Stud. Alc.*, 35, 106-30

McCord, W., McCord, J. and Gudeman, J. (1960). *Origins of Alcoholism*, Stamford Univ. Press, Stamford

Macdonald E.B. and Patel, A.R. (1975). 'Attitudes Towards Alcoholism', *Brit. Med. J.*, May, 430-1

Mackey R.A. (1969). 'Views of Care-giving and Mental Health Groups about Alcoholics', *Quart. J. Stud. Alc.*, 30, 665-71

McKinlay, J.B. (1973). 'Social Networks, Lay Consultation and Help-seeking Behaviour', *Social Forces*, 51, 275-91

Mäkëla, K. (1975). 'Consumption Level and Cultural Drinking Patterns as Determinants of Alcohol Problems', *J. Drug. Issues*, 5, 344

Maling, H.M. (1970). 'Toxicology of Single Doses of Ethyl Alcohol'. *International Encyclopedia of Pharmacology and Therapeutics* Vol. 2. Tremiolieres, J. (ed.) *Alcohols and Derivations*, Pergamon, New York

Mann, M. (1952.) *Primer on Alcoholism*, Gollancz, London

Mapother, E. (1928). In a discussion on 'The Aetiology of Alcoholism', *Proc. Royal Soc. Med.*, 21, 1346

Mello, N.K. and Mendelson, J.H. (1965). 'Operant Analysis of Drinking Patterns of Chronic Alcoholics', *Nature*, 206, 43-6

Mello, N.K. and Mendelson, J.H. (1966). 'Experimental Analysis of Drinking Behaviour of Chronic Alcoholics', *Academy of Science Annals*, 133, 828-45, New York

Mello, N.K., and Mendelson, J.H. (1970). 'Drinking Patterns During Work: Contingent and Non-Contingent Alcohol Acquisiton', *Recent Advances in Alcoholism*, National Institute of Mental Health, Washington, DC

Meltzoff, J. and Kornreich, M. (1970). *Research in Psychotherapy*,

Atherton Press, New York

Mendelson, J.H., Wexler, D., Kubzorsky, P.E., Harrison, R., Leiderman, G. and Solomon P. (1964). 'Physicians' Attitudes Towards Alcoholic Patients', *Archives of General Psychiatry*, 11, 392-9

Merry, J. (1966). 'The "Loss of Control" Myth', *Lancet*, 1, 1257-8

Merseyside, Lancashire and Cheshire Council on Alcoholism (1975). *Alcoholism and its Variations*, Twelfth Annual Report, Liverpool

Miller, C.H. and Agnew, N. (1974). 'The Ledermann Model of Alcohol Consumption: Description, Implications and Assessment', *Quart. J. Stud. Alc.*, 35, 877-98.

Ministry of Health (1962). Memorandum HM. (62) 43, *Hospital Treatment for Alcoholics*, London

Ministry of Health (1968). Memorandum HM. (68) 37, *The Treatment of Alcoholism*, London

Moore, R.A., (1961). 'Reaction Formation as a Counter-Transference Phenomenon in the Treatment of Alcoholism', *Quart. J. Stud. Alc.*, 22, 481-6

Morse, J.B. and Gordon, A. *Don't Tell me I'm not an Alcoholic!*, Hazelden Foundation Pamphlet, Center City, Minn

Murray, R.M. (1975). 'Alcoholism and Employment', *J. Alcoholism*, 10, 23-5

National Council on Alcoholism Criteria Committee (1972). 'Criteria for the Diagnosis of Alcoholism', *Amer. J. Psychiat.*, 129, 127

Office of Health Economics (1970). *Alcohol Abuse*, Office of Health Economics Studies in Current Health Problems, No. 34, London

Parades, A., Ludwig, K.D., Hassenfield, I.N. and Cornelison, F.S. (1969). A Clinical Study of Alcoholics Using Audiovisual Self-Image Feedback'. *J. Amer. Nerv. Dis.*, 148, 449-56

Pattison, E.M. (1966). 'A Critique of Alcoholism Treatment Concepts with Special Reference to Abstinence,' *Quart. J. Stud. Alc.*, 27, 49-71

Pattison, E.M. (1969). 'Comment on the Alcoholic Game', *Quart. J. Stud. Alc.*, 33, 1049

Pittman, D.J. and Snyder, C.R. (eds.) (1962). *Society, Culture and Drinking Patterns*, John Wiley and Sons, New York

Poley, W. (1975). 'Evaluation of a Workshop for Armed Services Personnel: Attitude Change and the Role of Authoritarianism',

J. Alc. and Drug Educ., 20, No. 3, 1-9

Rankin, J.G., Schmidt, W., Popham, R.E. and De Lint, J. (1975). 'Epidemiology of Alcoholic Liver Disease: Insights and Problems', in Khanna, J.M. (ed.) (1975). *Alcoholic Liver Pathology*, International Symposium on Alcohol and Drug Addiction Series, Alcoholism and Drug Addiction Research Foundation of Ontario, Toronto

Reinehr, R.C. (1969). 'Therapist and Patient Perception of Hospitalized Alcoholics', *J. Clin. Psychol.*, 25, 443-5

Ritson, E.B. (1968). 'The Prognosis of Alcohol Addicts Treated by a Specialist Unit', *Brit. J. Psychiat.*, 144, 1019-29

Robinson, D. (1972). 'The Alcoholigist's Addiction', *Quart. J. Stud. Alc.*, 33, 4, 1028-42

Robinson, D. (1976). *From Drinking to Alcoholism: A Sociological Commentary*, John Wiley & Sons, London

Robinson, L.H. and Podnos, B. (1966). 'Resistance of Psychiatrists in the Treatment of Alcoholism', *J. Nerv. Ment. Dis.*, 143, 220-5

Roebuck, J.B., and Kessler, R.G. (1972). *The Etiology of Alcoholism*, Charles C. Thomas, Springfield, Illinois

Roizen, R. (1977). In 'the Rand Report: Some Comments and a Response', *J. Stud. Alc.*, (1977), 38, 1, 170-8

Room, R. (1972). 'Comment on the alcohologists addiction', *Quart. J. Stud. Alc.*, 30, 953

Room, R. (1977). 'Measurement and Distribution of Drink Patterns and Problems in General Populations' in Edwards, G. *et al.* (eds.) (1977). *Alcohol Related Disabilities*, WHO Offset Publication No. 32, Geneva

Roueche, B. (1960). *The Neutral Spirit – A Portrait of Alcohol*, Little, Brown & Co, Boston

Rush, B. Corig. 1785). *An Inquiry into the Effects of Ardent Spirits upon the Human Body and Mind*, Brookfield, Mass 1814, reprinted *Quart. J. Stud. Alc.*, (1943), 4 324-431

Satin, D.G. (1971). 'Help! Prevalence and Disposition of Psycho-Social Problems in the Hospital Emergency Unit', *Socl. Psychiat.*, 6, 105-12

Steiner, C.M. (1969). 'The Alcoholic Game', *Quart. J. Stud. Alc.*, 30, 920-38

Straus, R. and Bacon, S.D. (1953). *Drinking in College*, Yale Univ. Press, New Haven

Strupp, H.H., Fox, R.E. and Lessler, K.J. (1969). *Patients View Their Psychotherapy*, Johns Hopkins Press, Baltimore

Sulkunen, P. (1976). 'Drinking Patterns and the Level of Alcohol

Consumption: An International Overview', in Gibbins, R.J. *et al.*
(eds.) (1976). *Research Advances in Alcohol and Drug Problems*,
Vol. 3, John Wiley and Sons, New York
Swenson, C.H. (1971). 'Commitment and the Personality of the
Successful Therapist', *Psychotherapy Theory, Research and Practice*,
8, 31-6

Todd, J.E. (1882). *Drunkenness a Vice, not a Disease*, Case, Lockwood,
and Brainard, Hartford, Conn.
Trotter, T. (orig. 1788). *The Habit of Drunkenness is a Disease of the
Mind*, Edinburgh, 1804

Wilkins, R.H. (1974). *The Hidden Alcoholic in General Practice*, Elek
(Scientific Books), London
Willems, T.J., Letemendia, F.J. and Arroyabe, F., (1973). 'A Two-Year
Follow-up Study Comparing Short with Long Term In-Patient
Treatment of Alcoholics', *Brit. J. Psychiat.*, 122, 637-48
Wilson, G.B. (1939). *Alcohol and the Nation*, Nicholson and Watson,
London
World Health Organization (1951). Technical Report Series No. 42,
Geneva
World Health Organization (1952). Technical Report Series No. 48,
Geneva
World Health Organization (1977). *International Classification of
Diseases*, (9th Revision), Geneva

Ziegler, S.L. (1921). 'The Ocular Menace of Wood Alcohol Poisoning',
J. Amer. Med. Ass., 77, 1160

INDEX

For Product Safety Concerns and Information please contact our EU
representative GPSR@taylorandfrancis.com
Taylor & Francis Verlag GmbH, Kaufingerstraße 24, 80331 München, Germany